Michael

On the W...
in France

Gill Charlton studied history at Exeter University and went on to work as a commissioning editor at the *Telegraph Weekend Magazine*. In 1987, she joined the *London Daily News* as Travel Editor, before becoming a freelance travel writer and editor. She has visited more than 50 countries on assignment for a wide variety of national newspapers and magazines. She is currently travel consultant of the *Telegraph Magazine* and writes regularly for the travel pages of the *Daily* and *Sunday Telegraph*.

On the Waterfront in France 1993

Edited by
Gill Charlton

Photographs by John Brunton

Maps by Anthony Sidwell and Michael Hill
Researchers: Abigael Brisou-Nowik, Joanna Brooking,
Chantal Chenédé, Alice Loftie, Rachel Perkin, Ian Powys,
Alun Rhydderch, Jane Schofield, Nicci Selby, Rod Shepherd,
Kate Valentine, Tim Ware, Rafael Winer, Kate Wright

With thanks to
Nigel Horne, Editor of
the Telegraph Magazine,
whose idea this originally was

Fontana
An Imprint of HarperCollins*Publishers*

Fontana
An Imprint of HarperCollins *Publishers*,
77–88 Fulham Palace Road,
Hammersmith, London

A Fontana Original 1993

1 3 5 7 9 10 8 6 4 2

A catalogue record for book is
available from the British Library

ISBN 0 00 637819 6

Set in Monotype Bembo by
Hewer Text Composition Services, Edinburgh
Printed in Great Britain by
HarperCollins Manufacturing, Glasgow

Contents

Notes for Readers

Locations

We have listed establishments under the name of their town or village. Small villages may not appear in road atlas indexes, therefore, we have also included the name of the nearby town in the postal address. The village is usually within 10km of its postcode town.

Accommodation Categories

Where hotels contain restaurants open to non–residents entries show both hotel and restaurant symbols. Restaurants with rooms often require overnight guests to dine in the restaurant. Chambres d'Hote are the French equivalent of bed and breakfast and range from private chateaux taking in paying guests to seaside guesthouses.

Reservations

Essential for many hotels and restaurants, especially in summer and for Sunday lunch. Some hotels request clients to take half-board in high season or for stays of more than three nights. Bear in mind that you may be asked to quote a credit card number or write a letter of confirmation to secure your reservation.

Prices

The price range quoted for hotels is for a room sleeping two people, from the cheapest low-season rate to the most expensive high-season rate. Restaurant set menu prices are per person for lunch and dinner and usually include the cost of a half-bottle of house wine. The cheapest set menus may not be available at weekends. A la carte prices are for a three-course dinner without wine, per person.

Credit Cards
Often only Visa (Carte Bleu) and Access cards are accepted; only more expensive establishments tend to take American Express and Diners Club charge cards.

Opening Times
It is wise to telephone ahead as many establishments are family owned and run and may close unexpectedly, especially in winter. Where possible we have given precise dates for annual closing and the days of the week when restaurants are closed. However, these are subject to change at short notice.

Some small hotels also close for a night or two each week. What this means is that you cannot arrive on these days, and if you are already staying at the hotel expect reduced services.

Disabled Facilities
Where hotels have specially equipped rooms for wheelchair-bound clients, this is mentioned in the text of the entry. It is always best to check exact facilities offered before reserving a room or booking a restaurant table.

Each hotel, restaurant and cafe has been visited by a researcher. Wherever possible we have avoided places beside noisy main roads or in busy resort centres. No hospitality has been accepted and no entry in this guide has been paid for. All information was correct at the time of going to press.

Key to Symbols

🏨	Hotel
🍴	Restaurant
🛎	Restaurant with rooms
🛏	Chambres d'Hote
🍷	Cafe–bar
12/24	Number of rooms out of total with water view
💳	Credit cards accepted
🚫	No credit cards accepted
£	Inexpensive
££	Moderate
£££	Expensive
££££	Very expensive

North-West France

NORTH WEST FRANCE

Telegraph Guide

Le Tréport
Dieppe
Fécamp
Héricourt-en-Caux
Etretat
Ste-Adresse
Tancarville-Ecluse
Ile-sur-Mer
LE HAVRE
Deauville
Honfleur
Cabourg
Pont-Audemer
Caudebec-en-Caux
ROUEN
Jumièges
La Bouille
Sahurs
Rouen
Connelles
Les Andelys
St-Pierre-de-Vauvray
Fleury-sur-Orne
Pacy-sur-Eure
St-Aubin-le-Vertueux
Orne
Grèanges-Pont-Ecrepin
Seine
DIEPPE
Eure
PARIS
Balines
Ivry-la-Bataille
CHARTRES
Ecluzelles
Chartres
St-Symphorien-le-Chateau
Villeray
Sarthe
Neuville-sur-Sarthe
St-Christophe
LE MANS
ORLEANS
Bazouges-sur-le-Loir
Troo
Loir
St-Hilaire-St-Mesmin
Montreuil-sur-Loir
Loire
Gien
emy-le-Varenne
Nouan-le-Fuzelier
Briare
TOURS
Aubigny-sur-Nère
Chenehutte-les-Tuffeaux
see overleaf
St-Thibault
L'Ile-Bouchard
Loches
Fenestrelay
Indre
St Epain-Noyant
Henry
BOURGES
Cher
hasseneuil-du-Poitou
Creuse
Thaumiers
St-Benoît
Rivarennes
Bannegon
Meslon
Niort
La Chatre
Vienne
Melle
Confolens
Nieull
ANGOULEME
LIMOGES
Mosnee

Approx. 80 km.

see overleaf

Hotel   Chambres d'Hote
Hotel &   Restaurant
Restaurant   with rooms
Restaurant   Café-Bar
Where hotel and restaurant symbol is
indicated, there may be
several establishments included

AMBOISE

🏨 🍽 9/32 🛏 £££

Le Choiseuil, 36 Quai Charles Guinot, 37400 Amboise.
Tel: 47.30.45.45
Closed mid–November–mid-January
Dbl rm F680–F980

This lovely hotel set in Italianate gardens on the banks of the
Loire occupies several buildings. The elegant bedrooms are
beautifully decorated and very well equipped; the marble
bathrooms contain bathrobes, hairdryers and a selection of
toiletries. Nine rooms look out over the river, some enjoying views of the chateau as well. The large, airy dining-room
has panoramic views over the Loire through its large first-
floor windows. Creative modern cooking, attractively presented, with emphasis on fish and game. Last orders: lunch
2pm; dinner 9.15pm. Set menus from F200; à la carte
around F250.
Swimming pool, canoe and kayak hire, boat trips on Loire

AMBOISE

🏨 🍽 8/23 🛏 £

Hôtel du Lion d'Or, 17 Quai Charles Guinot,
37400 Amboise.   Tel: 47.57.00.23

Hotel and restaurant closed January 1–February 10,
Sunday and Monday nights November–March
Dbl rm F273–F314

This pleasant hotel is typical of those found in small pro-
vincial towns. It stands on the quieter south bank of the
Loire immediately below the ramparts of the Amboise
chateau. The big, creaky bedrooms are comfortable in an
old-fashioned way with heavy country furniture and sliding
doors partitioning off tiny shower rooms. It is owned by the
Renard family who welcome guests warmly and treat them
like friends of the family after a few days. Although the
restaurant has no river view it serves very good regional
country cooking – everything is freshly made – and the set
menu offers both excellent value and plenty of choice. A
particular speciality is *cassolette d'escargot aux champignons des
bois*, snails with wild mushrooms. Service is very efficient.
Last orders: lunch 2pm; dinner 9pm. Set menu F136; à la
carte around F150.
A convenient base for exploring historic Amboise on foot

AMBOISE

IOI ▭ ££

Les Bateliers, L'Entrepont, 7 Rue Commire,
37400 Amboise.   Tel: 47.30.49.49
Closed Sunday evening November–February

This unexceptional but pleasant restaurant sits on an island in
the Loire. Window tables in the two dining-rooms have
good river views, and in summer there is a pleasant waterside terrace next to an attractive *boules* park for meals or just
drinks. Good traditional regional cooking. Last orders: lunch
2.30pm; dinner 10pm. Set menus from F75; à la carte around
F230.

LES ANDELYS

🏚 ⎮○⎮ 6/10 ▭ £££

La Chaine d'Or, 27 Rue Grande, Petit-Andely,
27700 Les Andelys.   Tel: 32.54.00.31
Closed January, Sunday and Monday nights October–
March; restaurant closed Sunday evening and Monday
all year
Dbl rm F490–F740
Paris 1hr

Built in 1751 as a toll-house, its name comes from the chain
that used to hang across the Seine to force river traffic to pay
up. Now it is a charming inn with spacious bedrooms,
furnished in either 18th-century Norman or modern style.
The beamed restaurant is situated right alongside the Seine
and from the seven window tables there are tranquil rural
views across to a small island in the river. Specialities include
foie gras, pigeon and fish dishes. Drinks and coffee are served
on a garden terrace beside the river. Last orders: lunch 2pm;
dinner 9.30pm. Set menus from F135; à la carte around F300.
*Riverside walks; fishing (permit needed); Monet's house and lily-
ponds at Giverny 25km*

ANGERS

⎮○⎮ ▭ ££

La Terrasse, La Pointe Bouchemaine, 49080 Angers.
Tel: 41.77.11.96
Open all year
Angers 10km, follow signs for La Pointe

Beautifully situated in a quiet fishing hamlet at the confluence of the Loire and Maine rivers, this delightful restaurant
makes the most of its river panorama. In the smart, cheerfully
decorated dining-room you can taste a range of fish specialities – fish patés and pike, salmon and eels – some fished from
the Loire and cooked in embers. Very good *pâtisserie*. Ten

tables have good views over the Loire. Last orders: lunch 1.15pm; dinner 9.15pm. Set menus are available from F115; à la carte around F180.

Canoeing, fishing (permits sold in village) and riverbank walks. It is worth negotiating the modern urban sprawl of Angers to visit its impressive medieval old town dominated by a massive fortress which contains the famous 14th-century Apocalypse Tapestry

ARRADON

🏨 🍽 <u>11/12</u> 🛏 ££

Les Vénètes, Pointe d'Arradon, 56610 Arradon.
Tel: 97.44.03.11
Open April 1–September 30; restaurant closed Tuesday
Dbl rm F300–F450

Built out into the bay where the road ends, this pretty, modern hotel has expansive views over the bay of Morbihan and its islands which provide sheltered anchorages for yachts and fishing boats. Bedrooms are comfortable, well equipped and quiet; five have balconies. The restaurant specializes in fish and seafood, including grilled lobster and oysters fresh from local waters. All 20 tables have water views and aperitifs are served on an outdoor terrace, open to hotel and restaurant clients only. Last orders: lunch 1.30pm; dinner 9pm. Set menus from F140; à la carte around F200.

Small, adjacent sandy cove (swimming possible), boats for hire, walking path around Pointe d'Arradon starts beside hotel, boat trips to wooded islands from Vannes 9km away

ARROMANCHES-LES-BAINS

🏨 🍽 <u>32/32</u> 🛏 ££

La Marine, Quai du Canada, 14117
Arromanches-les-Bains.   Tel: 31.22.34.19
Open March 1–November 15
Dbl rm F330–F350

Arromanches is famous as an important D-Day landing beach for British troops and from the windows of this simple hotel–restaurant you can see the half-submerged remains of a war-time 'Mulberry' artificial harbour. Bedrooms are modern, clean and bright. All the tables in its popular promenade-side restaurant have views over the bay. Fresh fish and seafood are specialities. Lunch and drinks served at prom-side tables in summer. Last orders: lunch 2.30pm; dinner 9.30pm. Reservations advisable. Set menus from F90; à la carte around F280.

Safe sandy beach, windsurfing, waterskiing and cliff-top footpaths. The Musée de Débarquement contains models, photographs, dioramas, and Royal Navy film of the Allied Normandy Landings. Tennis and riding nearby

ARZAL

IOI ▭ ££

Anne de Bretagne, Armement Dréno, Arzal, 56190 Muzillac.   Tel: 97.45.02.81
Open March–Christmas

This modern riverboat operates popular lunch and dinner cruises along a particularly scenic stretch of the river Vilaine between the Arzal dam and the port of Foleux, 21km away. All the tables have good views through large picture windows and guests can take drinks up to the partly covered sun terrace on the deck above. The four-hour cruises with commentary depart daily at 12.30pm for lunch, and 8pm for dinner (Fridays and Saturdays only). Traditional French cooking, prepared on the boat. Seven-course lunch menus start at F164; dinner from F190. The price includes the cost of cruise.

ARZON

🏠 🍽 <u>120/120</u> 🛏 ££££

Hôtel Miramar, Port Crouesty, 56640 Arzon.
Tel: 97.67.68.00
Open all year
Dbl rm F950–F1475

This extraordinary modern hotel takes the form of an ocean liner in dock and, like a cruise ship, it is a complete resort in itself. It sits in the midst of an artificial lagoon behind a lovely sandy strand so every room has a water view, either over the lagoon or the open sea. The chic navy-and-white bedrooms are the height of pampered luxury with every modern convenience. Six rooms are specially equipped for the disabled. On the top 'deck' there is a large swimming pool and sunbathing terrace with panoramic views over the Gulf of Morbihan. Attached to the hotel is a thalassotherapy institute which offers health and beauty treatments based on the rejuvenating properties of seaweed and spa water with two trained doctors to advise on individual needs. There are two restaurants, one specializing in low-calorie menus. Last orders: lunch 2pm; dinner 10pm. Set menu F265; à la carte around F350.
Sauna, Turkish bath, heated seawater pools, gym, tennis, golf, riding, bicycle hire, watersports including scuba-diving

ARZON

🍽 🛏 £££

Le Grand Largue, 1 Rue du Phare, Port-Navalo, 56640 Arzon.   Tel: 97.53.71.58
Closed January, November 20–December 15, Monday evening and Tuesday all year

This enchanting restaurant almost encircled by the sea has a warm, romantic ambience. All 18 tables have views over the picturesque Gulf of Morbihan, and in fine weather both lunch and dinner are served on an outdoor terrace. Fish and crustaceans are kept in seawater tanks for freshness, and owner–chef Serge Adam makes a speciality of Lobster Kary, a Breton version of curry, using a recipe of herbs and spices handed on to him by a local pharmacist who had been an apothecary in the Far East. Last orders: lunch 2pm; dinner 10pm. Set menus from F125; à la carte around F280.

Boat excursions around gulf and its islands from nearby jetty, line fishing with local fishermen, small sandy beach 100m, riding nearby

ASNIERES-SUR-NOUERE

▥ ⦿ **20/20** ▭ £££

Le Moulin du Maine-Brun, La Vigerie,
Asnières–sur–Nouère, 16290 Hiersac.   Tel: 45.90.83.00
Closed November and December; restaurant closed
Sunday evening and Monday January–end March
Dbl rm F750
Turn right off N141 at La Vigerie

This large 16th-century flour mill has been transformed into an appealing hotel run by courteous, helpful staff. Both bedrooms and public rooms are handsomely decorated with smart soft furnishings and 18th- and 19th-century antiques. Each of the individually decorated rooms has a south–facing patio or balcony overlooking the tree–lined river Nouère. The highly acclaimed restaurant is a real treat, serving classic regional dishes in elegant but unpretentious surroundings. A particular house speciality is *L'Assiette du tout Canard Confit.* Magnificent grounds surround the hotel and include a deer park and a Cognac vineyard and distillery which produces a rare white Cognac, served as a delicious long drink with tonic. Last orders: lunch 1.30pm; dinner 9.15pm. Set menus from F175; à la carte around F300.

Outdoor unheated swimming pool, walks in delightful 100-acre park and private river fishing

AUBIGNY-SUR-NERE

▸━ ⏷❁ **6/11** ▭ ££££

Château de la Verrerie, Oizon, 18700 Aubigny-sur-Nère.
Tel: 48.58.06.91
Restaurant Maison d'Hélène.   Tel: 48.58.24.27
Open March 1–November 30; Restaurant closed Tuesday
excluding May–September
Dbl rm F880–F1300

This picture-postcard Renaissance castle stands on the edge
of a vast lake in a beautiful landscape. Built by the Stuart royal
family and for many years the home of the Duchess of
Portsmouth, mistress of Charles II, it is now owned by the
charming Comte de Vogué who speaks fluent English.
Bedrooms are spacious and decorated with great flair.
Throughout the castle there are fine examples of furniture,
tapestries, portraits and sculptures dating back to the 16th
century. In the grounds an independently run restaurant,
Maison d'Hélène, occupies a timber-frame cottage with a
lake-view dining terrace. The traditional cooking makes
good use of herbs, and the menu changes regularly, reflecting what is available in the local markets. Last orders: lunch
2pm; dinner 9pm. A la carte around F150.
In the park there is tennis, lake swimming, rowing boats, fishing and
riding (two horses for experienced riders only)

AUDIERNE

▥ ⏷❁ **23/29** ▭ £££

Le Goyen, Place Jean Simon, 29770 Audierne.
Tel: 98.70.08.88
Closed mid–November–mid–December and March 1–15;
restaurant closed Monday and Tuesday lunch out of season
Dbl rm F380–F680
Quimper 30km on D784

An immaculate hotel and restaurant overlooking Audierne's
busy fishing port, Le Goyen has been imaginatively

decorated with great attention to detail. Bedrooms are large, with well-equipped modern bathrooms and, often, separate sitting areas. In the restaurant, talented owner–chef Adolphe Bosser specializes in seafood, buying his lobster and crawfish direct from local fishermen. Guests can eat either in the formal dining-room or on the cool white verandah over-looking the sea. A speciality is *homard grillé à la Cornouaillaise aux morilles*, grilled lobster on a coulis of shellfish with wild mushrooms. A wide selection of Armagnacs, dating back as far as 1923, are available. Half-board preferred in high season. Last orders: lunch 2pm; dinner 9pm. Set menus from F160; à la carte around F300.

Beautiful long sandy beach around from port, two nautical clubs, scuba-diving and wide range of watersports, boats available for hire, interesting boat trips to Ile de Sein of Résistance fame

BALINES

🏠 🍽 8/12 🛏 ££

Moulin de Balines, RN12, Balines, 27130
Verneuil-sur-Avre.   Tel: 32.32.03.48
Open all year except Monday night October–April
Dbl rm F300–F350

Set in a tranquil rural landscape, water flows on either side of this pretty 18th-century mill. It is the pride and joy of Monsieur Gastaldi who bought it as a ruin 25 years ago. He has filled it with family antiques and bric-a-brac which, combined with his welcome, make you feel you have arrived to stay with an old friend. Bedrooms, reached by a sweeping stone staircase, are delightfully furnished in a refined French country style. The beamed restaurant serves creative versions of traditional dishes, and in summer 15 tables are set out on two terraces overlooking the river. Last orders: lunch 2pm; dinner 9.30pm. Set menus from F130 (children F65); à la carte around F220.

Fishing without permit in private park opposite, rowing boats for guests, lake swimming, tennis 300m

BANNEGON

🏠 ❘◎❘ 8/13 ⊟ ££

Moulin de Chaméron, Bannegon, 18210
Charenton-du-Cher.
Tel: hotel 48.61.83.80; restaurant 48.61.84.48
Closed mid-November–March 1 and Tuesday night
(excluding mid-June–mid-September)
Dbl rm F290–F420

This 18th-century mill sits in a tranquil rural landscape beside
the river Auron. The restaurant occupies the mill building
itself and in fine weather meals and drinks are served on a
canopied terrace built out over the water. Fresh local river
fish, game and fine *pâtisserie* are specialities. Do try the *sirop
aux aromates*, a delicious aperitif which is made here. On the
floors above, all the original mill machinery is preserved and
can be visited. The attractive, tastefully decorated bedrooms
occupy a separate building overlooking the garden which is
bounded by the river. Those on the ground floor have doors
opening directly on to a shared terrace and four are equipped
for disabled visitors. Service is friendly and attentive and the
English-speaking owners are keen to share their knowledge
of the area. Last orders: lunch 2pm; dinner 9pm. Set menus
from F135; à la carte around F250.
*Solar-heated outdoor pool, pond and river fishing (permits from
village), canal and riverbank walks*

BARFLEUR

� ⊟ £

Café de France, 12 Quai Charlot, 50760 Barfleur.
Tel: 33.54.00.38
Open all year
Cherbourg 27km

With its panelled bar and tiled floor, this is a real French café.
It overlooks the pretty lobster fishing port of Barfleur and is

often filled with fishermen and visiting yacht crews. The pleasant quayside terrace is perfect for breakfast in the early morning sun. From June to September a brasserie-style menu is available at lunchtimes offering dishes such as homemade marinated mackerel, fish soup, mussels and pizzas. Out of season simple omelettes and sandwiches are the order of the day. Try a glass of *Le Pommeau*, a Norman aperitif with calvados and cider. Opening hours 8am–9pm in winter; 8am–1am in summer.

Sandy beaches and watersports school nearby, coastal walk to Barfleur Point lighthouse for panoramic coastal views and pretty stone village of Gatteville

BARNEVILLE-CARTERET

🏠 🍴 15/35 ⊟ £

Hôtel Les Isles, 9 Boulevard Maritime, 50270
Barneville-Carteret.   Tel: 33.04.90.76
Closed mid–November–mid–February; restaurant
closed Monday lunch in winter
Dbl rm F300–F320

This attractive white beach-front hotel in the quietest part of the popular seaside resort of Barneville-Carteret is a friendly base for a family holiday. The clean, modern bedrooms, decorated in pinks and blues, have great views over the calm bay, especially from first-floor rooms where guests can see the sea while lying in bed. Only 11 rooms have attached bathrooms. Seven rooms have spacious balconies. The restaurant, where most tables enjoy sea views, specializes in fresh fish and seafood. Set menus from F85; à la carte around F150. Half-board compulsory in season.

Large, safe, sandy beach, windsurfing, fishing, marked walks through impressive sand dunes and forests, bicycles for hire, tennis 500m, golf and riding 1km. April–Sept catamaran to Jersey takes 30 mins

LA BAULE

🏨 🍽 130/222 ⊟ ££££

L'Hermitage, 5 Esplanade Francois André,
44504 La Baule.   Tel: 40.60.37.00
Open April–end October
Dbl rm F1370–F2110

This stately grand hotel, built in 1926, offers the height of
luxury in La Baule, one of France's smartest Atlantic coast
resorts. A chic but relaxed ambience pervades the public
rooms. The bedrooms, all decorated in different styles, are
extremely comfortable and well appointed. Those on the
fourth floor have small balconies with panoramic views over
the bay. It is the only hotel with direct access to the beautiful
9km strand of white sand that curves around the bay and its
smart beach restaurant, which specializes in fish and seafood,
is open to non-residents. Last orders: lunch 2.30pm; dinner
11.15pm. Set menus from F170; à la carte around F270.
Hotel facilities include heated seawater pool, fitness centre, sauna,
sailing, windsurfing, golf, tennis and riding

BAZOUGES-SUR-LE-LOIR

🍽 3/3 ⊟ ££

Moulin de la Barbée, Allée du Moulin,
Bazouges-sur-le-Loir, 72200 La Flèche.
Tel: 43.45.33.17
Closed mid-January–mid-February; Monday evening and
Tuesday November–March
Dbl rm F320
A11 exit Durtal 5kms

The great attraction of this ancient mill is its wonderful
outdoor terrace set above the river Loir. Protected from
showers by a canopy, all 16 tables look out over a weir
and a peaceful stretch of the river shaded by willows. Owner
Monsieur Doire is a keen sportsman, and game, freshwater

fish and eels which he has caught himself appear on the menu in traditional and regional dishes. Some inside tables also enjoy river views and in winter there is a large open fire in the middle of the dining room. There are three simply furnished bedrooms, all with en-suite bathrooms. Last orders: lunch 2.30pm; dinner 9.30pm. Set menus from F95; à la carte around F170.

Rowing boats, canoes for hire 6km, fishing (permits sold in village), marked footpaths, tennis and golf nearby

BEAUGENCY

🏠 ⬤ **18/18** 🛏 ££

Hôtel de L'Abbaye, 45190 Beaugency.   Tel: 38.44.67.35
Open all year
Dbl rm F540; four-person apartments F670

Occupying part of Beaugency's 17th-century abbey, this imposing hotel has a certain characterful austerity in keeping with its history. Bedrooms are spacious, with exposed beams, high ceilings and heavy old furniture, but nevertheless comfortable and well equipped. Six rooms have good views over the Loire towards a medieval stone bridge. The lofty dining room, with its black-and-white tiled floor, has lovely views over the river from window tables. Traditional regional cuisine. In summer, there is a garden terrace overlooking the cobbled quay for meals and drinks. Last orders: lunch 2pm; dinner 10pm. Set menus from F185; à la carte around F230.

Beaugency is a pretty, medieval town to explore; canoe and kayak hire; fishing

BEAUMONT HAGUE

🏠 **8/10** 🛏 ££

L'Erguillère, Port-Racine, St-Germain-des-Vaux, 50440 Beaumont Hague.   Tel: 33.52.75.31

Open mid–March–mid–November
Dbl rm F295–F330

At the end of a delightful country road winding through timeless farming villages, this attractive modern hotel built of local stone overlooks the tiny harbour of Port–Racine. Bedrooms are simply furnished, most with scenic views of the rocky coast and open sea. Breakfast and afternoon tea with homemade tarts and cakes are served on a pretty terrace overlooking the harbour; non–residents welcome for tea.
Interesting walks around coast and through Vallée des Sept Moulins, sandy beach in port and at Baie des Ecalgrain 5km away

BEAUMONT HAGUE

IOI ▭ ££

Auberge des Grottes, Nez de Jobourg, 50440
Beaumont Hague.   Tel: 33.52.71.44
Closed mid–October–mid–March; Monday evening and Tuesday except July and August and school holidays
Cherbourg 25km

Perched on top of 400ft cliffs, this solid stone house stands alone on the *chemin douanier*, the customs officers' path, defying the winds that sweep across this wild heathland. As a 15–year–old boy, the gregarious Monsieur Faurel helped build the auberge, and now runs a convivial restaurant specializing in lamb, seafood and crêpes including *homard Côtier*, local wild lobster with a warm mayonnaise. Do try the local clay–stoppered cider. Through the panoramic windows all diners can admire the seascape, especially magnificent at sunset and moonrise. Last orders: lunch 2pm (3pm when busy); dinner 9pm. Seafood platters are served all afternoon and crêpes and ice–creams in the tea room until 7pm. Set menus from F105; à la carte around F220.

BELLE-ILE-EN-MER

⌂ 𝟙◎ 31/43 ▭ ££££

Castel Clara, Port Goulphar, 56360 Le Palais,
Belle-Ile-en-Mer.   Tel: 97.31.84.21
Closed mid-December–mid-February
Dbl rm F1045; 4-person apartments F1490
Quiberon to Le Palais ferry takes 45 mins; 10-minute flight
from Lorient costs F150

Monet, Proust, Sarah Bernhardt and Dali all spent time on
Belle-Ile and today it is popular with writers seeking a
peaceful haven. Set on the cliffs overlooking pretty Port
Goulphar, Castel Clara is the island's best hotel. A handsome
modern building, it provides an oasis of calm in high season
when the island – and the less expensive hotels – fill with day-
trippers. Lamb and seafood – notably *Marmite de Goulphar*, a
fish casserole – are specialities in the restaurant where ten
tables overlook the fjord-like inlet. Lunch is also served on
the terrace by the pool. Last orders: lunch 1.30pm; dinner
9.30pm. Set menus from F160; à la carte around F350.
*Heated seawater pool, tennis courts, bicycles for hire. Nearby sandy
beaches and grottoes, watersports, golf, riding, thalassotherapy centre.
Walking and bicycling around craggy, broom- and heather-covered
west coast to tiny ports set in deep estuaries*

BLOIS

◎ ▭ £££

La Péniche, Promenade du Mail, 41000 Blois.
Tel: 54.74.37.23
Closed Sunday

Built in 1930 to transport grain along the Seine, this lovely
old barge has been converted into a floating restaurant by
Monsieur Bosque, who has added porthole windows to give
all diners a view of the river flowing past. Elegantly decorated
with crisp white linen, fresh flowers and tanks full of lobster,

it has a good local reputation for its fresh fish and seafood dishes. Good wine list, especially clarets. Last orders: lunch 2pm; dinner 9.30pm. Set menus from F150; à la carte around F270.

LA BOUILLE

🖰 ⚌ ▭ ℰℰℰ

Le Saint-Pierre, La Bouille, 76530 Grand Couronne.
Tel: 35.18.01.01
Open all year; closed Tuesday evening and
Wednesday November 1–April 1
Dbl rm F300–F400
From A13 exit Maison-Brulée

La Bouille, one of Claude Monet's favourite haunts, has a most attractive setting on the first concave bend of the Seine below Rouen. This pretty pink restaurant sits beside the river in the heart of this picturesque village of medieval half-timbered houses. Bedrooms are comfortable, three with particularly good river views. There are two smart dining-rooms and best river views are from tables near the large bay window on the first floor or, in summer, from the waterside terrace. Specialities include fish, local duck and *soufflé au calvados*. The owners speak fluent English. Last orders: lunch 2pm; dinner 9.30pm. Set menus from F140; à la carte around F200.
Lovely walks along banks of the Seine; river ferry across river for cars and foot passengers

BOYARDVILLE

🍴 ▭ ℰℰ

La Perrotine, 5 Rue des Quais, 17190 Boyardville,
St Georges d'Oléron.   Tel: 46.47.01.01
Closed January and Tuesday October–April
(except during school holidays)

Situated in a busy fishing port on the Ile d'Oléron, this agreeable quayside restaurant concentrates on regional seafood specialities such as sea bass, turbot, oysters and lobster. Crisp white linen and well-tended plants create a comfortable, relaxing ambience, in contrast to the often frenetic port activity being carried on outside. There is a bar and an outdoor terrace in summer. Last orders: lunch 2pm; dinner 9.30pm. Set menus from F130; à la carte around F220.
Bathing beach nearby, sailboards for hire, coastal and forest walks, excursions to neighbouring islands

ILE DE BREHAT

🏨 🍽 11/18 🛏 ££

Bellevue, Le Port Clos, 22870 Ile de Bréhat.
Tel: 96.20.00.05
Closed January 4–February 8
Half-board only, F375 per person
Ferry from L'Arcouest takes 10 minutes

Cars are banned on the pretty Ile de Bréhat where a tangle of paths threads past ancient stone houses and villas covered in honeysuckle. Ideal for an off-season weekend (the island is very popular with day-trippers in high summer), the Bellevue stands at the head of a picturesque cove next to the ferry jetty. Bedrooms are clean but small and sparsely furnished; bathrooms have showers only. The nicest rooms are those on the second floor which have small balconies. Most restaurant tables have expansive bay views. In good weather, meals and drinks are served on the quayside terrace. Last orders: lunch 2pm; dinner 9.30pm, although seafood platters served all day in summer. Set menus from F100; à la carte around F175.
Hotel rents bicycles and can arrange boat trips around the island, sailing lessons on catamarans, kayaks and sailboards; Guerzido beach 500m

BRIARE

ⅠOⅠ ▭ ££

Hostellerie Canal, 19 Rue de Pont-Canal, 45250 Briare.
Tel: 38.31.22.54
Closed mid–December–mid-January; Monday except
mid-June–end September

This pleasant restaurant overlooks the aqueduct which carries
a canal across the Loire. All tables have water views, and there
is an outdoor terrace for meals or drinks in fine weather. Fish
is a speciality with dishes such as *sandre au beurre de vanille* (pike
in vanilla butter) and *lotte à l'ananas* (monkfish with pine-
apple). Across from the restaurant a string of *bateaux mouches*
offers excursions and lunch and dinner cruises along the
Briare canal and the river Loire (tel: 38.37.12.75). Last
orders: lunch 2pm; dinner 9pm. Set menus from F100; à la
carte around F150.
Pleasant riverside walks

BRIGNOGAN-PLAGE

🏨 ⅠOⅠ 11/21 ▭ ££

Castel Regis, Plage du Garo, 29890 Brignogan-Plage.
Tel: 98.83.40.22
Open Easter–end September; restaurant closed
Wednesday lunch
Dbl rm F250–F420; 4–person apartments F360–F440

An enchanting place for a family holiday, the Castel Regis sits
right beside the sea in the quiet village of Brignogan which
has a magnificent, sheltered sandy beach bordered by strange-
ly shaped granite boulders. The bedrooms are contained in
rustic bungalows hidden among trees and five of these have
private Jacuzzis. Two rooms are specially adapted for disabled
guests. Much use is made of local granite in the public areas
giving them a cosy, intimate feel. The restaurant and breakfast
room sit on the water's edge, so there are expansive views

over the bay from all the tables. The fish, crustaceans and crêpes are prepared according to traditional Breton recipes. There is an outdoor terrace for drinks. Half-board is compulsory during July and August. Last orders: lunch 2pm; dinner 9pm. Set menus from F98 (children F70); à la carte around F300.

The hotel has a large heated swimming pool overlooking the bay, mini-golf course, tennis court and bicycles. The beach below the hotel is one of ten coves within walking distance; good coastal walks through dunes; boats and sand-yachts can be hired from nautical club

CABOURG

▦ ‖ᴑ‖ 34/70 ▭ ₤₤₤₤

Pullman Grand Hôtel, Promenade Marcel Proust, 14390 Cabourg.   Tel: 31.91.01.79
Open all year
Dbl rm F850

The Baroque facade of this grand 19th-century hotel dominates the seafront at Cabourg, a classier, less showy place than Deauville. Popular with Parisian weekenders, the hotel avoids formality, and the ambience is congenial and discreet. Marcel Proust often stayed here and his bedroom, now classed as an historic monument, retains its original furnishings. Guests can occupy it for F1200 a night. All the bedrooms are richly decorated, and many have sea-view balconies. Half the tables in the ornate Salle Balbec dining-room, which is used only during bank holidays, July and August, have good views over the beach and the sea. For *Proustmanes* there is also a bookshop selling his literary works and *tisane* and homemade *Madeleines* are served for tea. Last orders: lunch 2pm; dinner 10pm. Set menus from F190; à la carte around F300.

Good sandy beach, karting, promenade walks, sea fishing, casino

CANCALE

🏨 |O| 18/18 ▭ ££

Pointe du Grouin, 35260 Cancale.   Tel: 99.89.60.55
Open April 1–September 30; restaurant closed Tuesday
Dbl rm F260–F370

Spectacularly situated near the end of the Pointe du Grouin, a
wild rocky headland pounded by the waves, both the rooms
and restaurant of this large Breton house enjoy panoramic
views over the bay of Mont-St-Michel and the bird sanctuary
of the Iles des Landes. Bedrooms are furnished comfortably
rather than fashionably and most have en-suite bathrooms.
The restaurant has good sea views and specializes in lobster,
mussels and oysters which are collected from the proprietor's
own beds. Last orders: lunch 1.30pm; dinner 9pm. Set menus
from F120; à la carte around F200.
*Sandy beach 400m away with sailing school; good walks around
cliffs and to view oyster beds. The pretty port of Cancale can be
reached alongside the shore at low tide.*

CANCALE

🏨 |O| 6/6 ▭ £££

Hôtel de Bricourt, Rue des Rimains, 35260 Cancale.
Tel: hotel 99.89.61.22; restaurant 99.89.64.76
Closed January 1–March 7; restaurant closed
mid-December–mid-March, Tuesday and Wednesday
Dbl rms F650–F700

A delightful stone Breton house in a peaceful cliff-top location with uninterrupted views over Cancale's beaches to
Mont-St-Michel. The six bedrooms are charmingly furnished with great attention to detail and there is a croquet lawn
in the English garden. Only breakfast is served in the hotel as
the owners Olivier and Jane Roellinger have a separate
restaurant nearby, the Maison de Bricourt at 1 Rue Dugue-
sclin, in a wonderful 18th-century house furnished with

antiques. Seven tables look out over a small duck pond in the gardens. The cooking is imaginative and only fresh local produce, especially seafood, is used. Last orders: lunch 2pm; dinner 9.30pm. Set menus from F135; à la carte around F350. Gastronomic weekend menu F580.

Delightful woodland walks, boats are available for hire from the sailing club 2km, riding 6km, golf 15km

CANCALE

IOI ▭ ££

Le Narval, 20 Quai Gambetta, 35260 Cancale.
Tel: 99.89.63.12
Open all year; closed Monday

A magnificent display of shellfish at the restaurant entrance draws visitors in to Le Narval, one of many similar restaurants serving fresh fish and seafood on the quayside at Cancale, renowned as a centre for oyster cultivation since Roman times. Owned by the genial Monsieur Massé, it is a popular, lively place – even out of season. The restaurant has an upstairs dining-room with good views over the harbour rather than rows of parked cars. There is also an outdoor terrace which is open all year in good weather. Last orders: lunch 3pm; dinner 11pm. Set menus are available from F68; à la carte from around F150.

CARQUEFOU

IOI ▭ ££

Auberge du Vieux Gachet, Le Gachet, 44470 Carquefou.
Tel: 40.25.10.92
Open all year

This small tastefully decorated restaurant overlooks a pretty stretch of the river Erdre, a marina, and a chateau, La Gacherie, on the opposite bank. Only six tables have good water views, but in fine weather meals are served on an

attractive waterside terrace which is shaded by lime trees. The varied menu offers classic regional French dishes with light sauces. The service is friendly and very efficient. Last orders: lunch 2pm; dinner 9.30pm. Set menus available from F90 (lunch), F130 (dinner); à la carte around F170.
Good riverside walks, large public park nearby, riding and river fishing (permit needed)

CARQUEFOU

IOI 🖾 £

Pont de Bellevue, 47 Promenade de Bellevue, Ste-Luce, 44980 Carquefou.   Tel: 40.25.85.60
Lunch only; closed August and weekends except
during June, July and August
Near bridge across Loire at Bellevue

The best value lunch in France. At this simple workmen's restaurant and bar, the freshly prepared, four-course set menu costs under F50, with five choices in each course. Cheerfully decorated with very efficient service; visitors are usually shown to the smarter dining-room which overlooks the Loire and carries a F10 supplement. There is also a waterside terrace in summer. Open for lunch noon–2.30pm.

CAUDEBEC-EN-CAUX

IOI 5/5 🖾 £££

Le Manoir de Rétival, 2 Rue St-Clair, 76490
Caudebec-en-Caux.   Tel: 35.96.11.22
Closed all Sunday and for lunch on Monday and Tuesday
Dbl rm F300–F600

This 18th-century royal hunting lodge perched high above the Seine looks out over a graceful suspension bridge towards the Brotonne forest. It is essentially a restaurant (although bedrooms are kept for customers) and 27-year-old chef Jean-Luc Tartarin serves what he calls *cuisine contemporaine* using only fresh market produce and specializing in light, imaginative sauces. His brother is the in-house pastry chef. Four of the restaurant's 12 tables look out over the Seine, and there is a pretty terrace for breakfast and drinks. Last orders: lunch 1.30 pm (2pm at weekends); dinner 10pm. Set menus from F150 (lunch), F220 (dinner); à la carte around F350.

CAUREL

🏨 🍽 4/8 ⊟ ££

Beau-Rivage, Caurel, 22530 Mur-de-Bretagne.
Tel: 96.28.52.15
Closed mid-January–mid-February and last two weeks of November; restaurant only closed Monday evening and Tuesday except during July and August
Dbl rm F300

Situated on the beautiful Lake Guerlédan, this hotel is a simple, modern affair, but the fabulous views make up for that. This fjord-like lake, formed by the damming of the River Blavet, is one of the finest sights of inland Brittany and a popular place to camp in summer. Bedrooms are simply furnished but clean and all have en-suite bathrooms. The restaurant serves refined, lighter versions of traditional French dishes. In summer, cold meals are served outside on a terrace overlooking the lake. Last orders: lunch 2pm; dinner 9pm. Set menus from F85; à la carte F250.
Boat trips around the lake; lake swimming from beaches; canoes, pedalos and sailboards for hire; water-skiing

CHANTONNAY

🏨 🍽 35/60 ⊟ ££

Le Moulin Neuf, 85110 Chantonnay.   Tel: 51.94.30.27
Open all year
Dbl rm F220–F300

Set on the wooded shores of an attractive artificial lake (the Guignard dam is just down the road), this large white hotel is

a good place for an overnight stop, especially for families. Bedrooms are simply furnished but comfortable, many with French windows opening on to wrought-iron balconies. Three rooms are equipped for disabled visitors. The restaurant offers a varied menu, with freshwater fish a speciality. Both the restaurant and the large bar overlook the lake, and there is a terrace for meals and drinks in fine weather. Last orders: lunch 2pm; dinner 9.30pm. Set menus from F50 (children F35); à la carte around F100.
Hotel has heated swimming pool, pedalos for hire, sauna, tennis courts; good lake fishing (permit needed)

CHARGE

🏨 |◎| **7/15** ▭ ₤₤₤

Château-de-Pray, Chargé, 37400 Amboise.
Tel: 47.57.23.67
Closed January 1–February 15
Half-board only; F1130 for two people

This charming chateau, which dates back to the 13th century, provides a peaceful retreat high above the banks of the Loire. Furnished in baronial style, it is small enough to create the sort of friendly, homely atmosphere which induces guests to stay longer. The spacious bedrooms were all renovated last winter, and en-suite bathrooms added. The handsome dining-room serves traditional cuisine using only fresh market produce including river fish, and there are seven tables overlooking the valley of the Loire. In summer, there is a delightful garden terrace overlooking the river. Last orders: lunch 2pm; dinner 9pm. Set menus are on offer from F195; à la carte around F250.
Excellent base for visiting finest Loire chateaux and wine tasting in Montlouis and Vouvray. Woodland walks from chateau gardens, canoe and kayak hire nearby and boat trips in Amboise, balloon and helicopter rides from chateau grounds can be arranged

CHARTRES

IOI ▭ ££

Le Moulin de Ponceau, 21 Rue de la Tannerie, 28000
Chartres.   Tel: 37.35.87.87
Closed February; Sunday evening and Monday

The river Eure flows slowly under this pretty 16th-century
mill. Inside there is a classy rustic dining-room with polished
oak furnishings and log fire. Serge Guilleman and his wife
provide a warm welcome and traditional regional fare. Half
the tables have views over the river and, in summer, meals,
drinks and homemade pastries are also served on a very
pleasant wooden terrace overhanging the river. Last orders:
lunch 2.30pm; dinner 10.30pm. Tea room open 10am–
10pm in summer. Set menus from F145; à la carte around
F250.
Within walking distance of Chartres Cathedral and old town;
pedalos and rowing boats for hire on canal 800m away

CHASSENEUIL-DU-POITOU

▦ IOI 5/19 ▭ ££

Château du Clos de la Ribaudière, 86360
Chasseneuil-du-Poitou.   Tel: 49.52.86.66
Open all year
Dbl rm F280–F540

This attractive 19th-century chateau on the banks of the river
Clain just north of Poitiers has been tastefully renovated by its
charming owners, Philippe and Jeanine Bini. Marble bathrooms and parquet floors add to the air of luxury found in the
fashionably decorated bedrooms which look out over well-
tended grounds leading down to the river. The salon has the
air of an English club with comfortable leather chairs and a
bar serving Scotch whiskies. There are three dining-rooms
overlooking either the river or the ornamental lake set
beneath a castle. Traditional French cooking, using only

fresh local produce. Last orders: lunch 1.30pm; dinner 9.30pm. Set menus from F95 (lunch), F145 (dinner); à la carte around F250.
Futuroscope theme park 3km; leisure park with river beach, swimming and watersports at St-Cyr 10km; riding 8km

CHATEAU-GONTIER

▥ ◎ 13/14 ▭ £

Hostellerie de Mirwault, Rue de Val de Mayenne, Bazouges, 53200 Château-Gontier.   Tel: 43.07.13.17
Open all year; restaurant closed January 1–21 and Wednesday lunch
Dbl rm F230–F250

Owned by a British family, the Mitchells, this pleasant turn-of-the-century hotel sits on a peaceful stretch of the canalized river Mayenne. The recently refurbished bedrooms, all with attached bathrooms, have lovely views over the river to Mirwault castle. Small touches such as bowls of fruit and mineral water in the rooms show this to be a thoughtfully-run hotel. The chef is French and his menus are based around fresh produce from local markets; *côte de veau au cidre* (veal in cider) is a house speciality. Twelve tables have views over the canal and, in summer, meals and drinks are served on an outdoor terrace. Last orders: lunch 2.30pm; dinner 10pm (summer). Set menus from F75 (lunch), F110 (dinner); à la carte around F200.
Rowing boats and bicycles for hire, water-skiing, fishing (permits sold in town), swimming pool (a five-minute walk away), tow-path walks, famous Thursday cattle market in Château-Gontier

CHATEAUNEUF-SUR-SARTHE

▥ ◎ 7/7 ▭ ££

Hôtel de la Sarthe, 1 Rue du Port, 49330 Châteauneuf-sur-Sarthe.   Tel: 41.69.85.29

Closed October 8–30, February 12–26; restaurant closed
Sunday evening and Monday except during July and August
Dbl rm F170–F250

Ivy threatens to engulf this small hotel and restaurant on a
beautiful stretch of the river Sarthe. Bedrooms are fairly basic,
although all have bath or shower and WC, but the restaurant's reputation is very good. Traditional dishes based on
fresh market produce are served in both the rustic dining-
room and covered terraces which directly overlook the river.
In summer, there is a barbecue grill on the terrace; its
speciality is *fritures d'anguille à la Provençale* (fried eel in garlic
and parsley). Last orders: lunch 2pm; dinner 9pm. Set menus
from F89; à la carte around F200.
Canoes, kayaks and rowing boats for hire, river cruises from village
centre

CHATELAILLON-PLAGE

🏠 🍽 35/78 🛏 ££

Les Trois Iles, La Falaise, 17340 Chatelaillon-Plage.
Tel: 46.56.14.14
Open all year
Dbl rm F370–F495

Although this hotel belongs to the Altea chain, it is a striking
architect-designed building on a bluff above the resort with
views of the offshore islands. Bedrooms are tastefully decorated and include 17 superbly designed duplexes with
spacious balconies which cost F2500–F4150 a week. All
tables in the airy, modern dining-room enjoy sea views.
The menu focuses on dishes based around locally caught
fish and seafood. Last orders: lunch 2.30pm; dinner
10.30pm. Set menus from F130; à la carte around F200.
Swimming pool, tennis courts, nearby beaches with sailboard hire

CHATELAILLON-PLAGE

🏨 ⬛ 3/12 🛏 £

Le Saint Victor, 35 Boulevard de la Mer, 17340
Chatelaillon-Plage.   Tel: 46.56.25.13
Open all year; restaurant closed Sunday evening and
Monday in winter
Dbl rm F240–F270

This clean, comfortable hotel run by the helpful Monsieur
Blaineau, is separated from the beach by a small road. The
tastefully decorated bedrooms, all with en-suite bathrooms,
offer good value. Downstairs, the large, attractive restaurant
concentrates on fish and seafood. A particular speciality is *lotte
à la paysanne* (monkfish cooked in smoked ham in a *beurre
blanc* sauce). There are expansive views over the ocean and
offshore islands from window tables. Last orders: lunch 2pm;
dinner 9pm. Set menus from F85; à la carte around F150.

LA CHATRE

⬛ 🛏 ££

Auberge du Moulin-Bureau, 53 Rue du Faubourg
St-Abdon, 36400 La Châtre.   Tel: 54.48.04.20
Closed mid-December–end January, Sunday evening
and Monday

The river Indre flows slowly by this delightful 18th-century,
creeper-clad watermill in a tranquil countryside setting just
outside La Châtre. The mill machinery is still in working
order. Inside, only four tables have water views but from May
to September meals and drinks are served an attractive under
a giant willow on an island between the river and mill-race.
Simple traditional cooking, especially freshwater fish, duck,
terrines and local goat's cheese. Open for homemade pastries,
ice-creams and drinks all afternoon. Last orders: lunch
1.30pm; dinner 9pm. Set menus from F95; à la carte around
F150.

Children's play area and river swimming as mill is just 14km from source of Indre; nearby La Châtre is a picturesque village with homes dating back to medieval times and the castle keep contains a museum dedicated to writer George Sand

CHENEHUTTE-LES-TUFFEAUX

🏠 |O| 20/35 🛏 ££££

Château Le Prieuré, Chenehutte-les-Tuffeaux, 49350 Gennes.   Tel: 41.67.90.14
Closed early January—early March
Dbl rm F950—F1350

This former medieval priory and Renaissance chateau has been turned into a luxury hotel. It stands in a large wooded park and has commanding views over a wide, placid stretch of the river Loire as it meanders through the plain below. Bedrooms in the chateau itself are very spacious, comfortable and handsomely decorated in different period styles with appropriate antique pieces. Avoid the less expensive rooms in the modern bungalow-style annexe which, although nicely furnished, have less character and no water view. The conservatory-style restaurant sits right on the edge of the river cliff. The menu features both classic French and regional dishes based on fresh produce selected by the chef from nearby markets. A particular speciality is *terrine aux trois poissons Val de Loire* – a freshwater fish terrine. Last orders: lunch 2pm; dinner 9.30pm. Set menus from F250; à la carte around F300.
Heated outdoor pool, tennis court, fishing (permit from village), riding stables 3km

CHENILLE-CHANGE

|O| 🛏 ££

La Table du Meunier, Chenillé-Changé, 49220 Le Lion d'Angers.   Tel: 41.95.10.83

Closed mid-January–mid-February; Monday evening,
Tuesday evening and all Wednesday except July–September

Reaching across a meadow bordering the river Mayenne,
this delightful restaurant occupies a former walnut oil press.
An excellent lunch or dinner stop, it consists of five rooms
arranged on two floors which can seat over 200 diners. Two
outdoor terraces are also brought into use in fine weather.
There are several menus from which to choose – all *gastronomique*, which is the French term for dishes which use only
fresh market produce. Fish is a particular speciality. Open
noon–11pm for drinks and homemade pastries. Last orders:
lunch 2pm; dinner 10pm. Set menus from F98; à la carte
around F150.
*Fishing (permit from river beach café), tow-path walks, river swim-
ming and 18th-century windmill which can be visited*

CHERBOURG

🏨 🍽 56/84 🛏 ££

Mercure, Gare Maritime, 50100 Cherbourg.
Tel: 33.44.01.11
Open all year
Dbl rm F350–F580

A good overnight stop for those who do not want to drive
any further, this pleasant modern hotel – one of the Mercure
chain – overlooks both the yacht harbour and fishing port.
Bedrooms are comfortable and well equipped, but the best
water views are from the bar and restaurant which specializes
in traditional seafood dishes. Outdoor port-side terrace for
meals and drinks in summer. Last orders: lunch 2.30pm;
dinner 10.30pm. Set menus: from F98; à la carte around
F170.
*Ferry port for Portsmouth, Southampton, Poole, Rosslare (Eire) and
Channel Islands*

CHINON

🏨 ○| 9/18 ⌷ ££

La Boule d'Or, 66 Quai Jeanne-d'Arc, 37500 Chinon.
Tel: 47.93.03.13
Closed mid–December–end January; restaurant closed
Sunday evening and Monday mid–October–mid–April
Dbl rm F220–F320

A quayside road, which is fairly busy during the day, runs
between the river Vienne and this simple hotel in the heart of
medieval Chinon. A coaching inn dating back to the 18th
century, bedrooms at the front have good views across the
river to the Ile de Tours. The restaurant overlooks a pedestrianized street behind the hotel and its cooking enjoys a
good local reputation. *Coq au vin façon Boule d'Or* is a house
speciality, made to a secret recipe! The famous castle, where
Joan of Arc persuaded Charles VII to be crowned at Reims,
stands on a cliff behind the hotel. Last orders: lunch 2pm;
dinner 9.30pm. Set menus from F98; à la carte around F200.

CHOLET

🏨 ○| 4/8 ⌷ ££

Le Belvédère, Lac de Ribou, 49300 Cholet.
Tel: 41.62.14.02
Closed August and one week in February; restaurant
closed Sunday evening and Monday lunch
Dbl rm F295–F335
5km south-east of Cholet off D20

This attractive modern hotel stands on a rise above the Lac de
Ribou so that both the comfortable bedrooms and the
prettily furnished dining-rooms enjoy fine views of sailing
boats gliding across the lake. The talented Japanese chef,
Monsieur Inagaki, trained in France and is noted for his
delicately flavoured fish and seafood dishes. He will also
prepare Japanese specialities on request. In summer, meals

are also served on two outdoor terraces. Last orders: lunch 2.30pm; dinner 9.30pm. Set menus from F110 (Sunday F180); à la carte around F200.

Rowing boats, sailing dinghies, sailboards, pedalos, canoes and kayaks for hire; public tennis courts; golf course 3km

CLECY

🏠 🍽 <u>12/13</u> 🛏 ££

Moulin du Vey, Le Vey, 14570 Clécy.   Tel: 31.69.71.08
Closed December 1–28
Dbl rm F370–F460

This lovely creeper-covered watermill alongside the river Orne provides a tranquil retreat in the heart of Normandy. Bedrooms are handsomely decorated in different period styles, from rustic Norman to Louis XV, and below the windows a rushing stream gently turns the mill wheel. The restaurant occupies an old Norman barn adjacent to the mill, but it is far more pleasant to dine on the riverside terrace, which is used even on fine winter days. Refined versions of traditional regional dishes, including lobster in a creamy sauce. Half-board preferred in high season. Last orders: lunch 2pm; dinner 9.15pm. Set menus from F130; à la carte around F250.

Kayaks and canoes for hire, fishing (permits sold in the village), walks along the banks of the Orne; hang-gliding, tennis and riding within 1km

CLECY

☕ 🛏 £

La Potinière, 14570 Clécy.   Tel: 31.69.76.75
Open April 1–September 30
From Clécy follow the road towards the river, turn right just before bridge, then second left

Almost opposite the Moulin du Vey, this open-air café and crêperie occupies a wooden terrace overhanging a pretty part of the river Orne. It is a great place to relax and watch the boaters on the river. Brigitte Fraslin does a good trade in homemade cider as well as delicious crêpes, galettes, and salads, and a local speciality called *La Tourgoule*, a sort of rice pudding with cinammon. During July and August, there are live jazz or *café–théâtre* performances on Friday evenings. Open 10am–midnight.

Wooden Norman rowing boats and pedalos available for hire

CONCARNEAU

🏨 🍴 <u>43/48</u> 🛏 ££

Des Sables Blancs, Plage des Sables Blancs, 29900 Concarneau.   Tel: 98.97.01.39
Open April 1–October 31
Dbl rm F170–F290

A traditional seaside hotel with splendid views over the white sandy beach and the sea even from ground–floor bedrooms. Rooms are decorated in a simple homely style and would benefit from a facelift, but they offer good value for money. There are two dining-rooms, both specializing in fish and seafood dishes. There is also a beach–front terrace which operates as a bar–brasserie, open noon–10pm. Half-board is compulsory June 15–Sept 15. Last orders: lunch 1.45pm; dinner 9.15pm. Set menus from F80; à la carte around F110. *Concarneau is one of France's largest fishing ports and has a picturesque medieval walled town. Good safe swimming, boat hire, all watersports, hydrojet excursions to Iles de Glénan and along river Odet*

CONCARNEAU

🍴 🛏 £££

La Coquille, 1 Quai du Moros, 29900 Concarneau.
Tel: 98.97.08.52
Closed January, May 21–June 4 and Monday

Set directly on the quayside, with window tables overlooking the comings and goings in the busy commercial port, La Coquille is celebrated for its delicious fresh seafood dishes, especially lobster, prepared by owner–chef Jean-Francois Le Maitre. A particular speciality is *blanquettes de la mer*, a mixture of fish and seafood in a white sauce. There are three small, cosy dining-rooms. Do not pass up the opportunity to visit the bar where a highly entertaining parrot called Jacquot holds court, singing and whistling French wartime favourites and *La Marseillaise*. There is also a waterside terrace which is open in summer for both lunch and dinner. Last orders: lunch 2pm; dinner 9.30pm. Set menus from F150; à la carte around F250.

CONFOLENS

🏛 ΙΟΙ 5/14 🛏 £

Hôtel de Vienne, 4 Rue de la Ferrandie, 16500 Confolens. Tel: 45.84.09.24
Closed October 22–November 15, December 22–January 5; restaurant closed Saturday evening and Sunday (October–March), and Friday evening and Saturday (April–mid-June)
Dbl rm F250

This attractive 18th-century building backs on to the river Vienne where a large flower-decked terrace, where both meals and drinks are served, looks down over an old stone bridge across the river. Run by the charming and hospitable Dupré family, bedrooms are agreeably furnished, despite displaying that odd French habit of putting floral wallpaper on the ceilings. Nearly all have en-suite bathrooms. The restaurant serves traditional regional dishes including home-made terrines and *pâtisserie*. Last orders: lunch 2pm; dinner 9pm. Set menus from F58; à la carte around F150.
Confolens is a picturesque little town full of medieval and Renaissance buildings

CONNELLES

🏨 🍴 27/27 🛏 £££

Moulin de Connelles, Connelles, 27430
St-Pierre-du-Vauvray.   Tel: 32.59.53.33
Closed three weeks in November
Dbl rm F600–F850

This beautiful 19th-century half-timbered manor house and mill stand on a small island in the Seine with some rooms actually spanning the river. Completely renovated two years ago, the spacious bedrooms are extremely comfortable and tastefully decorated, their walls hung with copies of pictures by Impressionist painters associated with the area. All the restaurant's tables have water views. Chef Olivier Souyge trained under Paul Bocuse and his light modern versions of traditional Norman dishes are gaining a strong local following. In summer, outdoor barbecues are held. Last orders: lunch 2pm; dinner 9.30pm. Set menus from F140; à la carte around F300.
The hotel has a swimming pool, tennis court, rowing boats for guests, and offers fishing on a private island with permits purchased at reception

LE CONQUET

🏨 🍴 37/49 🛏 ££

Hôtel de la Pointe Sainte Barbe, BP 21, 29217
Le Conquet.   Tel: 98.89.00.26
Closed November 12–December 18; restaurant closed Monday excluding bank holidays and July 1–September 15
Dbl rm F169–F572

The brightness of the light on the Pointe Sainte Barbe attracts many film crews to this peninsula, the most westerly place on mainland France. The hotel sits on a bluff facing directly west, its rooms suffused with a clear, intense light reflected from the sparkling waters below. Clean, but unimaginatively decorated, this is a good overnight stop. Two rooms are specially equipped for the disabled. All the restaurant's tables have panoramic views over the port, beach and offshore islands. Fresh fish and seafood is the order of the day. There is also an outdoor terrace bar. Last orders: lunch 2pm; dinner 9.30pm. Set menus from F88; à la carte around F220.

Stairs to sandy beach (there are seven sandy coves in the vicinity); lovely walks along the coastal path to Pointe St Mathieu lighthouse and 13th-century abbey church

LE CONQUET

🏠 🍴 <u>12/28</u> 💳 £

Le Marianna, Plage du Trez–Hir, Plougonvelin, 29217 Le Conquet.   Tel: 98.48.30.02
Open Easter–Oct 30; restaurant closes beginning of September
Dbl rm F220–F230; family rooms F340

An ideal place for a family holiday with young children, the Marianna sits at one end of a beautiful long beach of white sand. Bedrooms are cheerfully decorated with attractive modern furnishings and pine ceilings, although the attached bathrooms are on the small side. There are separate children's rooms with bunk beds. First-floor rooms have access to a shared sun terrace. The restaurant does not face the sea, but the bar, decorated 1890s Louisiana saloon-style, has a panoramic view over the bay from its two terraces and is open for breakfast, drinks and ice-creams 8am–1am. Last orders: lunch 2pm; dinner 10.30pm. Set menus from F72; à la carte around F100.

Sandy beach; nautical centre offering sailing, windsurfing and scuba-diving lessons; local tennis courts; bicycles and sea canoes can be hired from hotel; boat excursions from Le Conquet to remote islands of Molène and Ouessant

LA COTINIERE

🏨 20/45 ▭ ££

Motel Ile de Lumière, La Cotinière, 17310
St-Pierre-d'Oléron.   Tel: 46.47.10.80
Open Easter–September 30
Dbl rm F450–F620; family apartments F900–F1100

Motel is a misnomer for this attractive collection of neat
white one- and two-storey units built around a good-sized
swimming pool on the largest of the offshore islands of
France's Atlantic coast. Bedrooms are spacious and comfortably furnished and have lovely views over a quiet dune-
backed beach, just outside the lively fishing port of La
Cotinière. The owners are welcoming and helpful in arran-
ging boat trips.
*Safe bathing beach; hotel tennis court, sauna and gym; watersports,
boat trips and riding in the resort, 9-hole golf course 8km*

COULON

🏨 |○| 5/11 ▭ ££

Au Marais, 46–48 Quai Louis Tardy, 79510 Coulon.
Tel: 49.35.90.43
Closed mid-November–Easter; restaurant closed
Sunday evening and Monday
Dbl rm F350
A11 exit Niort 23km

In the heart of the *Venise verte* of the Marais poitevin, this
charming stone hotel overlooks the river Sèvre Niortaise in
the exceptionally pretty village of Coulon. Bedrooms are
comfortable, unfussy and spotlessly clean. The intimate
quay-front restaurant serves imaginatively cooked *cuisine de
coeur*, using only fresh local produce. A particular speciality is
its delicious grapefruit tart. Guests staying at the hotel must
take one meal a day in the restaurant. Last orders: lunch 2pm;
dinner 9.30pm. Set menus from F98; à la carte around F300.

Small boats for hire and boat trips on the 'couches', a network of natural canals that criss-cross this region; mini-bus excursions to discover 'Le Marais Secret'

LE CROISIC

🏨 🍽 14/14 🛏 ££

Le Grand Hôtel de l'Océan, Place de Port-Lin, 44490 Le Croisic.   Tel: 40.62.90.03
Open all year
Dbl rm F420–F550

The sea foams against the rocks below this century-old hotel and restaurant built at the water's edge on a granite outcrop. Frequented by the rich and famous over the years, from Edith Piaf and Maurice Chevalier to the Rainers and President Mitterand, it is a peaceful seaside retreat. The large seaside resort of La Baule lies 10km away and a little further is the resort of St Marc-sur-Mer where the French classic *Les Vacances de Monsieur Hulot* was filmed. Most of the pleasantly decorated, comfortable bedrooms have balconies or terraces with panoramic views of the peninsula. The restaurant, specializing in fish and seafood (try the sea bass baked in salt), occupies an elegant enclosed verandah so all diners can enjoy the fabulous ocean views. A traditional English tea is served at 5pm. Last orders: lunch 2.30pm; dinner 10pm. No set menus; à la carte around F250.
Small sandy beach with safe swimming, fishing, watersports nearby

DAMGAN

🏨 🍽 16/24 🛏 ££

L'Albatros, 1 Boulevard de l'Océan, 56750 Damgan.
Tel: 97.41.16.85
Open April 1–early October
Dbl rm F230–F320
On beach 500m from town centre

An attractive modern hotel on a gorgeous stretch of Breton beach, L'Albatros provides a peaceful, value-for-money base for bucket-and-spade holidays. The bedrooms are very clean, prettily furnished and well equipped, although only half have en-suite bathrooms. One room is specially adapted for disabled guests. The two pleasant dining-rooms specialize in fish and seafood platters which are popular with locals and tourists alike, as is the outdoor terrace bar which overlooks the beach. Last orders: lunch 2pm; dinner 9pm. Set menus from F78; à la carte F150.

Good beach for swimming, tennis, windsurfing, sailing, riding 10km

DEAUVILLE

🏢 ⚬ 82/310 🛏 ££££

Hôtel Normandy, 38 Rue Jean Mermoz, 14800 Deauville.   Tel: 31.98.66.22
Open all year
Dbl rm F1270–F2000

While the gables, half-timbering, and cobbled courtyards create the impression of a rambling Norman manor, this hotel's interior is pure jet-set. During July and August, international celebrities, politicians and film stars come here to see and be seen. The luxurious bedrooms are decorated in a refined tasteful style and the recently renovated public rooms are cool and elegant. If you have children, a nursery, with qualified nanny, and membership of the Mickey Club on the beach are available free to guests. Although the hotel's dining rooms have no sea view, the same hotel group owns Ciro's, a smart beach restaurant on Deauville's famous *Planches*, a boardwalk that runs the length of the beach. Last orders: lunch 2.30pm, dinner 9.15pm. Set menus from F175; à la carte around F300. Tel. 31.88.18.10 for reservations at Ciro's.

Hotel has an indoor heated swimming pool, sauna, solarium and gym and offers a range of complimentary activities: tennis, bicycling,

golf lessons and free drinks and entry to weekend shows at casino.
Summer events include July jazz festival, Deauville races in August
and American film festival in September

DEAUVILLE

IOI ▭ ££

Bar du Soleil, Boulevard de la Mer, 14800 Deauville.
Tel: 31.88.04.74
Open all year; November 11–March 23 weekends only

Since 1925, the rich and famous have enjoyed watching the
world go by from this unpretentious bar and brasserie on the
Planches promenade opposite the casino. Surprisingly, prices
are not outrageous, and the best views are from the terrace,
which is protected from the wind by a glass screen. Here
breakfast, lunch and drinks are served; meat and fish kebabs
are a particular speciality. Open 9am–8pm. Weekday set
lunch F95 (children F55); à la carte around F200.
The bar has its own private beach opposite with loungers and parasols
for hire and waiter service

DIEPPE

▥ IOI **57/89** ▭ ££

La Présidence, 1 Boulevard de Verdun, 76200 Dieppe.
Tel: 35.84.31.31
Open all year
Dbl rm F350–F850

Wedged between an ancient town gate and the castle, the
functional facade of this modern hotel belies the warm
welcome and comfort found inside. The recently renovated
bedrooms are cheerfully decorated and well equipped. There
are also three rooms specially adapted for disabled guests. The
fourth-floor restaurant and grill makes the most of its elevated
position, with 16 tables enjoying expansive views over the
castle, the chalk cliffs and a broad sweep of bay. Last orders:

lunch 3pm; dinner 10pm (limited menu until 1am). Set menus from F150; à la carte around F200.

Heated swimming pool and good clay tennis courts at casino opposite, pebble beach, sea fishing

DINAN

🏨 8/8 ⊟ ££

Les Rossignols, Le Port de Dinan, 22100 Dinan.
Tel: 96.39.11.48
Open all year
Dbl rm F250; apartments (2-night minimum stay) from F400 a night

This 17th-century Breton manor enjoys beautiful views across the river Rance to the historic, walled town of Dinan on the opposite bank. Only a tow-path separates the hotel from the river, making it a much quieter base than hotels in Dinan itself. Painstakingly restored five years ago by the Leach family from Tunbridge Wells, who live on the premises, it comprises six apartments and two double bedrooms. Great care has been taken to preserve its original features, heavy wooden beams and granite walls, and the well-furnished apartments consist of two to four bedrooms, sitting/dining room and well-equipped kitchens with smart oak units. There is no restaurant but the *salon de thé* serves English teas and home-baked cakes, snacks and drinks, served on a terrace which benefits from the evening sun. Dinan's restaurants are just a few minutes' walk away. Book early for high season; children over 12 preferred due to the spiral staircases.

Electric boats, canoes and kayaks for hire; bicycles can be rented from hotel; good tow-path walks, fishing (no permit needed from hotel's pontoon) swimming pools nearby

DINARD

🏠 9/10 🛏 £££

Reine Hortense, 19 Rue de la Malouine, 35800 Dinard.
Tel: 99.46.54.31
Open April 1–November 15
Dbl rm F750–F1300

Built as a private villa for Queen Hortense, mother of
Napoleon III and Queen of Holland, this palatial yet small
hotel still evokes the *belle époque* although it is now surrounded by tall modern hotels and apartments. It stands
directly above the beach and has lovely views over the bay
and the fortifications of St Malo. Bedrooms are spacious and
richly decorated: No. 4 contains the Queen's elaborate
ballustraded bath; the rest have recent modern bathrooms
with Jacuzzis. The beautiful Salon contains some of the
Queen's belongings. No restaurant. If the Reine Hortense
is full, ask for a room in the new Castel Eugénie, its sister hotel
next door, which contains seven bedrooms romantically
furnished in Louis-Philippe style.
*Beach with charming old-fashioned changing cabins, large public pool
nearby, casino. Boat trips to St Malo (10 mins), Cap Fréhel,
Cézembre Island (good beach), Chaussey Islands, and up the river
Rance to Dinan*

DUCEY

🏠 21/28 🛏 ££

Le Moulin de Ducey, 1 Grande Rue, 50220 Ducey.
Tel: 33.60.25.25
Open all year
Dbl rm F360–F470

A working flour-mill until destroyed by fire five years ago, its
ancient walls now contain a comfortable hotel. Bedrooms are
spacious and furnished in a smart rustic style with pretty views
over a weir on the Sélune river, an islet, and a 16th-century

stone bridge. There are two rooms equipped for disabled guests. You can request a full English breakfast in the pretty breakfast room which has similar lovely river views.

Salmon and trout fishing (permits available in village), pleasant walks around lakes on dammed Sélune river 15km away

ECLUZELLES

🍽 🛏 £££

Le Saint Louis and L'Aquaparc, 28 Rue Etienne Malassis, 28500 Ecluzelles.   Tel: 37.43.74.75
Open all year

This smart modern restaurant complex opens on to a pretty, landscaped park of 25 acres leading down to a lake. Of the 30 tables in Le Saint Louis, 12 have lake views. The *gastronomique* cooking is based around seasonal market produce and has a good local reputation. Specialities include seafood, fresh-water fish and game. There is also an outdoor terrace for meals and drinks in fine weather. Last orders: lunch 2.15pm; dinner 10pm. Set menus from F120; à la carte around F250. Reservations advised.

Sailing boats and sail-boards for hire from school on other side of lake, free fishing for restaurant clients, lakeside promenade

ERQUY

🍽 🛏 £££

L'Escurial, Boulevard de la Mer, 22430 Erquy.
Tel: 96.72.31.56
Closed January 1–15; Tuesday evening and Wednesday except during July and August

All 11 round tables in this attractive restaurant overlook the bay of Erquy, the scallop-fishing capital of France. Presided over by talented female chef, Véronique Bernard, it has a peaceful, romantic ambience with dining by candle-light. Seafood, especially *Coquilles St Jacques* prepared in a tart with

mushrooms and a coulis of shellfish, is the speciality but the menus, unlike many on the Breton coast, also cater for meat lovers. Last orders: lunch 2pm; dinner 10pm (summer), 9pm (winter). Set menus from F98; à la carte around F250.
Good sandy swimming beaches, sailing school, scuba-diving, boat trips around coast, footpaths over Cap d'Erquy

ETABLES-SUR-MER

🏚 ⊙ 2/5 ▭ ₤₤

La Colombière, Boulevard du Littoral, 22680
Etables-sur-Mer.   Tel: 96.70.61.64
Closed Oct 1–15; restaurant closed Sunday evening
and Monday except mid-June–mid-September
Dbl rm F260–F495
Just off the N786 2km north of Etables at Notre-Dame-de-l'Espérance.

Situated on the edge of a cliff, this old Breton house has a bird's-eye view of the bay of St-Brieuc. The interior is cosy, with tiled floors, leather chairs, and beamed ceilings. Bedrooms are comfortably furnished with large, modern bathrooms although only two have good sea views. The restaurant occupies a large, airy verandah so all tables have magnificent coastal views and, in summer, a further five tables are set out on a terrace in the garden from where you can also see the sea. Fish and crustaceans are the specialities. Guests are requested to take half-board in season. Last orders: lunch 2.30pm; dinner 10pm. Set menus from F98; à la carte around F250.
Sheltered sandy beaches; sailing, windsurfing and scuba-diving nearby; riding 5km; daily ferry to Jersey takes 1hr 45mins each way

ETRETAT

🏚 ⊙ 4/8 ▭ ₤₤₤

Le Donjon, Chemin de St-Clair, 76790 Etretat.
Tel: 35.27.08.23

Open all year
Half-board only, F600–F800 per person

This charming hotel, covered in creepers, occupies a 10th-century fortified keep famous for its once-secret underground passageway to the beach, closed since the railway was built in 1900. In a quiet location above the resort, it has fabulous views over the chalk cliffs, weathered into arches and stacks. Madame Abo-Dib, who returned to her native Normandy from Australia, takes great care of guests, and public rooms are decorated with intriguing memorabilia from her travels. Bedrooms are beautifully decorated in different styles (l'Orientale and l'Horizon have best views). The restaurant, which specializes in seafood and duck (*canard à la presse*), has panoramic views of the bay. Last orders: lunch 2pm; dinner 10.30pm (summer). Set menus from F110; à la carte around F250.
Outdoor hotel swimming pool, nearby tennis and golf, good cliff-top walks

EVRON

🏨 🍴 12/26 🛏 ££

Relais du Gué de Selle, Mézangers, 53600 Evron.
Tel: 43.90.64.05
Closed two weeks in February, a week in November and over Christmas and New Year
Dbl rm F310–F420
Evron 5km

A good base for an active holiday, this old farmhouse and its outbuildings have been converted into an appealing hotel on the banks of a beautiful little lake. Bedrooms are comfortable and good value, all with satellite television. There are several family rooms sleeping up to four, and one equipped for disabled guests. The country-style restaurant serves fresh local produce – beef, lamb, chicken and pike – with *gâteau de brochet à l'avocat* (pike in avocado) a particular speciality.

Although the restaurant itself has no water views, there is a waterside terrace for drinks in fine weather and talk of allowing people to eat here too. Last orders: lunch 2pm; dinner 9pm. Set menus from F80; à la carte around F200
Beach for lake swimming (safe for children), sailing and windsurfing – hire and tuition at leisure centre, pedalo and bicycle hire, tennis, pike fishing permits F18 a day

FECAMP

IOI ▭ £££

Le Viking, 63 Boulevard Albert I, 76400 Fécamp.
Tel: 35.29.22.92
Open all year; closed Monday and, in winter,
Sunday evening

This comfortable, modern first-floor restaurant, with its Nordic decor and large tinted windows, stands on the seafront at Fécamp. Its elevated position affords stunning views of the high chalk cliffs stretching away towards Etretat and, on summer evenings, of sunset over the Channel. Fish and crustaceans are the specialities, also Benedictine soufflé. Downstairs there is a brasserie and self-service restaurant which enjoys similar good sea views. Last orders: lunch 2.30pm; dinner 9.30pm. Set menus from F105 (weekdays), F155 (weekends); à la carte around F200.
Safe shingle beach, fishing from rocks, ruined castle of Dukes of Normandy, guided tours of Benedictine distillery and museum, interesting municipal museum with beautiful ivory carvings, 12th-century abbey church

FENESTRELAY

IOI ▭ ££

Auberge du Vieux Moulin, Fenestrelay, 18390
St-Germain-du-Puy.   Tel: 48.24.60.45
Closed Sunday evening and Monday

This 16th-century watermill stands in lovely grounds on the outskirts of Bourges offers traditional regional cooking in a romantic setting. Tables in the charmingly arranged dining-room in the mill itself have no water views, but there is a large conservatory in an enchanting setting beneath an ancient willow on the riverbank where barbecued fish and meat are served. Last orders: lunch 1.45pm; dinner 9.45pm. Set menus from F90 (barbecue), F103 (restaurant); à la carte around F190.

FILLE-SUR-SARTHE

IOI ⊟ ££

Le Barrage, Fillé, 72210 La Suze-sur-Sarthe.
Tel: 43.87.14.40
Closed Sunday evening and Wednesday

This charming restaurant occupies a particularly tranquil spot on the banks of the river Sarthe in the pretty country village of Fillé. Most tables have a view of the river, but from April to September choose an outdoor table on the verandah or beside the tow-path. Imaginative *nouvelle cuisine* dishes based on fresh produce from local markets. Fish is a speciality; try the *rosace de melon et de saumon à l'huile d'olive*. Last orders: lunch 2pm; dinner 9pm. Set menus from F75; à la carte around F200. Reservations advised (owner Didier Loysance speaks English).
Pontoon for boaters to tie up to; tow-path to dam and old mill, pike fishing (permits are sold in the village)

FLAMANVILLE

IOI ⅔ ⊟ £

Le Sémaphore, Flamanville, 50340 Les Pieux.
Tel: 33.52.18.98
Closed November; restaurant closed Wednesday excluding July and August

Dbl rm F150–F200
Turn right after Château de Flamanville and follow signs

This pretty white house, formerly used as a naval signal
station, stands alone on a barren cliff-top. The simple restaurant occupies a semi-circular room with marvellous views
over the rugged coastline and the sea far below. Grilled fish,
salads, crêpes and galettes dominate the menu and, in summer, meals and drinks are also served on an outdoor terrace.
The two bedrooms are simple and neat (only one has an en-
suite bathroom) and there is also a small dormitory for
backpackers. Last orders: lunch 2pm; dinner 10.30pm (summer), 9pm (winter). Set menus from F78; à la carte around
F110.
*Sandy beach 20-minute walk; coastal footpath; fishing from rocks;
ferry from Diélette 3km away to Guernsey (75 minutes) and Sark (1
hour)*

FLEURY-SUR-ORNE

IOI ▭ ££

Auberge de l'Ile Enchantée, Fleury-sur-Orne, 14123 Ifs.
Tel: 31.52.15.52
Closed two weeks in February, Sunday evening and Monday

Just off a busy road on the outskirts of Caen, this appealing
restaurant has an unexpectedly quiet and charming riverside
location, looking across to the islet after which it is named. It
is a perfect place for that last French supper before taking the
ferry from Caen to Portsmouth. Arranged on two floors, the
dining-rooms have a comfortable, rustic ambience. Specialities include fish and homemade duck liver paté. Window
tables on both levels overlook the green, wooded banks of
the Orne and the islet. Last orders: lunch 2pm; dinner
9.30pm. Set menus available from F125; à la carte around
F250.

LA FLOTTE

🏨 ΙΟΙ <u>20/40</u> 🍽 £££

Le Richelieu, 44 Avenue de la Plage, 17630 La Flotte.
Tel: 46.09.60.70
Closed January
Dbl rm F500–F1400

This elegant modern villa offers the height of luxury on the
pretty Ile-de-Ré, joined by a causeway to La Rochelle. The
staff contribute to the discreet, relaxing ambience. Bedrooms
in the main villa are immaculate, furnished with reproduction Louis XV pieces, and 14 have large terraces overlooking
the sea. Three rooms are suitable for disabled guests. The
dining-room and its beautiful covered terrace overlook the
bay and the first-class seafood is the thing to order here. Half-
board is compulsory in high season, at weekends and over
national holidays. Last orders: lunch 2.30pm; dinner
10.30pm. Set menus from F220; à la carte around F400.
*Hotel has heated outdoor pool, tennis court, billiard room and thalass-
otherapy and aromatherapy health and beauty treatment centre.
Nearby watersports school and riding. Bicycles can be rented from
the village to follow the cycling track around this picturesque island*

FOURAS

ΙΟΙ 🍽 ££

La Jetée, Pointe de la Fumée, 17450 Fouras.
Tel: 46.84.60.43
Closed two weeks in January, December 1–15 and Tuesday
except July 1–September 15

While not the most attractive looking building, this is a
popular and lively seafood restaurant in a busy fishing
port. Specialities include *la chaudré de la Mère Bichaud*, a
pan of mixed fish in a white wine and garlic sauce, which
is still made by the owner's mother. Around ten tables have
spectacular views over the Ile-d'Aix and the Ile-de-Ré. The

Ile-d'Aix ferry leaves from the jetty opposite every hour in summer and three times a day in winter. Last orders: lunch 3pm; dinner 9.30pm. Set menus from F85; à la carte around F250.

FREHEL

IOI ▭ £

La Fauconnière, Le Cap Fréhel, 22240 Fréhel.
Tel: 96.41.54.20
Open April 1–September 30

Clinging to the cliff edge at the end of the Cap Fréhel point, this simple restaurant and bar offers a stunning panorama of the coast around St Malo. Popular with sightseers and walkers, it serves omelettes, fresh fish and seafood cooked with herbs and spices. The pastries are also delicious. Open 10am–7pm daily. Dinner served July 10–August 20; last orders 9pm. Set menus from F100; à la carte around F130.
A path beside the restaurant leads down to a platform where cormorants and seagulls nest on mauve rocks; from the lighthouse opposite there are views as far as the Channel Islands; Les Sables d'Or, a lovely beach with safe swimming, lies 3km away

GIEN

▦ IOI <u>13/19</u> ▭ ££

Hôtel du Rivage, 1 Quai de Nice, 45500 Gien.
Tel: 38.67.20.53
Closed mid-February–mid-March
Dbl rm F350–F500

This chic hotel enjoys beautiful views over the Loire down to an old humpbacked stone bridge. Bedrooms, decorated in relaxing pastels, are very comfortable and include three family apartments. Facilities include an indoor pool. The prettily decorated restaurant is a romantic place for dinner by candle-light. It serves modern versions of classic French dishes including freshwater fish: *millefeuille de sandre et salmon aux genièvre et lie de vin* is a particular speciality. There are river views from window tables. Half-board is preferred between June and September. Last orders: lunch 2pm; dinner 9.15pm. Set menus from F155; à la carte around F300.

Sights of historic Gien include an international hunting museum and a famous earthenware factory and museum

ILE DE GROIX

🏨 🍴 10/12 🛏 ££

Hôtel de la Marine, 7 Rue du Général-de-Gaulle, 56590 Ile de Groix.   Tel: 97.86.80.05
Closed January; restaurant closed Sunday evening and Monday October–March
Dbl rm F209–F328
Ferry from Lorient takes 45 minutes; advance booking for cars advised

A 10-minute walk uphill from Port-Tudy, this hotel is a quieter base than those right on the port, and stands in a lovely garden dotted with sun loungers. The Hubert family provide a warm, friendly welcome. North-facing bedrooms on the upper floors, all recently renovated, have sea views. The restaurant has no water views but it does serve inventive fish and seafood dishes such as *feuilleté de coquilles St Jacques* and *langoustine poilé en persillade*. Half-board is compulsory during July and August. Last orders: lunch 2pm; dinner 10pm. Set menus from F68; à la carte around F150.

The Ile de Groix is a relaxing retreat best explored on foot or by hired bicycle. There are some lovely sandy beaches including Les Sables Blancs, an unusual convex-shaped beach which is famous for its rare minerals such as garnets found in the sand and on the rocks. Sailing, windsurfing and scuba-diving are on offer

GUISCRIFF

📶 ▬ £

La Salmonière, St-Eloi, 56560 Guiscriff.   Tel: 97.34.09.30
Closed mid-January–mid-February, Monday and Tuesday
Located 12km south of Guiscriff on road to St Thurien;
follow yellow signs 'La Salmonière'

Set in the middle of the countryside in a remote rural spot,
this flower-decked Breton stone mill complete with water-
wheel overlooks two private lakes and a stream. Most restaurant tables have some water view and in fine weather further
tables are set out on a small terrace under trees by the lakes.
Traditional French cooking; local river trout is a speciality.
Try the *truite rose aux pétoncles à la crème*, pink trout with little
scallops in a cream sauce. Last orders: lunch 2pm; dinner
9.30pm. Set menus from F75; à la carte around F150.
Trout fishing

HEDE

📶 ▬ ££

La Vieille Auberge, Route de St-Malo, 35630 Hédé.
Tel: 99.45.46.25
Closed mid-January – mid-February, last week of
August, Sunday evening and Monday
On N137 1km north of Hédé

A charming stone house set in a colourful garden overlooking a pond, this restaurant is popular with locals from nearby
Rennes. Although the view from the main dining-room is
obscured by shrubs, there are good views from the tables in
the *salon*. In summer, tables are set out on a waterside terrace,
providing the perfect setting for a romantic candle-lit dinner.
Lobster, crawfish, crab and homemade *fois gras* are the house
specialities. Last orders: lunch 1.30pm; dinner 9.30pm. Set
menus from F100; à la carte around F200.

HENNEBONT

🏠 🍽 15/24 🛏 £££

Château de Locguénolé, Route de Port-Louis, Kervignac,
56700 Hennebont.   Tel: 97.76.29.04
Closed January 2–February 8; restaurant closed Monday
and Tuesday lunch October–March
Dbl rm F620–F1300
From Hennebont take the D781 south (signposted Port-
Louis) for 4.5km

This solid early 19th-century manor in a pretty woodland
setting has commanding views over the estuary of the Blavet.
Madame de la Sablière's family has lived on the estate for
more than 500 years, and they have operated a prestigious
hotel and restaurant here since 1968. Bedrooms are spacious
and tastefully furnished with elegant antiques and Persian
carpets, as are the sitting rooms. Eight of the restaurant's
tables have water views and, in summer, meals are also
served on a terrace overlooking the estuary. The *cuisine
moderne* ensures lighter, innovative versions of traditional
French dishes, especially fish, while retaining decent-sized
portions. Half-board preferred July–September. Last orders:
lunch 2pm; dinner 9pm. Set menus from F190; à la carte
around F350.
*Chateau's 500-acre grounds contain marked walking trails, heated
outdoor pool, sauna, Turkish bath and tennis court; bicycles free of
charge; mooring for yachts available below chateau*

HERICOURT-EN-CAUX

🏠 🍽 8/13 🛏 £

Auberge de la Durdent, Route de Cany,
Héricourt-en-Caux, 76560 Doudeville.   Tel: 35.96.42.44
Closed one week in February and two weeks in November;
restaurant closed Monday during July and August;
Wednesday and Thursday lunch rest of the year
Dbl rm F220

The Durdent river actually runs beneath the dining-room of this delightful country inn, and diners can watch trout swim past through glass panels in the floor. Bedrooms are simply but nicely furnished, some with French windows which open out on to the lawn so that guests can enjoy breakfast overlooking the river. All the bedrooms have en-suite bathrooms. Specialities in the restaurant include smoked trout and salmon, which are farmed in the river, and cider-based sauces. There is also a waterside terrace open 8am–10pm in summer for drinks and snacks. Last orders: lunch 2pm; dinner 10pm. Set menus from F70; à la carte around F250.

Trout fishing in hotel grounds, mountain bikes for hire, pretty walks along the Durdent and nearby forest (hotel provides picnic hampers), riding 3km

HERRY

🍽 🛏 ££

Le Haut Berry, 48 Rue de Prieuré, 18140 Herry.
Tel: 48.79.51.56
Open March 1–October 31

This tastefully renovated barge takes visitors along the canal which runs alongside the Loire between Sancerre and La Charité, stopping off to taste some of the region's excellent wines and explore Sancerre's old town. Afterwards guests enjoy a good five-course lunch while cruising gently along the canal back to St Satur near Sancerre. The day trip lasts from 9am–5pm and costs about F265 including lunch. There are also half-day cruises and evening dinner and dance events on a moored boat.

HONFLEUR

🏚 33/33 🛏 ££

Le Cheval Blanc, 2 Quai des Passagers, 14600 Honfleur.
Tel: 31.89.13.49

Closed January
Dbl rm F356–F550

A hostelry since the 15th century, this appealing hotel stands at the entrance to the *Vieux Bassin*, Honfleur's impossibly picturesque inner harbour which is lined with tall, narrow dwellings hung with slates. Bedrooms, furnished in country floral prints, are quiet and comfortable with views either over the old fishing harbour or the more modern outer yacht harbour. Breakfast is included in the room price.
Fishing from jetty, sail-boats for hire, boat trips along the coast and down the River Seine.

HONFLEUR

▦ ◯ <u>24/39</u> ▭ ££££

Ferme Saint-Siméon, Rue Adolphe Marais, 14600 Honfleur.   Tel: 31.89.23.61
Open all year
Dbl rm F1750

Things have changed somewhat since Monet, Corot and Sisley came to paint at a simple farmhouse high above the estuary of the Seine. Though it is now an exclusive hotel, you can still sleep in the cosy *atelier* which was once Corot's studio and enjoy a fine view of the sea through its bay window. More spacious and luxurious accommodation is found in Le Pressoir, a stylish modern addition, and in an 18th-century manor house set in beautifully landscaped grounds. The farmhouse restaurant offers gastronomic cooking and, in summer, meals are served on a shady terrace overlooking the wide estuary. Last orders: lunch 2pm; dinner 9.30pm. Set menus from F240 (lunch), F420 (dinner); à la carte around F450.
Heated indoor pool with sea view; sauna, steam bath and hydro-massage, solarium, gym; tennis court in grounds; Seine cruises and yacht hire can be arranged.

HUISSEAU-SUR-COSSON

🏨 🍽 <u>10/10</u> 🛏 ££

Château de Nanteuil, Huisseau-sur-Cosson, 41350
Vineuil.   Tel: 54.42.61.98
Closed January 2–February 5, third week of November;
restaurant closed Monday and Tuesday lunch
Dbl rm F190–F350

The river Cosson, diverted into a mill-stream, runs past this
18th-century chateau built beside the source of a sacred
spring in a seven-acre park. Bedrooms are simply but attractively furnished, most with attached bath or shower and WC.
However, owner Frédéric Théry's main activity is his restaurant which seats 60 on its lovely waterside terrace. The menus
are well chosen and the accent is on fish, game in season, and
regional specialities. If you are here in May, seek out the
Asperges de Vineuil – the most expensive asparagus in France –
which is grown in this area. Monsieur Théry serves them
warm with a *sauce mousseline*, Hollandaise with lemon juice.
Guests must dine in the restaurant; half-board from F300 a
person. Last orders: lunch 2pm; dinner 9.30pm (summer).
Set menus from F110; à la carte around F200.

L'ILE BOUCHARD

🍽 🛏 ££

Auberge de l'Ile, 3 Place Bouchard, 37220 L'Ile Bouchard.
Tel: 47.58.51.07
Closed February, Sunday evening and Monday

Set on an island in the river Vienne, this unpretentious
restaurant serves imaginative and well-presented food, a
mixture of *cuisine moderne* and traditional regional favourites
such as freshly made ravioli stuffed with lobster and black
chanterelle mushrooms. In summer, French windows open
out on to a terrace overlooking a wide stretch of the river as it
flows under two bridges in the centre of this beautiful small

town. Very good, extensive wine list. Last orders: lunch 2pm; dinner 9pm. Set menus from F95 (weekday lunch), F160 (dinner); à la carte around F250.

Canoe and kayak hire, water-skiing, Loire chateaux and wine cellars nearby

LES ILES CHAUSEY

🏨 🍴 5/8 ✉ ♒

Hôtel du Fort et des Iles, 50400 Les Iles Chausey.
Tel: 33.50.25.02
Open mid-April–mid-September; restaurant closed
Monday for non-residents
Half-board only; from F240 per person
Ferry from Granville takes 1 hour

Built on one of the 70 islets that make up the Chausey archipelago, this delightful hotel is a perfect place to unwind. No cars or bicycles are allowed on the island and the hotel does not have a television set. It is a popular landfall for cross-Channel yachtsmen and although credit cards are not accepted you can pay with an English cheque supported by a banker's card. Owner Bernard Pichard, whose grandfather opened the hotel in 1928, sailed around the world before settling here. The panelled bedrooms, furnished in a simple nautical style, have breathtaking views over a seascape that changes dramatically as 40ft tides recede to reveal craggy granite outcrops, bays of white sand and rock pools teeming with marine life. Locally caught seafood – lobster, crab, oysters and mussels – is served in the cosy dining-room where all tables have sea views. Booking is essential for non-residents. There is a garden terrace for drinks. Last orders: lunch 2pm; dinner 9pm. Set menus from F95; à la carte around F250.

Several sandy beaches (one with lifeguard); hotel rents motorboats; beautiful coastal walks

IVRY-LA-BATAILLE

⫿◎ ▭ ⛢

Le Moulin d'Ivry, 10 Rue Henri IV, 27540
Ivry-la-Bataille.   Tel: 32.36.40.51
Closed one week in October and all February

Alone on an island in the middle of the river Eure, the water
flows both around and through this splendid old watermill in
a sleepy village. The dining-room is decorated in country
style with large old beams, an open fire, and crisp pink table
linen. Ten tables have lovely views across the river to some
old Norman houses and, in the summer, meals are served on
an open-air verandah which overhangs the water. Specialities
include duck in cider, monkfish curry, and game in season.
Last orders: lunch 2.30pm; dinner 10pm. Set menus from
F160; à la carte around F300.
Fishing (permits sold in village); lovely riverbank walks

JOSSELIN

⛫ ◎ **18/36** ▭ £

Hôtel du Château, 1 Rue Général-de-Gaulle, 56120
Josselin.   Tel: 97.22.20.11
Closed Christmas and February
Dbl rm F185–F280

This simple hotel–restaurant has a wonderful view over the
river Oust to the impressive battlements of Josselin castle,
built between the 11th and 15th centuries, directly opposite.
Bedrooms are clean and comfortable, most with attached
bathrooms. The castle, reflected in the still waters below,
soars above the restaurant's large windows, providing a
dramatic backdrop for lunch or a value-for-money overnight stop. Last orders: lunch 2pm; dinner 9pm. Set menus
from F70; à la carte around F150.
*Josselin is a picturesque old town with an early medieval basilica and
chapel, streets of 17th-century houses; the castle is open to the public*

JULLOUVILLE-LES-PINS

IOI ▭ ££

Le Casino, Place du Casino, 50160 Jullouville-les-Pins.
Tel: 33.61.82.82
Open April 1–November 15; closed Monday evening and
Tuesday except July–mid-September

Its days as a casino long gone, this seafront building now
houses a pleasant seafood restaurant and a brasserie. Both are
flooded with light and look out over a beautiful sandy beach,
crowded with holidaymakers in high summer. In the stylish
formal dining-room, menus concentrate on fresh fish and
seafood and locally reared meat. In fine weather, meals and
drinks are also served on a promenade-side terrace. Last
orders: lunch 2pm; dinner 10pm. Brasserie open noon–
11pm. Set menus from F95; à la carte around F160 (more
for seafood).
Safe sandy beach, sailing and windsurfing school, motorboats for hire;
tourist train and delta-plane for another view of the resort

JUMIEGES

IOI ▭ ££

L'Auberge du Bac, Jumièges, 76480 Duclair.
Tel: 35.37.24.16
Closed three weeks during January and February, Tuesday
evening and Wednesday except during July and August

A half-timbered farmhouse has been converted into this
friendly, intimate restaurant at a ferry-crossing point on the
Seine. Most tables in the dining-room have a river view, and
passing tankers and barges fill the windows as they sail from
Rouen to Le Havre and the open sea. There is a large
waterfront terrace open for meals and drinks which is enclosed and heated in winter months. Inventive regional
cooking including *blanquette de veau à l'ancienne*, a traditional
veal dish allowed to simmer for hours. Salmon, fish and game
is smoked in the auberge's own smokehouse. Try the *foie de*

lotte fumé – smoked turbot's liver. Last orders: lunch 2.30pm; dinner 9.30pm. Terrace bar open 9.30am–11pm. Set menus from F80; à la carte around F250.

Impressive ruins of Jumièges Abbey, riverside walks, car ferry across to Brotonne forest; situated on Routes des Fruits where you can pick your own fruit in summer

LOCHES

🏠 🍴 <u>9/20</u> 🛏 ££

Hôtel George Sand, 39 Rue Quintefol, 37600 Loches.
Tel: 47.59.39.74
Closed November 27–December 27
Dbl rm F200–F400

This 15th-century post-house stands on the main road beneath the castle. Many of the original beams and stone fireplaces were retained when it was restored in 1981 and a 15th-century spiral staircase leads up to the very comfortable bedrooms, each furnished in a different colour scheme. Ask for one overlooking the river as those on the road side can be noisy. There is also one ground-floor room suitable for disabled guests. The restaurant occupies the former stables where the eccentric novelist George Sand used to keep her horse. Virtually all the tables overlook the river Indre and there is a delightful riverside terrace in summer. Good regional cooking based on fresh market produce: *sandre au beurre de Chinon* (a sort of pike in a buttery red wine sauce) is a speciality. Last orders: lunch 2pm; dinner 9.30pm. Set menus from F85; à la carte around F200.

Fishing (permits are sold in town), municipal swimming pool and tennis courts 200m, convenient base for touring the Loire Valley

LOMENER

🏠 🍴 <u>14/14</u> 🛏 ££

Le Vivier, Lomener, 56270 Ploemeur.   Tel: 97.82.99.60

Closed January 1–15; restaurant closed Sunday
evening except during July and August
Dbl rm F330; four–person apartment F500
D163 4km south from Ploemeur

This attractive modern hotel built into the rocks on the edge
of the sea enjoys marvellous views from both rooms and
restaurant across to the Ile de Groix. Bedrooms are fairly
basic with modern furniture and showers not baths; two have
good balconies. Ten of the restaurant's tables directly overlook the sea and this, combined with its seafood specialities,
makes it a popular lunch venue with locals. There is a tank
containing live lobsters and crawfish. Last orders: lunch 2pm;
dinner 10.30pm. Set menus from F100; à la carte around
F200.
Small sandy coves popular with families, all watersports, fishing;
motorboats, sail-boards, canoes and kayaks for hire at Guidel-Plage
10km; golf and riding nearby; Oceanis centre (pool with water slides)
in Ploemeur

LORIENT

ⓘ ▭ ££

Café Leffe 'Le Skipper', Maison de la Mer, Quai de Rohan,
56100 Lorient.   Tel: 97.21.21.30
Open all year

Situated on the quayside of Lorient's large yacht harbour, this
is a good place to stop for a drink, a snack or a meal before
taking the ferry across to Belle-Ile or Ile de Groix. On the
ground floor there is an airy brasserie and café, open from
7.30am–2am in summer, with a large covered terrace. The
restaurant occupies a glass conservatory on the first floor and
specializes in seafood. You can also find delicious homemade
ice-cream here with a choice of over 30 flavours and a range
of Belgian draught beers. Last orders: lunch 2.30pm; dinner
11pm. Set menus from F78; à la carte around F200.
Boats for Port Louis and islands leave from in front of the restaurant

LUYNES

🏨 ○| 22/40 ▭ ₤₤₤

Domaine de Beauvois, 37230 Luynes.
Tel: 47.55.50.11
Closed January 15–March 15
Dbl rm F660–F1360
On D49 2km north of Luynes, signposted Cléré-les-Pins

Sumptuously furnished in mainly 18th-century style, this elegant chateau surmounted with a 15th-century tower overlooks the valley of the river Bresme and a pond. It stands on an ancient estate where King Louis XIII used to enjoy hawking with the Duc de Luynes. The concièrge, Bryan Byron, is Welsh so English-only speakers will have no problems. The cuisine and the wine cellar are outstanding, although none of the restaurant's tables have water views. Last orders: lunch 2pm; dinner 9.15pm. Set menus from F190 (lunch), F260 (dinner); à la carte around F320.
Heated outdoor pool and tennis court; hotel lends bicycles and tackle for fishing; walks in 400 acres of woodland alongside the river Bresme; helicopter and hot-air balloon flights over Loire chateaux can be organized from hotel; riding 3km; golf 12km

MANSLE

🏨 ○| 10/10 ▭ ₤

Les Trois Saules, St-Groux, 16230 Mansle.
Tel: 45.20.31.40
Closed February 21–March 7, October 31–November 15; restaurant closed Sunday evening and Monday lunch October–Easter
Dbl rm F190–F240
Mansle 3km

Attractively situated on the banks of an arm of the river Charente in the tiny village of St-Groux, this charming hotel has been a family concern for three generations and is a particularly good place to stay if you have young children. Bedrooms are simply but comfortably furnished, all with showers, and all enjoy views over the river. An open wood fire burns in the restaurant on cool evenings. The menus concentrate on simple hearty fare at very good prices, and drinks are served on a terrace overlooking its pretty grounds leading down to the river. Children's playground in the gardens. Last orders: lunch 1.45pm; dinner 9pm. Set menus from F58; à la carte around F120.

In village, rowing boats, bicycles and canoes for hire, public swimming pool, fishing (permits sold in Mansle), shady riverbank walks

MANSLE

🏨 🍽 16/32 🛏 £

Hôtel Beau Rivage, 16230 Mansle.   Tel: 45.20.31.26
Closed three weeks in November; restaurant closed Sunday evening October–May
Dbl rm F215–F230
Angoulême 26km south

This large modern hotel on the banks of the river Charente is a good value stopover. The spacious, airy bedrooms are adequately furnished, half with en-suite bathrooms, and all with balconies overlooking either the river or a bridge. There is a prettily decorated restaurant and, in summer, meals are served on a terrace beside Monsieur Louis' beautiful rose garden which runs down to the river. Last orders: lunch 1.30pm; dinner 9.30pm. Set menus from F64; à la carte around F145.

Rowing boats, canoes and mountain bikes free for guests; lovely riverside walks; fishing (permit available in village)

MANSLE

🍽 🛏 £

La Marmite, 16230 Mansle.   Tel: 45.22.20.48

Closed 10 days in February, first two weeks of October and Monday except during July and August

Close to the Charente river, La Marmite is the ideal restaurant in the area for a relaxed meal – particularly for families. Stone built, the restaurant's interior is spacious and rustic, while the large outdoor terrace by the stream is well protected from the sun by parasols. It adjoins a play area for children which has swings, as well as ducks, chickens and other assorted birds; adults can supervise their offspring without stirring from their chairs. The unflappable patrons, Helena and Renée Riffaud, who have two young children of their own, cook and serve hearty traditional fare at reasonable prices – salmon trout with sorrel is a speciality – and simple children's meals are also available. Helena is English, so although the restaurant is typically French, translation is readily available. Last orders: lunch 2pm; dinner 9pm. Set menus from F53 (children F32); à la carte around F120.

MELLE

2/4 £

Le Moulin de Gennebrie, 79500 Melle.   Tel: 49.07.11.96
Open all year
Dbl rm F140
From Melle take D950 to Brioux. After 10km turn right to Périgné; mill 1.5km further on

This 400-year-old mill, covered in ivy, is lovingly looked after by Monsieur Merigeau who will set its wheels in motion for interested guests. Two of the four bedrooms are in the attic, and all prettily decorated with wonderful antique furniture. Bathroom facilities are shared. Winding paths thread across the lush, tranquil grounds to shady arbours. Breakfast is served under tall willows beside the stream. There is also cheaper dormitory-style accommodation for

walkers and cyclists which costs F25 a night, but you will need to bring your own sleeping bag.
Private 50-acre park, fishing (permits sold in village), rowing boats lent by owner

MESCHERS-SUR-GIRONDE

🏨 ○| **6/6** 🛏 ££

Les Grottes de Matata, 17132 Meschers-sur-Gironde.
Tel: 46.02.70.02
Hotel open all year; restaurant open June 1–Sept 15
Dbl rm F250–F350

This is rather a special place, literally carved into the cliffs with delightful views over the estuary of the Gironde. The small hotel opened last summer and all the rooms have sea views through bay windows. Dug into the cliffs below, the long-established restaurant is a convivial place, popular with locals as well as tourists. All the tables have water views and there is an outdoor dining terrace on the cliff's edge. Seafood is the order of the day. There is also a crêperie and cocktail bar open 11am–midnight in summer. Last orders: lunch 1.30pm; dinner 10.30pm. Set menus from F120; à la carte around F200.

MESLON

○| 🛏 ££

La Source, Meslon, 18210 Coust.   Tel: 48.63.53.80
Open all year
A71 Exit 9, 20km south on N144

This simple auberge sits beside a small lake and provides a tranquil stop for a meal or a drink. Although none of the inside tables have water views, you can dine on a lakeside terrace which is open whenever the weather is fine. Freshly prepared dishes using seasonal produce. Last orders: lunch

2pm; dinner 10.30pm. Drinks and snacks available 9am—
midnight. Set menus from F60; à la carte around F130.
Nearby beautiful ancient Troncais forest with lake for windsurfing

MOELAN-SUR-MER

🏠 |○| 23/27 ⊟ £££

Les Moulins du Duc, 29350 Moelan-sur-Mer.
Tel: 98.39.60.73
Closed January 15—March 1; restaurant open all year
Dbl rm F420—F850
N165 exit Quinterlé

Two 16th-century watermills and their granite outbuildings
have been tastefully converted into comfortable cottage-style
accommodation. Popular with the rich and famous — past
guests include Willy Brandt, the Queen Mother and Remy
Schneider — the spacious, well-equipped bedrooms and
apartments, all with satellite television, look out either over
a mill-pond or the Belon river which runs through the hotel's
extensive secluded grounds. The restaurant comprises four
intimate dining-rooms in the mill itself. Some window tables
have river views and, in summer, there is an outdoor dining
terrace. The fish and seafood are obtained directly from local
fishermen in Moelan-sur-Mer, and specialities include the
famous Belon oysters. Guests are asked to take one meal a day
in the hotel. Last orders: lunch 2.30pm; dinner 10pm. Set
menus from F140; à la carte around F280.
*Heated indoor swimming pool, sauna and gym; free salmon and trout
fishing; beach with watersports 5km*

MONTBAZON

🏠 |○| 6/12 ⊟ £

Le Moulin Fleuri, Route du Ripault, Montbazon, 37250
Veigné.   Tel: 47.26.01.12

Closed Oct 15–30, restaurant closed Sunday evening
and Monday in winter
Dbl rm F165–F255 ⸀

An arm of the river Indre flows around this characterful 16th-
century mill which offers excellent value as a base for touring
the Loire Valley. Bedrooms are comfortable, clean and
prettily furnished; eight with attached bathrooms. Half the
restaurant's tables overlook the mill-pond and there is a
waterside terrace for drinks and breakfast. Owner Alain
Chaplin cooks traditional regional dishes in his charming
rustic dining-room. Excellent Loire wine list. Guests asked
to dine in restaurant or take half-board March 1–November
15. Last orders: lunch 2pm; dinner 9pm. Set menus from
F145 (children F50); à la carte around F220.
Riverside walks, fishing in 9-acre grounds

MONTBAZON

🏠 🍽 8/21 ▭ £££

Domaine de la Tortinière, Les Gués de Veigné, 37250
Montbazon.   Tel: 47.26.00.19
Closed December 20–March 1
Dbl rm F660–F1100

Set in 30 acres of grounds sweeping down to the river Indre,
Denise Oliverau-Capron and her family provide a warm
welcome at their beautiful Second Empire chateau. Bedrooms are handsomely furnished and have been recently
renovated, including the installation of Jacuzzi baths.
Rooms in the chateau's turrets are much sought-after and
the most expensive. The elegant, conservatory-style dining-
room serves classic regional dishes: *la coratinée de sandre aux
poireaux* (Loire pike with leeks) and *pigeon de Tourenne farcie au
St Maure* (pigeon stuffed with goat's cheese) are among the
specialities. There are magnificent views over the valley of
the Indre from the terrace where breakfast and drinks are
served. Half-board preferred June–September. Last orders:

lunch 1.30pm, dinner 9.15pm. Set menus from F205; à la carte around F300.
Solar-heated outdoor pool, tennis court, free fishing, private boat for river trips

MONTLOUIS-SUR-LOIRE

IOI ⊟ £££

Roc en Val, 4 Quai de la Loire, 37270
Montlouis–sur–Loire.   Tel: 47.50.81.96
Closed January 2–17, Sunday evening and Monday
(open Monday evening April–September)

An attractive white 18th-century mansion provides a hand-some setting for this refined and stylish restaurant. It is slightly raised above road level, so most tables enjoy expansive views over the Loire. Modern interpretations of traditional regional dishes are the hallmark of chef Bernard Bach. A particular speciality is ravioli of rabbit in a nut sauce. Last orders: lunch 1.45pm; dinner 9.30pm. Set menus from F150 (lunch), F165 (dinner); à la carte around F250.
Walks in wooded grounds; wine caves and chateaux of Chenonceau and Amboise nearby

MONTREUIL-SUR-LOIR

⊨ 2/3 ⊞ £

Château de Montreuil, Montreuil–sur–Loir, 49140
Seiches–sur–le–Loir.   Tel: 41.76.21.03.
Open mid-March–mid-October
Dbl rm F270–F320

This handsome neo-Gothic chateau has a magnificent setting on a bluff above the river Loir. Farmer and local mayor, Jacques Bailliou, and his wife Marie are friendly, welcoming hosts who encourage guests to make themselves at home in the spacious panelled sitting-room. Bedrooms are very sim-ply furnished with shower cubicles and WCs. Breakfast is

included, and on request Madame Bailliou serves a delicious four-course dinner (using home-grown produce) with wine, for around F100. A steep path leads down to an old mill and pleasant riverside walks.
Boats for hire

MONT-ST-MICHEL

🏚 |O| 15/27 ▭ £££

La Mère Poulard, Grand-Rue, 50116
Le Mont-St-Michel.   Tel: 33.60.14.01
Open all year
Dbl rm F750–F950

Rising above the ramparts that surround Mont-St-Michel, this attractive hotel has been famous for its omelettes, mixed and cooked in cast-iron pans over an open wood fire, since it opened for business in the 19th century. Bedrooms are handsomely decorated in various styles and many enjoy views over the shallow bay to the mainland. Eight tables in the second-floor dining-room have water views. Omelettes filled with salmon, or flambé are the house speciality, but the menu also includes *gigot pré salé*, lamb grazed on the local salt-water meadows. Last orders: lunch 2pm; dinner 9.30pm. Set menu F250 (lunch), F450 (dinner); à la carte around F400.
Medieval church and abbey; son-et-lumière tableaux depicting island's history, daily June–September, except Sundays

MONT-ST-MICHEL

🏚 |O| 8/28 ▭ ££

Le Mouton Blanc, Grand-Rue, 50116
Le Mont-St-Michel.   Tel: 33.60.14.08
Closed November 15–February 1
Dbl rm F250–F480

A friendly atmosphere pervades this unpretentious hotel and restaurant. One of the oldest medieval houses on Mont-St-Michel, it is designated a historic monument and rooms contain the original 14th-century beamed ceilings. Only a few of the small but recently renovated, comfortable rooms have water views, but all offer good value for such a tourist magnet. There are four dining-rooms, but only the large open-air terrace has views over the bay to the *prés salés*, salt meadows grazed by sheep. Lamb reared on this salty grass is a speciality. Last orders: lunch 2.30pm; dinner 9pm. Set menus from F85; à la carte around F200.

MONTSOREAU

🏠 ○ 9/12 🛏 ££

Le Bussy, 49730 Montsoreau.   Tel: 41.51.70.18
Closed December 15–January 31; restaurant closed
Tuesday lunch June–September, Monday evening
and Tuesday October–May
Dbl rm F270–F300

This charming inn set in terraced gardens has beautiful views down over the Loire and towards Montsoreau castle. Bedrooms are comfortable with rustic decor, all with en-suite bathrooms. Its restaurant, Diane de Méridor, is 200m below, overlooking the river, but also a fairly busy road. All diners enjoy river views, even those with their backs to the windows, thanks to a wall of mirrors. Last orders: lunch 2.30pm; dinner 9.30pm. Set menus from F75; à la carte around F130. *Good base for touring Loire chateaux and Saumur, Bourgueil and Chinon vineyards*

MOSNAC

🏠 ○ 5/10 🛏 £££

Le Moulin de Marcouze, Mosnac, 17240
St-Genis-de-Saintonge.   Tel: 46.70.46.16
Closed February and one week during November;
restaurant closed Tuesday and Wednesday lunch except
June 15–September 15
Dbl rm F650–F700

An outstanding stylish conversion of a watermill on the river Seugne, the large bedrooms with their smart terracotta-tiled floors and antique furniture provide everything guests could need, even towelling robes in the bathrooms. Five have terraces overlooking the river and one room is specially equipped for disabled guests. All rooms are air-conditioned. The elegant simplicity is carried through into the waterside restaurant where diners can enjoy classic regional dishes prepared by owner Dominique Bouchet, award-winning chef from the prestigious Tour d'Argent in Paris. A particular speciality is *le gigot de sept heures*, lamb marinated in Bordeaux wine for seven hours to an old recipe followed hardly anywhere in France now. There are excellent clarets among the 600 wines on the wine list. Last orders: lunch 2pm; dinner 9.30pm. Set menus from F190; à la carte around F350.

Outdoor hotel pool, fishing, walks through riverside park, private helicopter for visits to vineyards and chateaux

MUIDES-SUR-LOIRE

🛏 **5/5** 🛏 £££

Château de Colliers, Muides-sur-Loire, 41500 Mer.
Tel: 54.87.50.75
Closed November–February
Dbl rm F750

This pretty 17th-century chateau, set in a peaceful park, has been in the de Gélis family since 1779. Family furniture, antique objets d'art and portraits fill the rooms, and guests are made to feel part of the family by Christian and Marie-France de Gélis. All the comfortably furnished bedrooms enjoy views down over the river towards a bird sanctuary on a small island mid-river. On prior reservation guests can enjoy dinner *en famille* cooked by the enthusiastic Madame de Gélis, from F200 including Cheverny wines. Lovely gravel terrace on riverbank for aperitifs.

Walking paths along the Loire and to Château de Chambord; riding, golf and tennis 5km

MUZILLAC

🏠 🍽 23/28 ▭ ₤₤₤

Domaine de Rochevilaine, Pointe de Pen-Lan, Billiers,
56190 Muzillac.   Tel: 97.41.69.27
Closed January 6–February 24
Dbl rm F580–F1100

This fine old Breton customs house and its fortified hamlet,
built to defend the estuary against English smugglers, perch
on the edge of a rocky promontory where the Vilaine estuary
meets the sea. Most bedrooms have spectacular water views
and guests are lulled to sleep by the sound of the sea. Two
family apartments occupy converted houses in the hamlet.
The attractive sitting rooms have a shipboard feel. Their
polished wooden floors are covered with Persian rugs and
the large windows provide splendid views out to sea. All the
restaurant's tables have sea views, and chef Patrice Caillaut is
widely acclaimed for his imaginative seafood dishes, especially his *Menu Homard*. Last orders: lunch 2pm; dinner
9.30pm. Set menus from F250; à la carte around F350.
Non-residents must book.
Outdoor heated pool and natural seawater pool in rocks below, sandy
beaches, fishing, tennis 500m

NANTES

🏠 🍽 58/100 ▭ ₤₤

Sofitel, 15 Boulevard Alexandre Millerand, 44200 Nantes.
Tel: 40.47.61.03
Open all year
Dbl rm F615

On a large island in the river Loire, two miles from the centre
of Nantes, this modern hotel offers the kind of well-equipped
bedrooms and efficient service associated with the Sofitel
chain. (One room specially equipped for disabled guests.)
Half the bedrooms, including 18 non-smoking rooms, have

expansive views over the Loire, wide at this point and quite busy with river traffic. Its 'Tilbury' restaurant specializes in fish but has no river views. There is 24-hour room service. Last orders: lunch 2.30pm; dinner 10.30pm. Set menus from F110; à la carte around F200.

Hotel has heated outdoor pool and tennis courts; river cruises 3km away

NANTES

IOI ⊟ ££££

Torigai, Ile de Versailles, 44000 Nantes.   Tel: 40.37.06.37
Closed August 15–September 4 and Sunday

This intriguingly designed modern restaurant sits in a Japanese garden on an island in the river Erdre which flows through the centre of Nantes. Built conservatory-style with walls of plate glass, it is decorated with exotic plants. Twelve tables enjoy views out over the river towards the cathedral. Talented Japanese chef, Shigeo Torigai, successfully blends French and oriental cuisine; seafood is a speciality. A waterside terrace is used in good weather. Last orders: lunch 2pm; dinner 10pm. Set menus from F180 (lunch with wine), F240 (dinner); à la carte around F400.

NERSAC

IOI ⊟ ££

Auberge du Pont de la Meure, Route Hiersac, Nersac, 16440 Roullet-St-Estaphe.   Tel: 45.90.60.48
Closed August; Friday evening and Saturday
Angoulême 8km

This charming small restaurant sits beside the river Charente in Cognac country, popular for barge-cruising holidays. Five tables overlook a peaceful river scene, and the menus concentrate on traditional French cooking such as peppered steak *flambé* in cognac and *brochette de langoustine*. Reservations essential. Last orders: lunch 2pm; dinner 10pm. Set menus from F110; à la carte around F200.

Tours of Cognac distilleries and chocolate factory; motorboat hire; fishing

NEUVILLE-SUR-SARTHE

🏠 ⊟ £££

Le Vieux Moulin, Neuville-sur-Sarthe, 72190 Coulaines.
Tel: 43.25.31.84
Closed January, October 15–31, Sunday evening and Monday
A11 exit Le Mans-Nord-Alencon 4km

This atmospheric 17th-century watermill is set in tranquil grounds astride the river Sarthe, and one of the big wheels still turns to provide the restaurant's electricity. There are two dining-rooms, a rustic room in the mill itself where three tables enjoy water views, and a large heated conservatory 300m away overlooking the mill wheel, weir and a stretch of river. Classic French cooking with the accent on fish. An old presbytery has been renovated to provide accommodation and should be ready to take in guests this summer. Last orders: lunch 2.15pm; dinner 10pm. Set menus from F120; à la carte around F320.

Tow-path walks, fishing (permits sold in town)

NIEUIL

🏰 🍽 10/14 ⊟ £££

Château de Nieuil, Nieuil, 16270 Roumazières Loubert.
Tel: 45.71.36.38
Closed November 5–April 26
Dbl rm F550–F1200

This palatial 16th-century chateau, built as a hunting lodge for Francis I, is surrounded by a wide moat, its water

channelled from a river. It was opened in 1937, as the first chateau–hotel in France, and the present owners Jean–Michel and Luce Bodinaud are charming and helpful hosts. Bedrooms, decorated in different styles, are richly furnished with antiques, paintings and tapestries. Bathrooms are luxurious and there are two rooms specially equipped for disabled guests. In the panelled dining-room, chef Madame Bodinaud serves delicious regional dishes prepared according to ancient recipes, using vegetables from the chateau's own kitchen gardens. Last orders: lunch 2pm; dinner 9pm. Set menus from F220; à la carte around F320.
Swimming pool, tennis court, fishing in the moat and 10-acre lake, walks in the extensive grounds

NIORT

IOI ⊟ ££

La Belle Etoile, 115 Quai Maurice Metayer, 79000 Niort. Tel: 49.73.31.29
Open all year; closed Sunday evening and Monday
A11 exit 22/23 11km

This charming restaurant on the banks of the Sèvre contains two elegant and spacious dining-rooms. Most tables have river views, and there is a waterside garden terrace for summer dining. Owner–chef Claude Guignard offers a diverse menu based on fresh local produce, mixing traditional regional recipes with lighter seafood dishes. Popular with locals. Last orders: lunch 2pm; dinner 9.30pm. Set menus are available from F120; à la carte around F250.
Canoes and kayaks for hire; river boat trips 2km away; fishing with permit

ILE DE NOIRMOUTIER

🏠 12/22 ⊟ ££

Bord à Bord, 6 Rue de la Linière, L'Herbaudière, 85330 Ile de Noirmoutier.   Tel: 51.39.27.92

Open all year
Dbl rm F300–F410

Built five years ago, this simple but attractive hotel overlooks
the marina at L'Herbaudière, an important fishing and pleasure port which is less touristy than the resort of Noirmoutier. Bedrooms, which contain kitchenettes, are large and
cheerfully decorated in primary colours. Nine rooms have
decent-sized terraces overlooking the harbour. There are
also apartments for four to six people. There is no restaurant, but a bar and breakfast room with sea views.
*Heated outdoor pool, sandy beaches and watersports nearby, fishing
trips with fishermen or in rock pools, bicycle hire, interesting woodland and salt marsh walks*

NOTRE-DAME-DES-MONTS

🏨 🍽 **25/40** 🛏 ££

Hôtel de la Plage, 2 Avenue de la Mer, 85690
Notre-Dame-des-Monts.   Tel: 51.58.83.09
Closed November 1–January 31; restaurant closed Sunday
evening and Monday except June–October and school holi-
days
Dbl rm F330–F440

This sleek white seaside hotel overlooks the promenade
gardens and a good sandy beach in a pleasant family resort.
Public rooms and bedrooms are stylishly decorated. All sea-
view rooms have French windows leading on to pleasant
terraces with tables and chairs. The restaurant looks out over
the bay and serves ample helpings of locally-caught seafood as
well as meat dishes. Meals are also served on a beachside
terrace. During July and August guests must take half-board
and stay for a minimum of three nights. Last orders: lunch
2pm; dinner 9.30pm. Set menus from F96–F350; à la carte
around F250.
*Safe sandy beach, watersports facilities during July and August, hotel
golf packages for ocean-side dune course at St-Jean-de-Monts*

NOUAN-LE-FUZELIER

🏠 🍴 <u>12/20</u> 🚪 ££

Le Moulin de Villiers, Nouan-le-Fuzelier, 41600
Lamotte-Beuvron.   Tel: 54.88.72.27
Closed January 2–March 20, first two weeks of September,
Tuesday evening and Wednesday during November and
December
Half-board only F190–F250 a person
A71 Exit 3, 10km away

This beautiful 19th-century watermill sits beside an attractive
lake in the heart of a forest. Gérard and Gladys Andrieux are
very friendly and welcoming, and the bar is popular with
locals as well as residents. Bedrooms are modest but comfortable and the parquet-floored restaurant serves seasonal fish
and game. There is a pretty waterside terrace for drinks and
breakfast in summer. Last orders: lunch 2pm; dinner 8.45pm.
Set menus from F72; à la carte around F150.
*Fishing for hotel guests, village tennis courts, exploring forests and
lakes of the off-the-beaten-track Sologne region*

OLIVET

🏠 🍴 <u>6/10</u> 🚪 ££

Les Quatre Saisons, 351 Rue de la Reine Blanche,
45160 Olivet.   Tel: 38.66.14.30
Closed two weeks in January or early February; restaurant
closed Sunday evening and Tuesday October–March
Dbl rm F350–F400

On the quiet wooded banks of the river Loiret this wonderful
hotel – formerly a shipyard building turned open-air dance
hall – is a classified historic monument. Bedrooms, all fashionably decorated in different styles, are well appointed. The
restaurant occupies a large airy hall overlooking the river but,
in summer, be sure to book a table on the wonderful waterside verandah. Specialities include game and fish, including

lobster and crayfish kept in a tank. Last orders: lunch 2pm; dinner 9.30pm. Set menus from F165; à la carte around F220. *Rowing boats for hire, boat trips down Loiret, tow-path walks, fishing (with a licence), convenient base to explore Sologne forests and Loire chateaux*

PACY-SUR-EURE

🏠 🍽 16/17 ▭ ££

L'Etape, 1 Rue Isambard, 27120 Pacy-sur-Eure.
Tel: 32.36.12.77
Open all year
Dbl rm F265–F280

This white manor house stands in a small park on the banks of the river Eure. Bedrooms are quiet, spacious and pleasantly decorated, with lovely views over the river. The restaurant's large windows look directly on to the water and give the impression of dining on a boat. All the tables have pretty outlooks, and the specialities on offer include freshwater fish, *foie gras* and seasonal game. Last orders: lunch 2pm; dinner 9pm. Set menus are available from F95; à la carte around F250.
Good trout fishing (permits are sold in Pacy), riverside walks, Monet's home at Giverny is just 15km away

PAIMPOL

🏠 🍽 7/7 ▭ ££

Le Repaire de Kerroc'h, 29 Quai Morand, 22500
Paimpol.   Tel: 96.20.50.13
Open all year; restaurant closed first two weeks of February and December and first week of June; Tuesday and Wednesday lunch October–April
Dbl rm F390–F450; family apartments F580

This 18th-century stone house, right on the port at Paimpol, was built by Pierre Coronge Kersaut, a notorious pirate. It is

now a comfortable, seaside hotel with two pretty and convivial dining-rooms which serve freshly caught seafood and oysters; both are well frequented by locals. A particular speciality is *canneton au miel et aux épices*, duck with honey and spices. In summer, meals and drinks are also served on an open-air terrace which faces the port. Bedrooms are quite small but have high ceilings and are full of character, with fine views over this little fishing port. A good place for an overnight stop. Last orders: lunch 1.30pm; dinner 9.30pm. Set menus are available from F95; à la carte around F250.
Boat excursions to Ile de Bréhat, fishing trips with local fishermen

PENESTIN

🏠 |○| 10/16 🛏 ££

Hôtel Loscolo, 56760 Pénestin.   Tel: 99.90.31.90
Closed November 3–Easter; restaurant closed Tuesday and Wednesday lunch excluding July 1–September 15
Dbl rm F480

Splendidly situated at the tip of a narrow peninsula beside a lovely sandy beach, this unpretentious seaside hotel enjoys a particularly tranquil location. Recently renovated, it is tastefully decorated throughout and first-floor bedrooms share a terrace. The restaurant, which specializes in seafood (with a tank for live lobster and crawfish), has an excellent reputation. Those with a good appetite should try the house speciality, *ragoût Breton*. Last orders: lunch 1.30pm; dinner 10pm. Set menus from F125; à la carte around F250.
Hotel offers sailing, windsurfing and water-skiing

PERROS-GUIREC

🏠 |○| 21/21 🛏 ££

Le Sphinx, 67 Chemin de la Messe, 22700 Perros-Guirec.
Tel: 96.23.25.42

Closed January 6–February 15; restaurant closed
Monday lunch
Half-board preferred; F430–F470 per person

This tall, thin, turn-of-the-century house makes the most of
its cramped site, between the hillside and rocks below. The
11 comfortable bedrooms in the main house (nine with
balconies) enjoy splendid views over the open sea towards
Ile Tomé and its neighbours. A new extension contains a
further 10 rooms, decorated in a modern English country
style with large windows making the most of the sea view.
The spacious bar, lounge and dining-room, are decorated in
traditional French country style with high wood-beamed
ceilings. A path leads down along the rocks to a small sandy
cove. Seafood dominates the menu and there is a tank with
live lobsters and crawfish. Last orders: lunch 1.30pm; dinner
9.30pm. Set menus are on offer from F115; à la carte around
F250.
Good swimming beaches; boat excursions to Sept Iles; sailing boats
and windsurfers for rent 100m, tennis courts in town

PLENEUF-VAL-ANDRE

IOI ▭ ₤₤₤

La Cotriade, Port de Piégu, 22370 Pléneuf-Val-André.
Tel: 96.72.20.26.
Closed January 15–February 15, Monday evening and
Tuesday

A small unpretentious restaurant, all its 14 tables look out
across the bay of St-Brieuc. Prize-winning master chef
Jean-Jacques Le Saout, who worked in New York for ten
years, prepares only the catch of the day – sole, turbot, St
Pierre – and fresh seafood, cooked in light sauces. There is
also a small bar which serves fishy snacks. Last orders: lunch
2pm; dinner 9pm. Set menus from F170; à la carte around
F370.

PLEUGEUNEUC

🏚 🍽 6/8 🛏 £££

Château de la Motte–Beaumanoir, Pleugeuneuc, 35720
St–Pierre–de–Plesguen.   Tel: 99.69.46.01
Closed December 23–January 2 (maybe until March);
restaurant closed Monday and Tuesday June–September;
Tuesday only in winter
Dbl rm F680–F780
St–Malo 32km north on RN137

This splendid 15th–century moated manor house set in a 60–
acre park overlooks a small lake. The home of the Bernard
family since 1978, it has been extensively renovated but
remains a quiet, atmospheric retreat with polished flagstone
floors, heavy oak beams and enormous fireplaces. The bedrooms, reached by the original stone staircase, are very
spacious and decorated in mock baronial style. Lunch and
candle–lit dinners are served in the summery dining–room
with the emphasis on fish and seafood. In fine weather, meals
are also served on a lakeside terrace. Last orders: lunch 2pm;
dinner 10pm (non–residents must make a reservation). Set
menus from F135; à la carte around F350.
*Swimming, fishing, 16th–century Château de la Bourbansais with
safari park nearby*

PLOUGUERNEAU

🏚 🍽 24/29 🛏 £

Castel Ac'h, Plage de Lilia, 29880 Plouguerneau.
Tel: 98.04.70.11.
Open all year; restaurant closed Christmas and January 31
Dbl rm F150–F245

Set in farmland beside a beautiful beach of fine sand, this
modern seaside hotel is an inexpensive base to enjoy a family
bucket–and–spade holiday. The bedrooms are small but
cheerfully decorated – some sleeping four – and bathrooms

are functional. The restaurant serves mediocre food but service is efficient and there are wonderful views across the bay. Last orders: lunch 1.30pm; dinner 9.30pm. Set menus are on offer from F75 (children's menu F45); à la carte around F200.

Six sandy beaches within 2km of hotel, dune areas, rich fossil deposits, watersports, hotel tennis court, visits to tallest lighthouse in Europe, boat hire

PONT-AUDEMER

🏨 🍽 **14/14** 🛏 £££

Belle-Isle sur Risle, 112 Route de Rouen, 27500 Pont-Audemer.   Tel: 32.56.96.22
Closed January–mid-February; restaurant closed
Sunday evening and Monday except June–September
Half-board only; F680–F980 per person

This attractive 19th-century mansion stands in a five-acre park on a private island in the river Risle. A discreet, tranquil retreat, bedrooms are spacious and handsomely furnished. In the restaurant, ask for a table in the airy rotunda overlooking lawns leading down to the river. A particular speciality is *fricassé de homard au Sauternes*. Last orders: lunch 2pm; dinner 9.30pm (10.30pm weekends). Set menus F189 lunch, F380 weekend dinner; à la carte around F350.

Swimming pool, tennis court, canoes and kayaks are available for hire; good pike and trout fishing

PONT-AVEN

🍽 **4/4** 🛏 £££

Moulin de Rosmadec, 29930 Pont-Aven.
Tel: 98.06.00.22
Closed February, October 15–30, Sunday evening
(except during July and August), and Wednesday
Dbl rm F450

In a characterful village famous for its mills and association with Paul Gauguin, this 15th-century stone mill, surrounded on three sides by a rushing stream, has an enchanting setting. The dining-room is quite dark with polished wooden floors and heavy beams so that from the 12 tables you hear, rather than see, the water. However, there are water views from a small conservatory called La Serre. Acclaimed owner–chef Pierre Sébilleau specializes in classic fish and seafood dishes. A particular speciality is *turbot roti au coulis de langoustine*. There is a waterside terrace for drinks and seafood platters. The four prettily furnished bedrooms look over the stream. Last orders: lunch 2pm; dinner 9.30pm. Set menus from F150; à la carte around F320.

Canoe and kayak hire, boat trips along Aven, river fishing, lovely riverbank walks past ruined mills and to Bois d'Amour, inspiration for many artists

PONT-AVEN

🏠 🍽 11/26 🛏 ££

Hôtel Roz-Aven, 11 Quai Théodore Botrel, 29930 Pont-Aven.   Tel: 98.06.13.06
Closed November 15–February 15 and Monday nights except June–mid-September; restaurant open June 15–September 15 except Tuesday
Dbl rm F340–F600

This picture-postcard thatched house sits on the quayside overlooking the river Aven where it widens into an estuary. In the main building, there are 11 comfortable bedrooms, some with Louis XIV reproduction beds. Eleven of these have pretty harbour views. The hotel has recently opened a modern annexe 50 metres away and rooms have views over the port. Across the road, on the water's edge, there is a terrace for meals and drinks where guests can relax and watch the comings and goings of boats and feed the swans. Fish and seafood are the order of the day. Last orders: lunch 1pm; dinner 9pm. Set menus are available from F85; à la carte around F150.

LES PONTS-DE-CE

🏚 IOI 6/11 ⊟ £

Le Bosquet, 49130 Les Ponts-de-Cé.   Tel: 41.57.72.42
Hotel and restaurant closed February 14–28,
August 16–31, Sunday night and all Monday
Dbl rm F220–F250
On N160 5km S Angers

The Loire splits briefly into three here, and this unpretentious
hotel stands on the southernmost arm, the Louet. Bedrooms
are small and simply furnished, but directly overlook a
pleasant stretch of river (a busy main road runs behind the
hotel). The restaurant is typically French – starched white
tablecloths, tapestry chairs and arrangements of fresh flowers
– and the varied menu, concentrating on fresh produce, is
popular with locals. Seven tables enjoy river views, and there
is a shady riverbank terrace for drinks. Guests must dine in
restaurant. Last orders: lunch 1.45pm; dinner 9.15pm. Set
menus from F95; à la carte around F250.
*Good base for touring Loire chateaux, river swimming, bicycles for
hire*

PORNIC

IOI ⊟ £££

Beau Rivage, Plage de la Birochère, 44210 Pornic.
Tel: 40.82.03.08
Closed January, October 15–27, Monday evening and
Tuesday October–March

This unprepossessing building set in the rocks above a small
sandy cove contains a convivial restaurant, popular with
locals. The light, creative cuisine concentrates on fresh fish
and seafood, and as half the tables are on a raised platform, all
enjoy excellent sea views. There is an outdoor terrace for
snacks, drinks and ice-creams in summer. Open 8am–10pm.

Last orders: lunch 2.30pm; dinner 9.30pm. Set menus from
F135; à la carte around F300.
Sandy bathing beach directly below

PUTANGES-PONT-ECREPIN

🏨 ⏐◯⏐ 6/20 🛏 £

Hôtel du Lion Verd, Place du Pont, 61210
Putanges-Pont-Ecrepin.   Tel: 33.35.01.86
Closed December 23–January 31
Dbl rm F240–F300

A very attractive modern stone building alongside the river
Orne, this hotel offers good value with clean, quiet, comfortable rooms (Nos 7, 8 and 10 enjoy the best river views).
Tapestries hang all around, woven by Madame Guillais, the
owner, in her increasingly rare spare time. The restaurant is
prettily decorated with views over the fast-flowing river, and
there is an outdoor waterside terrace for drinks, breakfast and
snacks. Fresh local produce – ham, trout, pork, cider and
cream – used for classic Norman dishes; tank containing live
lobsters. Last orders: lunch 2pm; dinner 9.30pm. Set menus
from F65; à la carte around F150.
*Rowing boats, canoes and pedalos for hire, fishing (permits sold next
door), many signposted walks around Orne valley*

QUIBERON

🏨 10/27 🛏 ££

Le Gulf Stream, 17 Boulevard Chanard, 56170 Quiberon.
Tel: 97.50.16.96
Closed December and January
Dbl rm F350–F580

Set in the middle of a long south-facing sandy beach in the
popular resort of Quiberon, this seafront hotel has retained
the character of its former life as two private homes. There are
four attractive first-floor rooms with French windows opening on to a wide terrace. In high summer, when the beach is

crowded, guests can retreat to a tree-shaded garden at the rear. Breakfast included in the room price.

Good beach with swimming school for children, sailing, windsurfing, fishing excursions, boat trips to Belle-Ile, Hoedic and Houat islands, interesting walks around the rocky headlands of Coté Sauvage

QUIMPER

🏠 <u>10/13</u> 🛏 ££

Château de Kerambleis, Plomelin, 29700 Quimper.
Tel: 98.94.23.42
Open July 1–Aug 30
Dbl rm F350–F650
East of Plomelin, 8km south of Quimper

Set in parkland overlooking the high wooded cliffs of the river Odet, this late 19th-century chateau was completely renovated in 1985. The public rooms with their parquet floors and wood-panelling are decorated in period style. Bedrooms are comfortable but more sparsely furnished, with bathrooms or small sitting-rooms in round turrets. Breakfast only.

Small swimming pool, fishing from riverbank, motorboats for hire nearby. In Quimper, sights include old town, cathedral, fine arts museum, potteries; boat trips down the Odet

REDON

🏠 🍽 <u>3/5</u> 🛏 £

La Belle Anguille, Route de Ste-Marie, 35600 Redon.
Tel: 99.72.31.02
Closed two weeks February and first week of November; restaurant closed Wednesday
Dbl rm F185–F200
Redon 2km

This stone-faced Breton house stands beside a wonderfully tranquil stretch of the river Vilaine. The Robert family

extends visitors a warm welcome at this small, unpretentious
hotel. Bedrooms are freshly decorated, and at night the
sounds of the river's wildlife on the prowl can be heard
drifting up into the rooms. The restaurant (eight tables have
water views) is very popular with locals; specialities include
pike and perch from the river, as well as eels and game. In
summer, meals and drinks are also served on the riverbank.
Last orders: lunch 1.30pm; dinner 9pm. Set menus from F55
(F75 at weekends); à la carte around F120.
*Freshwater fishing (permits are sold in Redon), mini-golf, woodland
walks, riding 1km*

LA REMIGEASSE

🏨 ΙΟΙ 11/26 🛏 ££££

Le Grand Large, Baie de la Remigeasse, 17550
La Remigeasse.   Tel: 46.75.37.89
Open April 1–September 30
Dbl rm F630–F1110

In a beautiful, secluded spot with magnificent views of the
ocean and sand dunes, this modern ivy-covered building
offers a tranquil refuge on the Ile-d'Oléron. Bedrooms are
extremely comfortable and well appointed. There are panoramic views over the coast from all tables in the pleasant
dining-room. Fish and seafood dominate the menus and *sole
braisée et dorée au Champagne* is a particularly speciality. Half-
board is compulsory mid–June–end Sept and costs F1480–
F1810 a night for two people. Last orders: lunch 2pm; dinner
9.15pm. Set menus from F230; à la carte around F270.
*Covered heated pool, tennis court, bicycles and sail-boards for hire;
riding nearby*

RIVARENNES

🛏 9/10 🛏 £££

Château de la Tour, Rivarennes, 36800 St-Gaultier.
Tel: 54.47.06.12

Open all year
Dbl rm F350–F800

Guests are made to feel completely at ease in this imposing
chateau, parts of which date back to the 14th century,
although it was remodelled in the 18th century. Beautifully
situated on the banks of the river Creuse, it has been the
home of the Dukes of Clermont-Tonnerre for generations.
Bedrooms are elegantly furnished with antiques and pretty
wallpapers. Dinner is served on request from F350 including
wine. Drinks are served on a small riverside terrace. Cookery
and porcelain painting courses occasionally take place.
*Nearby riding, fishing, tennis, golf and kayaking; horse-drawn
carriage day trips*

RIVEDOUX-PLAGE

🏠 🍽 **10/34** 🛏 ££

Auberge de la Marée, 17940 Rivedoux-Plage.
Tel: 46.09.80.02
Open Easter–October; restaurant closed Monday lunch
and Tuesday lunch except June–October
Dbl rm F300–F600

This pretty hotel sits beside Rivedoux harbour on the Ile-de-
Ré. Andalusian in style, its delightful garden with swimming
pool, fountain and patio provides a quiet sanctuary on busy
days. Bedrooms are comfortable and nicely decorated, all
with en-suite bathrooms. Most tables in its restaurant enjoy
lovely views over the fishing harbour. Freshly caught seafood
is a speciality. Last orders: lunch 2pm; dinner 9.30pm. Set
menus from F85 (lunch), F155 (dinner); à la carte around
F300.
Sandy beaches, tennis and watersports nearby; horse-riding 5km

LA ROCHE-BERNARD

○| ▭ £

La Douanerie, Quai de la Douane, 56130
La Roche-Bernard.   Tel: 99.90.62.57
Closed January 1–February 15 and Tuesday
June 1–September 15

This low, white-washed restaurant, pizzeria and café–bar
looks directly out over the wide river Vilaine. Relaxed and
casual, it is popular with yachtsmen who can drop anchor in
mid-river. The first-floor Cardinal restaurant specializes in
fresh seafood with six tables overlooking the river. Pizzas,
pasta dishes, drinks and ice-cream sundaes are served downstairs and out on the quayside terrace in summer. Café–bar
open 9.30am–midnight; pizzas around F40. Last orders in
Cardinal: lunch 2.30pm; dinner 10.30pm. Set menus from
F90 (children F50).
Boat trips along the Vilaine, sailing boats for hire, water-skiing, fish-
ing, exploring historic port town of La Roche-Bernard, riverside walks

ROCHECORBON

▦ ○| 11/11 ▭ £££££

Les Hautes Roches, 86 Quai de la Loire, Rochecorbon,
37210 Vouvray.   Tel: 47.52.88.88
Closed mid-January–mid-March; restaurant closed Sunday
evening and Monday November–April
Dbl rm F995–F1300

Like many homes built along the Loire's cliff faces, this hotel
is troglodytic, with bedrooms which have been gouged out
of the rock. But there is nothing primitive about these cave-
dwellings: rooms are extremely spacious and luxurious, with
marble bathrooms, stylish reproduction furniture and soft
lighting. For the claustrophobic, there are more bedrooms
in the main house, which also contains an elegant dining-
room where French windows open on to a terrace over-

looking the river. Fish is a speciality. Last orders: lunch 1.30pm; dinner 9.30pm. Set menus from F160; à la carte around F250.

Vouvray wine caves, fishing, golf and riding nearby

LA ROCHELLE

Saint-Jean d'Acre, 4 Place de la Chaine, 17000 La Rochelle.   Tel: 46.41.73.33
Hotel open all year; restaurant closed Friday evening and Saturday lunch November–end March
Dbl rm F480–F590

This pleasant hotel sits in the heart of the Vieux Port, facing the medieval towers that frame the entrance to the harbour. Bedrooms are all comfortably furnished, some with balconies, and three are equipped for disabled visitors. The restaurant serves beautifully presented *nouvelle cuisine*, and there is also a large quayside terrace for meals and drinks in summer. Last orders: lunch 2pm; dinner 10.30pm. Set menus from F75; à la carte around F240.

Watersports and jet-ski hire nearby

LA ROCHELLE

Les Brises, Chemin de la Digue Richelieu, 17000 La Rochelle.   Tel: 46.43.89.37
Open all year
Dbl rm F360–F550

In a quiet location facing the open sea with the yacht harbour opposite, this neat modern hotel, surrounded by parkland, is an oasis of calm and comfort. Spacious bedrooms are pleasantly decorated with good quality furnishings including wild-cherry fitted units. All sea-view rooms have balconies. There is also a splendid south-facing terrace above a small pebble beach. Decent parking facilities – a great advantage in La Rochelle.

LA ROCHELLE

IOI ▭ ££££

Richard Coutanceau, Plage de la Concurrence, 17000
La Rochelle.   Tel: 46.41.48.19
Closed Sunday all year and Monday evening out of season

Situated just outside the busy Vieux Port, this elegant restaurant, decorated in soothing pastels, is regarded as the best in the region, and specializes in imaginative and beautifully presented seafood dishes. All tables enjoy panoramic views of the bay, and the courteous and enthusiastic staff add just a little more atmosphere to the experience of dining in a place already heaped with culinary accolades. *Homard rôti dans sa coque*, lobster baked in its shell, is a particular speciality. Last orders: lunch 1.30pm; dinner 9.30pm. Reservations essential. Set menus from F200; à la carte around F380.

RONCE-LES-BAINS

🏨 IOI 12/28 ▭ ££

Le Grand Chalet, 2 Avenue de la Cèpe, Ronce-les-Bains,
17390 La Tremblade.   Tel: 46.36.06.41
Open March 1–November 15; restaurant closed Tuesday
Dbl rm F260
La Rochelle 60km

This pleasant modern hotel offers good value for the area. Although bedrooms are decorated in old-fashioned beiges, they are spacious and clean, all with en-suite bathrooms. Most sea-view rooms have good balconies with spectacular views of the Ile-d'Oléron. The seafood restaurant, which specializes in oyster and lobster salads and seafood ravioli, enjoys similar views, and there is an outdoor terrace for drinks. Half-board compulsory in July and August. Last

orders: lunch 2pm; dinner 9pm. Set menus from F79
(lunch), F130 (dinner); à la carte around F220.
*Steps into the sea from patio, good sandy beaches, watersports school
and tennis nearby*

ROSCOFF

🏨 🍽 6/25 💳 ££

Hôtel Brittany, Boulevard Ste-Barbe, 29681 Roscoff.
Tel: 98.69.70.78
Closed November 15–March 15
Dbl rm F390–F480

Originally a 17th-century manor house, the building has been
reconstructed stone by stone to create this large, comfortable
hotel overlooking the harbour. It is tastefully furnished
throughout, but bedrooms in the old part have more character than those in the modern, purpose-built extension. The
elegant seafood restaurant occupies a splendid stone loggia
with expansive sea views through the glassed-in arches. Half-
board is compulsory in July and August and costs F390–F440
per person. Last orders: lunch 2pm; dinner 9.30pm. Set
menus are available from F115; à la carte around F250.
*Hotel has heated covered swimming pool and sauna; sail-boards for
hire; ferries for Plymouth and Cork*

ROSCOFF

🏨 🍽 14/20 💳 ££

Hôtel Bellevue, Boulevard Jeanne-d'Arc, 29680 Roscoff.
Tel: 98.61.23.38
Hotel closed November 10–March 20; restaurant closed
February 1–March 20 and Wednesday except
June–mid-September
Dbl rm F230–F350

Almost next-door to the Brittany, this is a simple modern
establishment with small, comfortable bedrooms, immaculate

bathrooms, and a pleasant seafood restaurant whose tables have expansive views over the port and across to the Ile de Batz. There is a small outdoor terrace where drinks and meals can be served in summer. Last orders: lunch 2pm; dinner 9.30pm. Set menus from F98; à la carte around F150.

ROUEN

🏨 22/37 ▭ ££

Le Viking, 21 Quai du Havre, 76000 Rouen.
Tel: 35.70.34.95
Open all year
Dbl rm F300

This modern hotel sits on the banks of the Seine in the heart of Rouen, near its famous cathedral. Bedrooms are clean and comfortable, and those with Seine views have balconies. Top-floor rooms enjoy the best views with double-glazed sliding doors to cut down on the noise from traffic passing below. There is no restaurant but the owner, Monsieur Delage, will always rustle up a snack for late-night arrivals and help with sightseeing itineraries.
Rouen old town, especially Notre Dame Cathedral; botanical gardens; wonderful views down over Seine valley from Corniche road; cruises along Seine; canoes for hire

ROYAN

🏨 13/27 ▭ ££

Hôtel Miramar, 173 Avenue de Pontaillac, 17200 Royan.
Tel: 46.39.03.64
Open Easter–October 15
Dbl rm F360–F380

At the quieter, smarter end of Royan, this is one of its prettiest hotels providing an air of tranquillity amid this thriving holiday resort. Bedrooms are decorated in different styles, mostly with floral fabrics, and French windows open

on to small balconies. Madame Milliot is exceptionally charming and very happy to organize and advise on excursions and local facilities. Breakfast only.
Safe sandy beaches, all watersports, boat trips along the Gironde and around the Ile-d'Oléron; tennis, golf and riding nearby

ROYAN

IOI ▭ £££

La Jabotière, Esplanade de Pontaillac, 17200 Royan.
Tel: 46.39.91.29
Closed Christmas and January, Sunday evening and
Monday except June 20–August 31

Located next to the casino, this elegant restaurant sits right on the beach with a large wooden terrace reserved for light meals and drinks. All inside tables enjoy a magnificent view across the bay. Its *nouvelle cuisine* fish and seafood specialities come highly recommended and the menu changes seven times a year. Good Bordeaux wine list. Last orders: lunch 2pm; dinner 10pm. Set menus from F100; à la carte around F300.

LES SABLES-D'OLONNE

▦ IOI **8/18** ▭ ££

Beau Rivage, 40 Promenade de Clemenceau, 85100
Les Sables-d'Olonne.   Tel: 51.32.03.01
Hotel and restaurant closed two weeks in October,
mid-December–mid-January, Sunday and Monday nights
except June–September
Dbl rm F350–F500

A busy road runs in front of all the hotels in this popular high-rise resort, but the Beau Rivage's restaurant is a culinary treat. Only the freshest local produce, cooked in light sauces, is served in the airy, salmon-pink dining-room with its panoramic views over the sandy beach and the bay. *Feuilleté de homard aux morilles,* lobster in puff pastry with wild mushrooms, is a particular speciality. Very good wine list and selection of Armagnacs. Bedrooms are comfortable but simply furnished, all with en-suite bathrooms, and six have French windows opening on to balconies. Last orders: lunch 2.30pm; dinner 9.30pm. Set menus from F170; à la carte around F370. *Safe sandy beach, all watersports, fishing from rocks*

SAHURS

⌂▼ ▭ £

Champetre du Passage du Bac, 76113 Sahurs.
Tel: 35.32.45.15
Closed November 1–January 31
Beside car ferry crossing point

Excellent for breakfast or a quick lunch, this café–bar has a wonderful tree-shaded terrace on the banks of the Seine opposite the medieval old town of La Bouille. The menu includes pizzas and crêpes as well as sandwiches and drinks. There is a children's playground at the end of the terrace and, in winter, the glassed-in verandah also enjoys good river views. Open 9am–10pm in summer, 9am–8pm in winter.

STE-ADRESSE

IOI ▭ £££

Le Beau Séjour, 3 Place Clemenceau, 76310 Ste-Adresse.
Tel: 35.46.19.69
Open all year
Le Havre 5km

There is a breathtaking view over the Seine estuary towards Deauville through the floor-to-ceiling windows in this attractive restaurant on a hillside above the beach. On windy days, diners are entertained by windsurfers flying through the waves. A famous Second World War cabaret club, it retains an atmospheric mahogany-panelled interior with thick wall-to-wall carpeting and bistro-style furnishings. Fish and seafood

dominate the menus. Good wine list. Fine selection of cigars.
Last orders: lunch 2pm; dinner 9.30pm. Set menus from
F119; à la carte around F230.

STE-ANNE-LA-PALUD

🏨 🍽 <u>15/30</u> 🛏 £££

Hôtel de la Plage, Ste-Anne-la-Palud, Plonévez-Porzay,
29550 Plomodiern.   Tel: 98.92.50.12
Open Easter–October 15
Dbl rm F850–F900

This beautiful white hotel, built in the style of a manor, is the
only building on Douarnenez Bay, one of the finest beaches
in Brittany. Surrounded by sand dunes and heathland, the
hotel's isolated position makes it an ideal retreat and the sea-
view bedrooms look out over a long sandy beach as far as the
eye can see. The comfortable bedrooms are tastefully furnished, some with antique pieces, and all have well-equipped
modern bathrooms. The restaurant serves traditional fish and
seafood dishes and nearly all the tables enjoy magnificent
seascape panoramas. Guests are asked to take half-board
during July and August. Last orders: lunch 1.30pm; dinner
9pm. Set menus from F190; à la carte around F300.
*Tennis court, swimming pool, sauna; fishing; windsurfing and
sailing 15km*

ST-AUBIN-LE-VERTUEUX

🏨 🍽 <u>7/8</u> 🛏 £

Hostellerie du Moulin-Fouret, Route de
St-Quentin-des-Iles, St-Aubin-le-Vertueux,
27300 Bernay.   Tel: 32.43.19.95
Hotel and restaurant closed Sunday and Monday nights
Dbl rm F230

This 16th-century, creeper-clad mill, bounded by the Char-
entonne river on three sides, sits in a beautiful and tranquil

landscape. Although the mill wheel no longer turns, its mechanism frames the cosy bar. Bedrooms are simply furnished with pretty views over the lawn to the river. Lovely old Norman furniture and a big open fire on cold evenings create an inviting dining-room where traditional regional dishes are freshly interpreted by owner—chef Francois Deduit. Try the speciality pudding, *Gustave Chauvel*, named after Monsieur Deduit's grandfather. In good weather, meals are served on the pink-gravelled terrace overlooking the river. Last orders: lunch 2pm; dinner 9.30pm. Set menus from F98; à la carte around F220.

Trout fishing in grounds (F100 a day), Bernay's medieval abbey and houses

ST-AUBIN-SUR-MER

🏨 🍽 <u>15/29</u> 🛏 ££

Le Clos Normand, Promenade Guynemer, 14750 St-Aubin-sur-Mer.   Tel: 31.97.30.47
Open Easter—October 31
Dbl rm F270–F315

On the beachfront in this pretty seaside town, which is somewhat quieter than its neighbours in high season, this Caen-stone hotel has a warm, congenial atmosphere. Bedrooms are comfortable, although on the small side, and enjoy lovely views over the beach and the open sea. The bay-windowed dining-room specializes in seafood and duck cooked in cider and calvados. Last orders: lunch 2pm; dinner 9pm. Set menus from F128; à la carte around F170.

Windsurfing, sailing, fishing from jetty, sand and shingle beach, bicycles for hire, tennis courts; convenient for touring Second World War landing beaches

ST-BENOIT

🏠 🍽 **8/10** 🛏 £

Le Chalet de Venise, 6 Rue du Square, 86280 St-Benoit.
Tel: 49.88.45.07
Hotel and restaurant closed three weeks in January, one
week in September and Sunday and Monday nights
Dbl rm F200
A10 exit 20 Poitiers 5km

A relaxed, informal atmosphere pervades this attractive small
hotel set in an oasis of greenery beside the river Miosson.
Bedrooms are nicely decorated, all with en-suite bathrooms.
The restaurant, popular with locals, has fine views over the
river and the gardens beyond. Its terrace is a delightfully
tranquil spot for a drink or a meal in summer. Last orders:
lunch 2pm; dinner 9.30pm. Set menus from F99 (weekdays),
F159 (weekends); à la carte around F250.
*Canoeing, river-swimming 500m, fishing (permits sold in St-Be-
noit), Futuroscope theme park 25km*

ST-CHRISTOPHE

🍽 🛏 £

Auberge du Gué, 3 Place St-Ouen, St-Christophe, 28200
Châteaudun.   Tel: 37.45.75.01
Open all year

This simple country restaurant and bar occupies an attractive
former mill – once the village stores – on the banks of the
river Loir. There are limited water views from the interior
dining-room which is decorated in a modern rustic style, its
centrepiece a large open fireplace where a fire is lit on cool
days. However, the flower-decked riverside terrace overlooks a tranquil pastoral scene and is a lovely place for a meal
or simply a drink whenever the weather is fine. Last orders:
lunch 2pm; dinner 9.30pm. Terrace open all day for drinks,
pastries and ice-creams in summer. Set menus from F75; à la
carte around F130.

ST-DYE-SUR-LOIRE

🏚 🍽 **30/40** 🛏 ££

Manoir Bel Air, St-Dyé-sur-Loire, 41500 Mer.
Tel: 54.81.60.10
Closed January 15–February 20
Dbl rm F320–F380

This attractive 17th-century manor backs on to the Loire,
separated from the river's edge only by a small country lane.
There is a modern extension, almost indistinguishable from
the original house, which contains very comfortable, spacious bedrooms with the best river views, while those in the
old part tend to be small, although they are furnished with
genuine antiques. The attractive restaurant serves traditional
seasonal dishes including game in season. Ten tables enjoy
panoramic river views and there is a delightful outdoor
terrace for meals, drinks and high tea in summer. Last
orders: lunch 2.30pm; dinner 9.30pm. Set menus from
F118; à la carte around F200.
Riverside walks, fishing

ST EPAIN-NOYANT

🍽 🛏 ££

Auberge du Moulin des Roches, St Epain–Noyant, 37800
Ste-Maure.   Tel: 47.65.80.47
Closed October 31–March 15 and Monday except
June–August
A10 exit, 5km away

The machinery of this squat 17th-century watermill is in
perfect working order and guests can watch it in motion
while eating. Although diners hear rather than see the mill
stream from the restaurant and cocktail bar, there is an open-
air grill on a terrace beside the mill pond. Traditional regional
food is served in the restaurant; grilled meats and salads only

on the terrace. Last orders: lunch 2.30pm; dinner 9.30pm.
Set menus from F98; à la carte around F150.
Fishing (no permit needed), restaurant has five horses for hire

ST-FLORENT-LE-VIEIL

🏠 �🍴 <u>14/19</u> 🛏 £

L'Hostellerie de la Gabelle, 12 Quai de la Loire, 49410
St-Florent-le-Vieil.   Tel: 41.72.50.19
Open all year except November 1
Dbl rm F180–F250

On the south bank of the Loire, 40km downstream from
Angers, this pleasant hotel has a clear view over the river.
Bedrooms are simple, clean and well equipped, with en-suite
bathrooms. The restaurant serves regional specialities, including freshwater fish, eels and sweetbreads, in comfortable
surroundings; eight tables have good river views. In summer,
there are waterside terraces on both banks for drinks and
breakfast. Last orders: lunch 2pm; dinner 9pm. Set menus
from F65 (weekdays), F90 (weekends); à la carte from F150.
*Attractive town and riverside walks, fishing, rowing and motorboat
hire*

ST-FORT-SUR-LE-NE

🏠 🍴 <u>5/10</u> 🛏 ££

Le Moulin de Cierzac, St-Fort-sur-le-Né, 16630
Segonzac.   Tel: 45.83.01.32
Hotel and restaurant closed February and Monday
except during July and August
Dbl rm F350–F520
A10 exit 26, 30km away

This handsome 18th-century stone mill with tall white
shutters sits in lush grounds where the only sound is that
of the mill-stream tumbling past. Bedrooms are exceptionally
spacious with exposed beams and antique furniture. The

lounge and restaurant have exposed beams and stone walls and are comfortable and convivial with lovely views of the garden. Imaginative menus concentrate on fresh seasonal produce. Last orders: lunch 2pm; dinner 9.45pm. Set menus from F180; à la carte around F300.
Fishing (permits sold in Segonzac), swimming pool and tennis 4km

ST-HILAIRE-ST-MESMIN

🏨 🍽 14/20 🛏 ££

L'Escale du Port Arthur, 205 Rue de l'Eglise, 45160 St-Hilaire-St-Mesmin.   Tel: 38.76.30.36
Hotel closed January 1–15
Dbl rm F260–F300
Orleans 5km

In a quiet wooded location on the banks of the river Loiret, this pleasant modern hotel provides a good value base for exploring the Loire valley. Bedrooms are clean and comfortable, and all have en-suite bathrooms. The restaurant has floor-to-ceiling windows which make the most of the river views, and there is a delightful tree-shaded waterside terrace. Specialities include *coquilles St-Jacques* in artichoke sauce, freshwater fish and duck dishes. Last orders: lunch 2pm; dinner 9.30pm. Set menus from F110; à la carte around F200.
Pretty old village, walks along Loiret, free hotel canoe, fishing (permit F30)

ST-MALO

🏨 🍽 88/189 🛏 ££££

Grand Hôtel des Thermes, 100 Boulevard Hébert, 35401 St-Malo.   Tel: 99.40.75.75
Open all year
Dbl rm F920–F1060

Built in the tradition of 19th-century grand hotels, this elegant seafront hotel has been completely renovated in

the past few years and a stylish modern extension opened.
The public rooms are sumptuous and the bedrooms are all
well designed and tastefully furnished. Three have also been
specially adapted for the disabled. Attached to the hotel is a
thalassotherapy health spa offering a wide range of medical
and beauty treatments. There is also a children's club. The
conservatory-style Cap Horn restaurant enjoys fabulous sea
views. Last orders: lunch 2pm; dinner 9.15pm. Set menus
from F125 (lunch), F185 (dinner); à la carte around F300.
*Heated indoor seawater pool, health spa, gym; promenade and
beach; sand-yachts, sail-boards and boats for hire*

ST-MALO

🏨 12/23 🛏 ££

Hôtel Châteaubriand, 8 Boulevard Hébert, 35400
St-Malo.   Tel: 99.56.01.19
Closed January 7–February 4 and November
15–December 20
Dbl rm F320–F400

One of many similar sea-front establishments in St-Malo, this
simple, relaxing hotel is at the quieter end of town, away
from the worst of the traffic noise. Bedrooms are fairly basic
but clean and comfortable, six with French windows opening out on to small balconies. There is no restaurant, just a
pleasant bar with an outdoor terrace leading down to the
promenade that skirts the wide, sandy beach.
*Boat trips: down the river Rance to Dinan, around the coast to Cap
Fréhel and Cézembre island with its popular sandy beach*

ST-MALO

🍴 🛏 ££

Les Ecluses, Gare Maritime de la Bourse, 35400 St-Malo.
Tel: 99.56.81.00

Closed mid-November–mid-December and Monday
September–May
Opposite ferry terminal for Channel Islands

This surprisingly pleasant restaurant inside the port is conveniently situated for a meal prior to departure, or on arrival
by ferry. It is designed in the style of a conservatory and the
interior is decorated with all manner of nautical bric-a-brac.
All the tables have expansive water views either over the
harbour towards the walled city of St-Malo or across the bay
to Dinard. Last orders: lunch 2.30pm; dinner 9.30pm
(10.30pm in summer). Set menus are available from F92
(children F50); à la carte around F250.
Ferry port for Portsmouth, Guernsey and Jersey

ST-MAIXENT-L'ECOLE

🏨 🍽 10/10 🛏 ££

Logis Saint-Martin, Chemin de Pissot, 79400
St-Maixent-L'Ecole.   Tel: 49.05.58.68
Closed November 15–March 15
Dbl rm F300–F380
A10 exit 21, 10km away

This characterful 17th-century stone house, nestling in gardens bordering the river Sèvre, is presided over by the kind-
hearted and hospitable Madame Verdier. Decorated in coun-
try-cottage style, with tiled floors, old furniture and exposed
beams, the bedrooms are surprisingly spacious and tasteful,
and all have en-suite bathrooms. The pleasant restaurant
serves seasonal fish and game. Last orders: lunch 1.30pm;
dinner 9.30pm. Set menus from F98; à la carte around F150.
*Beautiful riverside walks, swimming pool in village; tennis, riding
and canoeing nearby. Convenient touring base for Marais Potevin
and Cognac country*

ST-PAIR-SUR-MER

🏚 <u>6/14</u> ▭ £

Pension Simone et Thérèse, 520 Rue du Fourneau,
St-Pair-sur-Mer, 50400 Granville.   Tel: 33.50.11.27
Open June 15–September 1
Half-board only, F195pp

This pleasant boarding house is one of many old seafront
mansions, built in all shapes and sizes, lining the promenade
of this attractive beach resort. It is full of old paintings,
furniture and bric-a-brac, and maintains a faithful clientele
who appreciate its good value. Bathroom facilities are shared.
A neat gravelled yard opens directly on to the beach which,
even in high summer, remains much quieter than its neighbours.
Safe sandy beach with sea-water swimming pool, fishing, water-
sports, golf and riding in Granville 3km

ST-PALAIS-SUR-MER

🏚 |○| <u>17/46</u> ▭ ££

Primavera, 12 Rue du Brick, 17420 St-Palais-sur-Mer.
Tel: 46.23.20.35
Closed December and two weeks in February;
restaurant closed Tuesday evening and Wednesday
October 1–April 30
Dbl rm F360–F480

Right on the sea's edge, in an isolated and picturesque
setting, the Primavera is a charming turn-of-the-century
neo-Romanesque folly. The spacious bedrooms, most in a
modern wing, are handsomely decorated, each in a different
style. Sea-view rooms have sliding doors opening on to
balconies. The pretty dining-room also has splendid sea
views. Seafood specialities. Half-board is compulsory during
July and August, costing F315–F425 per person. Last orders:

lunch 1.30pm; dinner 10pm. Set menus are available from
F108; à la carte around F220.
*Indoor heated pool, private tennis court; nearby sandy beaches with
naturist areas, windsurfing school and offshore fishing*

ST-PIERRE-DU-VAUVRAY

🏠 🍴 **8/14** 🛏 £££

Hostellerie St-Pierre, 1 Chemin des Amoureux, 27430
St-Pierre-du-Vauvray.   Tel: 32.59.93.29
Closed January and February; restaurant closed Tuesday
and Wednesday lunch
Half-board only; F525–F645 per person

This bizarre triangular-shaped, mock–Norman manor stands
on a beautiful stretch of the Seine, just a short drive from the
Paris–Rouen motorway. Bedrooms are tastefully furnished
in different styles, some with private patios overlooking the
river. All the restaurant's 14 tables enjoy river views, and chef
Alain Potier is known for his modern interpretations of
classic French dishes. Breakfast, drinks and pastries are
served on the lawn just feet from the Seine. Last orders:
lunch 1.30pm; dinner 9pm. Set menus from F160; à la carte
around F300.
*Tow-path walks, sailing boats, sail-boards and pedalos for hire at
marina 3km*

ST-REMY-LA-VARENNE

🍴 🛏 ££

La Riviera, 49250 St-Rémy-la-Varenne.
Tel: 41.57.02.19
Open April 1–September 30
On D120 25km east of Angers

Located on the peaceful south bank of the Loire, this simple
neat restaurant on the riverbank serves very good, well-
prepared regional food. Freshwater fish are the speciality –

eel, pike and salmon – and the *fritures de Loire*, deep-fried eels and other small fish, are particularly popular with locals. There are 15 tables in the pleasant, pink-and-white dining-room, all with views over the river, together with a further 20 tables on an outdoor terrace when the weather is fine. The bar is open for drinks and ice-creams 10am–10pm. Last orders: lunch 2.30pm; dinner 10pm. Set menus from F105; à la carte around F150.

ST-SAVINIEN

IOI ▭ £

Le Bec Fin, Etang de la Grande Thibaudière, 17350 St-Savinien.   Tel: 46.90.28.44
Closed two weeks in January, Tuesday all year and Monday evening out of season
A10 exit 23/24, 20km away

This simple, comfortable restaurant, bar and ice-cream parlour sits beside a pretty pond in tranquil countryside just a half-hour's drive from the motorway. It is an excellent value-for-money lunch stop. All the tables enjoy water views and there is also an outdoor terrace in summer. Specialities include fresh local duck and fish. Open 9.30am–2am in summer. Last orders: lunch 1.30pm; dinner 9.30pm. Set menus are available from F55 (children's menu F35); à la carte around F160.

ST-SYMPHORIEN-LE-CHATEAU

▥ IOI 14/54 ▭ ££££

Château d'Esclimont, St-Symphorien-le-Château, 28700 Auneau.   Tel: 37.31.15.15
Open all year
Dbl rm F1050–F1650
A11 Exit Ablis 5km

Built in 1543 for the Archbishop of Tours, this stunning Renaissance castle is surrounded by a moat crossed by stone bridges. Just 60km from Paris, it is a perfect weekend retreat. The spacious bedrooms are elegantly furnished, each in a different style, and overlook the beautiful grounds. Window tables in the three sumptuous dining-rooms all look out over a lake. Traditional French dishes based on seasonal produce. Drinks are served on a terrace overlooking the moat. The bar stocks more than 50 cognacs and armagnacs. Last orders: lunch 2.30pm; dinner 9.30pm. Set menus from F300; à la carte around F450.

The 140-acre park contains a heated outdoor pool, rowing boats and tennis courts. Ballooning trips from the chateau can be arranged

ST-THIBAULT

📷 <u>10/10</u> ✉ £

L'Etoile, 2 Quai de Loire, St-Thibault, St-Satur, 18300 Sancerre.   Tel: 48.54.12.15
Closed December 1–February 28 and Wednesday except during July and August
Dbl rm F130–F230

This restaurant has a magnificent setting with all tables enjoying expansive views over the Loire. Madame Boursin cooks good regional fare, including Loire eels and chicken liver paté with truffles. Two mouth-watering puddings are named after her granddaughters – *Delice de Stefanie*, a chocolate gateau, and *Sourire de Berengère*, a Cointreau soufflé. There is a lovely waterside terrace for meals in summer. Bedrooms are basic, only two with en-suite bathrooms. Guests must take dinner in restaurant. Last orders: lunch 2pm; dinner 9pm. Set menus from F95; à la carte around F230.

Pike, eel and perch fishing, riverside walks, visits to nearby Sancerre vineyards

SAINTES

🏨 🍴 <u>11/32</u> 💳 £££

Relais du Bois St Georges, Rue de Royan, Cours Genet,
17100 Saintes.   Tel: 46.93.50.99
Open all year
Dbl rm F600–F900

Old and new have been successfully blended to create this
elegant hotel just outside Saintes. Set around a small lake in
beautifully tended gardens, the opulent bedrooms are works
of art with themes including English country house, ship's
cabin, and even Aphrodite's temple. Most have furnished
patios or balconies. The plush, country-style restaurant also
overlooks the lake. Last orders: lunch 2pm; dinner 9.30pm.
Set menus from F155; à la carte around F250.
Indoor heated pool, tennis court, croquet lawn

SAUMUR

🏨 🍴 <u>24/45</u> 💳 ££

Loire Hôtel, Rue du Vieux Pont, 49400 Saumur.
Tel: 41.67.22.42
Open all year
Dbl rm F475–F550

Peacefully situated on the Ile d'Offard, this modern hotel has
been designed to blend in with the historic buildings that
surround it. The comfortable, well-equipped bedrooms
enjoy magnificent views over the Loire towards the chateau
and the old town of Saumur on the opposite bank of the
river. Its restaurant, Les Mariniers, serves regional seasonal
produce; specialities may include *pigeon et sa pomme tapé* and
the classic Loire pike dish, *sandre au beurre blanc*. Nine of the
tables enjoy panoramic views over the Loire. Last orders:
lunch 2pm; dinner 9.30pm. Set menus from F98; à la carte
around F250.

Watersports in leisure park; Saumur's sights include National Academy of Riding and Horse Museum and hotel can arrange riding weekends

SIZUN

IOI 🗖 £

Restaurant de la Terrasse / Crêperie de Milin Kerroc'h,
29450 Sizun.   Tel: 98.68.81.56
Closed Tuesday September 15–January 1
Sizun 1km north

This old, hand-laid stone mill beside a long, narrow lake provides a pleasant lunch or dinner stop. The first-floor enclosed dining verandah has good water views and serves smoked ham, duck, grilled meats and salads as well as crêpes. On the ground floor there's a café–bar with several outside tables. Families are made very welcome and there is a children's playground, mini-golf course and miniature train which circles the lake. There are also ten nicely furnished self-catering bungalows on the property. Open 10am–midnight. Set menus from F45 (children F30); à la carte around F150.
Pedalos for hire, fishing (tackle for hire), woodland walks

SUCE-SUR-ERDRE

IOI 🗖 ££££

La Châtaigneraie, 156 Route de Carquefou,
Sucé-sur-Erdre, 44240 La Chapelle-sur-Erdre.
Tel: 40.77.90.95
Closed January, first two weeks of August, Sunday evening and Monday (open Monday evening June–August)
Nantes 15km

A 19th-century manor in grounds leading down to a lovely stretch of the river Erdre houses this highly-acclaimed restaurant. Everything is homemade, fresh from the markets and cooked to order by owner–chef Joseph Delphin. Half the tables in the comfortable Baroque dining-room enjoy views over the Erdre, and large mirrors also reflect views of the water, creating a light airy setting. Expect refined versions of regional dishes, beautifully presented. Freshwater fish and seafood dominate the menu. Good selection of local cheeses. Very good wine list, many locally produced. West-facing outdoor terrace for meals and aperitifs in summer. Last orders: lunch 2pm; dinner 9.30pm. Set menus from F170 (lunch), F235 (dinner); à la carte around F300. Booking advised.

TANCARVILLE-ECLUSE

La Marine, 76430 Tancarville-Ecluse.   Tel: 35.39.77.15
Closed July 15–August 12, Sunday evening and Monday
Dbl rm F320–F500
Le Havre 35km

A nice stopover outside Le Havre, this hotel–restaurant sits in a pretty garden beneath chalk cliffs from where the impressive Tancarville suspension bridge launches itself over the Seine towards Honfleur. Bedrooms are clean and comfortable, one with French windows opening on to a first-floor terrace. The buzz of traffic is always heard in the background. The airy verandah restaurant serves *nouvelle cuisine* and, in summer, opens out on to the lawn. Most tables have impressive river views. Last orders: lunch 2pm; dinner 9pm. Set menus from F130 (children F50); à la carte around F350.
Tow-path walks, fishing from the garden

THAUMIERS

Château de Thaumiers, Thaumiers, 18210
Charenton-sur-Cher.   Tel: 48.61.81.62

Open March 15–November 15
Dbl rm F800; 3/4 person apartments F1000

This charming 18th-century chateau, partly surrounded by a
wide moat, is owned by the Vicomte and Vicomtesse de
Bonneval who delight in sharing their home with guests.
Richly decorated with beautifully preserved antiques, every-
thing has a history, except for the modern bathrooms.
Dinner, served *en famille* with the owners, can be provided
on prior reservation and costs F220 including wine. A serene,
discreet retreat in the heart of pastoral Berry.
*Tennis, golf practice range, and forest walks in grounds. Nearby
Berry chateaux, Sancerre vineyards, George Sand's home in Nohant*

TORIGNI-SUR-VIRE

IOI ▭ £

Le New Jersey, 50160 Torigni-sur-Vire.   Tel: 33.56.92.27
Closed September 15–October 10 and Tuesday

On the banks of a lake in the attractive old town of Torigni,
this simple grill and crêperie is a good lunch-stop. Most tables
glimpse the lake through the horse-chestnut trees, and there's
a waterside terrace in summer. Grilled fish, seafood platters,
and a good choice of stuffed crêpes make up the menu. Open
noon–9.30pm for drinks and crêpes. Last orders: lunch 2pm;
dinner 9pm. Set menus from F69; à la carte around F110.
Pedalos and water-scooters for hire

TREBEURDEN

▥ IOI 18/30 ▭ £££

Ti Al Lannec, Allée de Mézo-guen, 22560 Trébeurden.
Tel: 96.23.57.26
Closed November 12–March 15
Dbl rm F680–F880

Standing in secluded wooded grounds high above the sea,
stylish decor and great attention to detail have turned this

100–year–old house into a delightful romantic retreat. Decorated like a comfortable English country house hotel, it is pervaded by a warm, cosseted ambience. Bedrooms were renovated last year (two specially adapted for disabled guests) and 12 have balconies or substantial verandahs. Most tables in both breakfast room and dining-room enjoy expansive views over an attractive seascape. Drinks are also served on the lawn terrace. Guests are asked to take one meal a day in the restaurant. Last orders: lunch 1.30pm; dinner 9.30pm. Set menus from F120 (lunch); F185 dinner; à la carte around F250.

Hotel has health spa with Jacuzzi, sauna, steam bath, massage salon, mud and algae treatments, solarium and gym; private path down to beach; coastal path

TREBEURDEN

🏨 🍽 **18/18** ▭ £££

Manoir de Lan Kerellec, Allée Centrale de Lan-Kerellec, 22560 Trébeurden.   Tel: 96.23.50.09
Closed November 15–March 15; restaurant closed
Monday and Tuesday lunch mid–September–mid–June
Half-board only; F1300–F2060 a night for two people

Formerly the private home of Monsieur Daubé's grandparents, this lovely stone manor house has been transformed into a very smart hotel. The coastal panorama from both bedrooms and public rooms is magnificent as the sea swirls around a collection of rocky islets. Bedrooms are spacious and elegantly furnished (seven have large sun-terraces) and bathrooms are luxurious. The dining-room has a 40ft-high vaulted wooden ceiling and large windows so all diners can admire the sea view. Seafood is a speciality. Last orders: lunch 2pm; dinner 10pm. Set menus from F140 (weekday lunch), F185 (weekends and dinner); à la carte around F300.

Hotel speedboat used for picnics, island excursions, fishing and water-skiing (M. Daubé is an enthusiast who encourages guests to have a go); beaches below hotel; coastal path walks

LE TREPORT

IOI ⊟ ££

Le Homard Bleu, 45 Quai Francois I, 76470 Le Tréport.
Tel: 35.86.15.89
Closed December 15–February 15

Very popular with French families for a blow-out Sunday lunch, this convivial restaurant overlooks the harbour at Le Tréport. The best tables are those in the conservatory-style verandah attached to the first-floor dining-room which look out over Mers beach and the cliffs across the bay, as well as the busy fishing harbour below. Fresh local fish, often cooked in creamy Norman sauces, and enormous seafood platters are the mainstays of the menu. Salmon steak tartare is a particular speciality. Last orders: lunch 3pm; dinner 11pm. Set menus from F92 (F145 on Sunday); à la carte around F150.
Beautiful cliff walks, sand and shingle beach, windsurfing club

TREVIERES

⊨ 2/3 ⊟ ££££

Château de Colombières, Colombières, 14710 Trévières.
Tel: 31.22.51.65
Open June 15–September 15
Suites F800–F1000

This romantic 14th-century castle is surrounded by a moat with a drawbridge leading to an inner courtyard. Guests are personally greeted by the Comte and Comtesse Etienne de Maupeou, whose family has lived here for more than 300 years. There are three handsomely decorated suites which overlook the beautifully kept grounds and a small lake graced by wild ducks, geese and swans. A table d'hote dinner can be provided on advance notice. Children older than 12 preferred. Occasional four-day cookery courses, with professional tuition, are held at the chateau. For further information contact British tour operator, La France des Villages on 0449 737678.

Rowing boat in the moat, pike fishing in lake and river on property, summer concerts in the castle; nearby Bayeux with famous tapestry of the Battle of Hastings

TREVOU-TREGUIGNEC

🏠 ⦿ 12/12 ⊟ ££

Le Trestel Bellevue, Route Trestel, Trevou-Treguignec, 22660 Trélévern.   Tel: 96.23.71.44
Open Easter–November 5
Dbl rm F300–F330

This pretty house, with its steep pitched roof and wooden balconies, sits high on a pine-covered hill overlooking the crescent-shaped beach of Trevou-Treguignec. The hotel has a pleasant old-fashioned feel about it. Bedrooms are simple but comfortable and those on the top two floors have balconies with panoramic views. Tables in the restaurant either overlook the beach or glimpse the ocean through trees. Most guests take the half-board option, which is compulsory in July and August. The charming owners, Fernand and Louisette Bricout, insist that none of the food served has ever been frozen or microwaved. Specialities include game hen, rabbit, duck, crêpes, and fish and seafood. Last orders: lunch 2pm; dinner 9pm. Set menus from F110; à la carte around F170.
Excellent beach 500m, sailing, windsurfing and scuba-diving, boat trips to Sept Iles bird reserve and neighbouring islands

LA TRINITE-SUR-MER

🛏 4/4 ⊟ £

La Maison du Latz, Le Latz, 56470 La Trinité-sur-Mer.
Tel: 97.55.80.91
Open all year
Dbl rm F240–F300
From La Trinité follow signs for Château du Lac

Nicole Le Rouzic welcomes visitors to her attractive modern home built on the bank of a quiet creek. The four bedrooms are tastefully decorated, and guests can relax and enjoy breakfast, included in the room price, in the south-facing conservatory. Dinner served on request for F70–F120.
Sandy beaches and watersports 3km

TROO

🛏 ¾ 🍽 ££

Château de la Voute, Troo, 41800 Montoire–sur–le–Loir.
Tel: 54.72.52.52
Open all year
Dbl rm F350–F450

An ideal base for exploring the Loire Valley, this beautiful 16th-century manor is owned by two antique dealers who live on the ground floor. The first-floor guest bedrooms are elegant, stylishly decorated, and spacious, with beautiful antique furniture and large old baths and basins. Everything is impeccably maintained and kept spotlessly clean. Breakfast is served in the bedrooms or on a gravel terrace overlooking the Loir.
Boat trips along Loir from Vendome, riverbank walks, tennis and riding in interesting troglodyte village of Troo

TROUVILLE-SUR-MER

🍽 🍽 ££

Le Galatée, Promenade des Planches, 14360
Trouville-sur-Mer.   Tel: 31.88.15.04
Closed January 1–February 15

Essentially a conservatory on the beach, this convivial restaurant offers unimpaired views of the sun setting over the sea. The food is fresh and homemade, with specialities including grilled fish and sirloin steaks, lobster and prawns. There is also an outdoor terrace for snacks and drinks, open 9am–2am

May–September. Set menus from F65; à la carte around F135. Booking advisable.

VANNES

🏨 🍽 <u>24/42</u> 💳 ££

Le Roof, Presqu'île de Conleau, 56000 Vannes.
Tel: 97.63.47.47
Open all year
Dbl rm F450–F600

This attractive hotel stands on a quiet rural peninsula just outside medieval Vannes. It faces directly out over the entrance to the Morbihan Gulf and provides a good touring base for those who like a smart, modern ambience. Bedrooms are fashionably decorated and well equipped, most with balconies. There are two restaurants, one formal (eight tables enjoy good water views), the other more of a brasserie with a waterside terrace for meals and drinks which is open June–September. Last orders in restaurant: lunch 2pm; dinner 9.30pm. Set menus from F140; à la carte around F250. *Estuary beaches; tennis, squash, solarium 2km; boat excursions of Morbihan Gulf and islands from Vannes; Vannes' aquarium, butterfly farm and walled medieval town*

VELLUIRE

🏨 🍽 <u>10/11</u> 💳 ££

Auberge de la Rivière, Velluire, 85770 Vix.
Tel: 51.52.32.15
Closed January and February; restaurant closed Sunday evening and Tuesday except July–September
Dbl rm F300–F360

This inn on the banks of the river Vendée is owned and run by Robert and Luce Pajot who provide a warm welcome and take great pride in their delightful establishment. Set in beautiful unspoilt countryside on the edge of the *Venise*

Verte, a land of canals, dykes and reclaimed farmland, it offers a quiet retreat from the world. The very comfortable and prettily decorated bedrooms look straight out over the river. The great attention to detail is carried through to the restaurant, where five tables have water views. Fish, seafood, beef and game form the basis of Madame Pajot's appetizing menus. Last orders: lunch 2pm; dinner 9.30pm. Set menus from F80 (F160 at weekends); à la carte around F225.
Rowing boats and bicycles for hire, fishing (permits sold in village), lovely walking country

VILLERAY

🏨 🍴 <u>10/10</u> 💳 £££

Moulin de Villeray, Villeray, 61100 Condeau.
Tel: 33.73.30.22
Closed January 3–February 15; restaurant closed
Monday except May 15–October 15
Dbl rm F530–F740
Exit A11 Luigny, 30-minute drive

This 19th-century corn mill astride the Huisne river has been tastefully converted into a delightful, peaceful hotel. Bedrooms are impeccably furnished, each in a different style, and some overlook the attractive grounds and an ancient castle as well as the river. The wonderfully rustic restaurant, decorated with carved oak beams, a clay-tiled floor and tapestry chairs, looks out over the mill wheel and serves classic French cooking prepared by a chef from the Dordogne. There is a riverside terrace for drinks and afternoon tea. Guests asked to dine in the restaurant. Last orders: lunch 2pm; dinner 9pm. Set menus from F130; à la carte around F250.
Fishing (permits sold in village), good walks along river and through medieval Villeray, riding and tennis courts 3km

South-West France

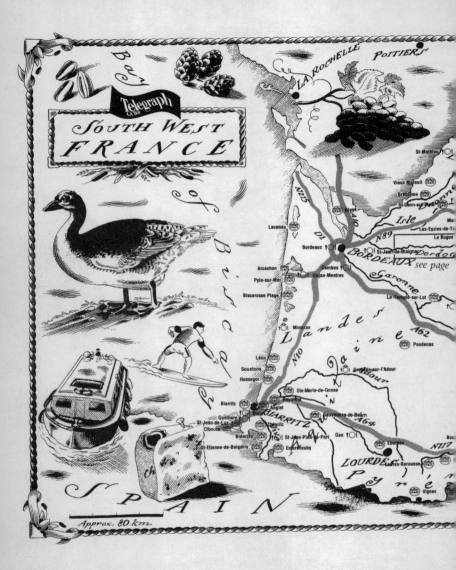

Telegraph GUIDE

SOUTH WEST
FRANCE

Bay of Biscay

SPAIN

Approx. 80 km.

LA ROCHELLE
POITIERS

St-Mathieu
Vieux Mareuil
Brantôme
St-Léon-sur-l'Isle
Blaye
Lacanau
Isle
Les-Eyzies-de-Ti
Le Bugue
Bordeaux
N89
BORDEAUX
St-Jean-de-Blaignac
Dordogne
see page
Arcachon
Cambes
Gujan-Mestras
Garonne
Pyla-sur-Mer
Biscarosse Plage
Le-Temple-sur-Lot
Landes
A62
Mimizan
Poudenas
Léon
Soustons
Grenade-sur-l'Adour
Hossegor
Ste-Marie-de-Gosse
Biarritz
Bayonne
Anglet
St-Jean-de-Luz
Guéthary
BIARRITZ
Sauveterre-de-Béarn
Ciboure
A64
Bidart
Bidarray
St-Jean-Pied-de-Port
Gan
Lourdes
St-Etienne-de-Baigorry
Esterencuby
N117
LOURDES
Pyré
Coates-Barousse
Vignec

ABREST

◻ 1/5 ▱ £

Les Eperons, 5 Avenue du Général de Gaulle, Abrest,
03200 Vichy.   Tel: 70.32.24.86
Open all year
Dbl rm F120

This simple restaurant stands on a pleasant wooded stretch of
the river Allier. Popular with local fishermen, it serves good
old-fashioned home cooking. In summer, meals can be served
on an outdoor terrace beneath large horse-chestnut trees on
the river bank. Bedrooms are modestly furnished but clean.
Last orders: lunch 2pm; dinner 9.30pm. Open all day for
drinks and snacks. Set menus from F60; à la carte around F120.

AGDE

▦ ⦿ 12/25 ▱ £££

La Tamarissière, 21 Quai Théophile-Cornu,
La Tamarissière, 34300 Agde.   Tel: 67.94.20.87
Closed October 15–April 1; restaurant closed Sunday
evening and Monday except June 15–September 15
when closed Monday lunch only
Dbl rm F410–F580
Take D32 from Agde

La Tamarissière is attractively situated on the banks of the
Hérault estuary, just south of the old fishing port of Agde.
The building itself is rather plain, but all the rooms are prettily
decorated and comfortably furnished; many have balconies
overlooking the river or the swimming-pool terrace and
garden. Weather permitting, meals are served on a shaded
riverside terrace – although the elegant dining-room is cool
and refreshing in summer. Nicolas Albano's menus mix classic
fish dishes with regional specialities such as *bouillabaisse*. Last
orders: lunch 1.30pm; dinner 9.30pm. Set menus from F140
(F220 at weekends); à la carte around F350.

Sandy beach 100m away at the end of the quay; water-skiing and sailing Cap d'Agde; fishing

AGDE

IOI ▭ ₤₤₤

Le Front de Mer, 2 Rue du Front de Mer, Cap d'Agde, 34300 Agde.   Tel: 67.26.75.75
Open all year for dinner and Sunday lunch

Surrounded by water on three sides, this small, imaginatively designed restaurant on the Cap d'Adge is a light airy place. All tables have splendid views over the sea through the large bay windows. Owner–chef, Monsieur Muroudot, takes great pride in his cooking, using only fresh seasonal produce, especially fish. There is a tank for live crustaceans. Imaginative fish specialities include *filets de rouget au caviar de légumes* and *salade de langoustines au beurre d'orange*. Last orders: Sunday lunch 2.30pm; dinner 10.30pm. Set menus are available from F180; à la carte around F300.

AGDE

🏨 IOI <u>20/55</u> ▭ ₤₤₤

Hôtel Capao, Avenue des Corsaires, Cap d'Agde, 34300 Agde.   Tel: 67.26.99.44
Open Easter–October 15
Dbl rm F480–F660; family rooms F750–F890

Set back on the nicest of Cap d'Agde's sandy beaches, Plage Richelieu, this well-equipped, modern hotel is particularly suitable for families with children. The comfortable, air-conditioned bedrooms are quiet and each has a private terrace overlooking either sand-dunes or the swimming pool set in lawns leading down to the beach. Two rooms are suitable for disabled guests. Extensive amenities including a crèche, fitness centre with saunas, Jacuzzi, and thalassotherapy health and beauty treatments, and a mini-bus service to the town and the marina. The dining-room has no water views, but there is a grill and snack bar on the beach.

Private sandy beach; windsurfing, water-skiing, sailing, pedalo and jet-ski hire; deep-sea fishing and glass-bottomed boat trips down Canal du Midi and to Etang du Thau to see oyster and mussel beds; golf and tennis

ALBI

🏨 |○| 15/24 ▭ ££££

La Reserve, Route de Cordes, 81000 Albi.
Tel: 63.47.60.22
Open May 1–October 31
Dbl rm F980–F1000

This beautiful white villa stands in secluded grounds leading down to the river Tarn. An exclusive establishment which takes itself very seriously, it is run by the Rieux family, master hoteliers since 1734. They pride themselves on their professional and courteous staff. Bedrooms are extremely tastefully decorated, eight with balconies overlooking the Tarn. There are also excellent river views from the restaurant and its outdoor terrace. Menus include a large choice of fish and specialities such as *terrine de foie gras* and *magret de canard*. Last orders: lunch 2pm; dinner 9pm. Set menus from F160; à la carte around F300.

Carp fishing excursions can be arranged; outdoor swimming pool and tennis court; golf 3km; riding 5km; watersports at Aigulèze 15km; heliport

ALBI

🏨 |○| 28/56 ▭ ££

Altea Hôtel, 41 Rue Porta, 81000 Albi.   Tel: 63.47.66.66
Open all year; restaurant closed Saturday
Dbl rm F340–F560

This stylish conversion of Albi's 18th-century bakery stands on the north bank of the Tarn with panoramic views over the river towards St Cécile Cathedral and the heart of the old town. Opened in 1987 after a two-year renovation programme, the hotel has preserved the impressive pink-brick facade, but the interior is modern and sophisticated. However, bedrooms are on the small side, although they are comfortable and attractively furnished in a simple modern style. In summer, guests can dine on an open-air terrace which overlooks the Tarn. Last orders: lunch 2pm; dinner 10.30pm. Set menus are on offer from F110; à la carte around F220.

Fishing 1km; exploring Albi's sights on foot; golf 3km; riding 5km; watersports at Aiguelèze 15km

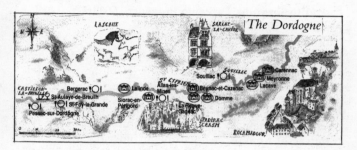

ALLAS-LES-MINES

🍽 ▭ ££

Le Gabarrier, Ldt. de Sandrou, 24220 Allas-les-Mines.
Tel: 53.29.22.51
Closed November 15–January 15 and Wednesday out of season

Set on the grassy riverbank of the Dordogne outside an otherwise uninteresting village, this sturdy stone restaurant recalls an old-style *guinguette*, or open-air dance hall. From tables on the flower-decked terrace there are fine views over a peaceful stretch of river and the flat rural landscape beyond. Meals are served outside whenever the weather is fine from mid-April–end September. Monsieur Besse's cooking has earned him a loyal local following. Calf sweetbreads with wild mushrooms is a particular speciality and the menu includes a wide choice of fresh fish dishes. Reserve ahead for a table on the terrace in high summer. Last orders: lunch 2pm; dinner 9pm. Set menus from F115; à la carte around F280.

AMELIE-LES-BAINS

🏠 🍴 30/59 🛏 ££

Castel Emeraude, La Petite Provence, 66110
Amélie-les-Bains.   Tel: 68.39.02.83
Closed December and January
Dbl rm F305–F340
Exit A9 Le Boulou 15km

The waterside location of the Castel Emeraude is enhanced by the privacy of its woodland setting on the banks of the river Tech. Originally a small 19th-century chateau – the two turrets at the front of the hotel give an indication of its former glory. The history of Amélie-les-Bains dates back to the Romans, who built the original spa, and its mineral waters are still recommended for invigorating the weary traveller. Bedrooms are spacious and quiet, 26 with patios on the water's edge. Two rooms have facilities for the disabled. Unfortunately, none of the tables in the restaurant have river views but, in good weather, meals are served on an outdoor terrace and drinks on the riverbank. Last orders: lunch 2.30pm; dinner 9pm. Set menus from F110; à la carte around F250.
Route maps for mountain-bike rides available from hotel; fishing; convenient base for exploring Pyrenees

LES ANCIZES-COMPS

🏰 🍴 <u>13/20</u> 🍽 £

Belle-Vue, Pont du Bouchet, 63770 Les Ancizes-Comps.
Tel: 73.86.80.39.
Hotel and restaurant closed mid-October–mid-February,
Tuesday and Wednesday nights excluding
June 15–September 15
Dbl rm F110–F160
Follow Pont du Bouchet signs from D19

This modern hotel stands alone on the banks of an artificial
lake, against a backdrop of wooded foothills and the Gorges
de la Sioule. Bedrooms are furnished simply but comfortably,
six with en-suite bathrooms, nine with bath or shower only.
The restaurant's menu is limited and the food is unadventurous but reasonably priced. Most tables have lake views and
there is a shaded wooden terrace which is used for meals in
summer. Last orders: lunch 1.30pm; dinner 8.30pm. Set
menus from F60; à la carte around F120.
*Fishing; lake swimming from beach 1km; boats, pedalos and sail-
boards for hire; forest walks*

ANGLET

🏰 🍴 <u>20/100</u> 🍽 £££

Atlanthal, 153 Boulevard des Plages, 64600 Anglet.
Tel: 59.52.75.75
Open all year
Dbl rm F615–F950
Follow signs 'Plage Nord'

This modern hotel sits beside a golf course just north of
Biarritz. Bedrooms, arranged around a central atrium, are
tastefully decorated in a warm modern style and particularly
well equipped. Some of those with sea views have floor-to-
ceiling windows and large balconies. The hotel contains a
thalassotherapy centre, where restorative health treatments

involve a course of seawater baths, massage and exercise. While catering for the health-conscious, the restaurant also provides for the discerning gourmet. Last orders: lunch 2pm; dinner 10pm. Set menus are available from F190; à la carte around F250.

Indoor and outdoor heated pools, sauna, Turkish baths, large gymnasium and exercise facilities; nearby golf and tennis; deep-sea fishing

ANGLET

🏠 🍴 7/14 ▭ ££££

Château de Brindos, Lac de Brindos, Route de l'Aviation, 64600 Anglet.   Tel: 59.23.17.68
Open all year
Dbl rm F1000–F1300

An Englishman built this handsome lakeside villa in the 1920s in the style of a Spanish Renaissance manor; this theme is carried through inside, with a medieval fireplace from Toledo and a Cordoba leather ceiling in the music-room. But there is nothing formal about the ambience, which is restful and welcoming. Bedrooms are spacious and elegantly furnished. Seven have peaceful open views over the pretty, private lake. The restaurant is highly regarded and has a similarly tranquil outlook across the water. Last orders: lunch 2.30pm; dinner 10pm. Set menus are available from F350; à la carte around F400.

Hotel swimming pool and tennis courts; pike and carp fishing in the lake

ARCACHON

🏠 15/29 ▭ £££

Les Vagues, 9 Boulevard de l'Océan, 33120 Arcachon.
Tel: 56.83.03.75
Open all year

Dbl rm F378–F710; half-board compulsory
July 2–September 9, F444–F584 per person

An interesting example of modern seaside architecture, this
stylish hotel enjoys splendid views across to Cap Ferret. The
bedrooms and public areas are all decorated in fashionable
pastel shades and immaculately maintained. Three first-floor
rooms have large terraces, and rooms at the top of the hotel
have enclosed glass verandahs. The restaurant, which is open
for breakfast and dinner only, is chiefly for hotel residents.
*Swimming from the small sandy beach; watersports, tennis, golf and
riding nearby*

ARCACHON

🏠 18/43 ▭ ££

Grand Hôtel Richelieu, 185 Boulevard de la Plage,
33120 Arcachon.   Tel: 56.83.16.50
Open March 15–October 31
Dbl rm F530–F600

This old-fashioned hotel overlooks the pier from where the
boats leave for Cap Ferret and the oyster beds. The fully
modernized bedrooms have quaint touches such as notepa-
per and envelopes in leather folders. Sea-view rooms enjoy
superb ocean views. The free parking for about ten cars is an
asset given the town's complicated one-way system. There is
no restaurant, but there is a wide choice of eating places
within walking distance.
*Fine sandy beach; boat trips around Arcachon lagoon, oyster-beds
and Ile aux Oiseaux; motorboats, sail-boats and windsurfers for hire
nearby*

ARGELES-SUR-MER

🏠 ⦿ 54/73 ▭ ££

Grand Hôtel du Lido, 50 Boulevard de la Mer, 66700
Argelès-sur-Mer.   Tel: 68.81.10.32

Open May 18–September 30
Dbl rm F400–F600
From Argelès follow signs to the beach

What sets this hotel apart from the many others on this stretch
of coastline is its location in a pleasant residential area on the
seafront. The Grand Hôtel du Lido, built in the 1950s, was
one of the first hotels in the area, and has since been pleasingly
modernized. Half the bedrooms have private verandahs with
good views of the coast. The pool area is hidden from public
view by tall trees and the proximity of a safe, sandy beach
makes the hotel particularly suitable for children. The varied
menu is reasonably priced and meals are served at the poolside or in the restaurant which overlooks the sea. Last orders:
lunch 2pm; dinner 9.30pm. Set menus from F130 (children
F65); à la carte around F250.
Sandy beach; watersports; organized excursions into the Pyrenees

ARGELIERS

IOI ▤ ££

Au Chat Qui Peche, Maison du Cantonniers, Argeliers,
11120 Ginestas.   Tel: 68.46.28.74
Open Easter–mid–October
A61 30 minutes away

On the banks of the Canal du Midi, Au Chat Qui Peche is
reminiscent of an English country pub. The restaurant has a
rustic charm with exposed beams, wooden tables and a
blackboard menu. Outside tables have the best canal views.
Popular with locals and travellers alike, it is ideally located for
a lunch stop while exploring the Canal du Midi or the
Minervois and Corbières vineyards. The menu includes
many traditional dishes of Languedoc-Roussillon. Last orders: lunch 2.30pm; dinner 9pm. Set menus from F85
(children F40); à la carte around F160.
Fishing, tow-path walks

ARGENTAT

¶◎| ▭ £

Auberge des Gabariers, 15 Quai Lestourgie, 19400
Argentat.   Tel: 55.28.05.87
Open all year; lunch only in winter, closed Saturday and
Sunday September–mid–June

A cosy, convivial restaurant situated in the heart of Argentat,
its quayside terrace overlooks the Dordogne and picturesque
old buildings on the far side of the river. The interior has been
prettily decorated, although only a few inside tables look out
over the river. Traditional regional cuisine. Last orders: lunch
2pm; dinner 9.15pm. Open all day in summer for drinks and
ice-creams. Set menus from F58; à la carte around F100.
Fishing; watersports nearby; pleasant riverside walks

ARGENTAT

◻▵ ▭ £

La Crêperie, 2 Rue Portsaulou, 19400 Argentat.
Tel: 55.28.80.43
Open daily mid–June–mid–September, otherwise
Friday–Sunday during school holidays

This simple crêperie is conveniently located in the cobbled
pedestrianized centre of Argentat where the bridge, Le Vieux
Pont, crosses the Dordogne. For anyone exploring this
charming village it is a good place to stop for a quick
lunch. An outdoor terrace overlooks the river. Open from
noon to midnight.

ARPHY

¶◎| ▭ £

Le Val d'Arphy, Arphy, 30120 Le Vigan.   Tel: 67.81.06.30
Open weekends only October–May
From Arphy follow signs for Aulas

The remote peak of Mont Aigoual, and the wooded valley below, provide an impressive backdrop to this rustic restaurant. Many of the inside tables look out over the river Coudoulous as it rushes down the valley and there is an open-air gravelled terrace on the water's edge. Madame Maurin provides a very reasonably priced and varied menu, inspired by the traditions of the Cévennes. *Ecrevisses*, local freshwater crayfish, are a particular speciality. Steak and chips, fresh trout and drinks available all day. Open from 8am until the early hours. Set menus from F79 (children F40); à la carte around F130.
Trout fishing; swimming in the river; interesting walks along mountain paths; riding in Le Vigan

BANYULS-SUR-MER

Les Elmes, Plage des Elmes, 66650 Banyuls-sur-Mer.
Tel: 68.88.03.12
Closed January 1–February 10
Dbl rm F250–F440

This simple seaside hotel stands beside a sandy cove near the main beach at Banyuls. Bedrooms are modestly furnished, most with air-conditioning. Seven have balconies with good sea views and these are also quieter than rooms overlooking the road, although some of these are new and have soundproofing. The restaurant, La Littorine, has a covered beachside terrace and serves the traditional *moules marinières* and *gigot de lotte* as well as the more adventurous creations of chef Daniel Brin based on fresh seasonal produce. The wine list includes 22 kinds of Banyuls, a fortified wine something like Port. Last orders: lunch 2pm; dinner 9.30pm. Set menus from F90; à la carte around F180.
Hotel hires sailing boats and sail-boards and arranges water-skiing and deep-sea fishing trips

BASSILAC

🏤 🍴 <u>10/12</u> 🛏 ££

Château du Rognac, Bassilac, 24330
St-Pierre-de-Chignac.   Tel: 53.54.40.78
Open April 12–October 15; restaurant closed Monday
except during July and August
Dbl rm F290–F365

Madame Daudrix inherited a wreck of a 16th-century chateau which, with the help of her husband, she has turned into
a charming hotel surrounded by the river Isle. Only the mill
turret has still to be re-roofed and restored. Each of the
comfortable bedrooms has its own character. Room No.
12 is topped with its own pepper-pot roof and has a circular
balcony overlooking the river. The restaurant's thick walls
prevent more than four tables from having good river views,
but the imaginative cooking is ample compensation. *Truite
aux cèpes* is a particular speciality. Last orders: lunch 2pm;
dinner 9.30pm. Set menus from F120; à la carte around F130.
River swimming, gliding from airfield next door, tennis and golf 8km

BAYONNE

🏤 🍴 <u>19/44</u> 🛏 ££

Hôtel Loustau, 1 Place de la République, 64110 Bayonne.
Tel: 59.55.16.74
Open all year; restaurant closed two weeks in January,
Saturday and Sunday in winter
Dbl rm F270–F390

Bayonne is an attractive place with an atmospheric old town
and this stylish modern hotel overlooks the confluence of the
Nive and Adour rivers. It is on the north bank, slightly to one
side of the main road through town and, therefore, not too
noisy, although there is a steady flow of traffic over the
nearby bridge. The neat, comfortable bedrooms are decorated in a relaxing peach and grey colour scheme and those

on the top two floors have excellent views across the Adour to the heart of old Bayonne with its cathedral and pretty shuttered homes. Window tables in the restaurant also overlook the river; fresh fish and regional specialities dominate the menu.

Bayonne is famous for its ham and an important fair is held during Easter week

BELCASTEL

IOI ▭ ££

Le Vieux Pont, Belcastel, 12390 Rignac.
Tel: 65.64.52.29
Closed January and February; Sunday evening and Monday

Named after the 15th-century bridge which crosses the Aveyron, the Vieux Pont's location at the heart of the tiny medieval village of Belcastel is peaceful and scenic. The decor is typically French, with starched white linen table-cloths and fresh flowers, but it has retained a medieval quality. Three large windows look out across the river to the 15th-century church and triple-arched bridge. It is advisable to arrive early to secure a window table. Innovative and imaginative cuisine reflects the availability of fresh seasonal produce. Last orders: lunch 1.30pm; dinner 9pm. Set menus from F120; à la carte around F275.

BELCASTEL

IOI ▱ £

Restaurant Couderc, Belcastel, 12390 Rignac.
Tel: 65.64.52.26
Open all year; closed Sunday evening out of season

This simple family-run restaurant and café–bar occupies one of Belcastel's many sensitively restored medieval buildings. It is situated on a tiny street which runs alongside a calm stretch of the river Aveyron. In summer, tables are also set out on a paved terrace which looks out over the old bridge spanning the river. Inexpensive regional fare. Last orders: lunch 2.30pm; dinner 9.30pm. Set menus from F65; à la carte around F110.

BERGERAC

IOI ▭ £

La Treille, 12 Quai Salvette, 24100 Bergerac.
Tel: 53.57.60.11
Closed January and Monday

Situated in the heart of medieval Bergerac, this timber-framed house has been restored to create a delightful upstairs dining-room. Eight tables have views over a wide, calm stretch of the river Dordogne and, in summer, meals are also served on a lovely vine-shaded terrace. Madame Maebe, who is not a native of the Périgord region, includes refreshingly different dishes on the menus such as baked trout with basil, alongside seemingly obligatory but nonetheless delicious Périgordine specialities of *foie gras* and *confit de canard*. Last orders: lunch 1.30pm; dinner 9.30pm. Set menus from F65 (lunch), F85 (dinner); à la carte around F130. *Fishing, tobacco and wine museums, canoes, kayaks and rowing boats for hire*

BERGERAC

IOI ▭ ££

Le Nautic, 12–14 Promenade Pierre Loti, 24100
Bergerac.   Tel: 53.57.03.27
Closed November and Monday

On the banks of the Dordogne outside Bergerac, this restaurant has views around a wide bend in the river, giving the impression of being deep in the countryside. Only tables on the verandah and the plane-tree-shaded riverbank terrace have water views, so in high summer it is worth booking in advance. Grilled langoustines are a house speciality, and for vegetarians there is an excellent hors-d'oeuvre buffet. English translation of menu. Open 9am–midnight for breakfast, snacks and drinks. Last orders: lunch 1.30pm, dinner 9.30pm. Set menus from F65; à la carte around F130.

BESSE-EN-CHANDESSE

🏨 🍽 6/18 🛏 £

Hostellerie du Pont du Roy, Besse-en-Chandesse, 63610 Besse-et-St-Anastaise.   Tel: 73.79.52.58
Closed November 15–December 15 and a week in April
Dbl rm F160–F195
NE of Besse on D5

On the grassy banks of a small fast-flowing stream at the edge of medieval Besse-en-Chandesse, this 17th-century former flour mill has an old-fashioned and rustic appeal with heavy oak furniture and lace curtains. Bedrooms are simply furnished, seven with en-suite bathrooms. Madame Reynaud makes her guests feel at home and nothing is too much trouble. The restaurant serves unpretentious regional farmhouse cooking; four tables have water views. Last orders: lunch 1.30pm; dinner 10pm. Set menus from F68; à la carte around F90.
Trout fishing in stream (permits easily obtainable); swimming and watersports on the lake at Super Besse holiday resort 7km; walks along the riverbank

BEYNAC-ET-CAZENAC

🏨 🍽 14/22 🛏 ££

Hôtel Bonnet, Beynac-et-Cazenac, 24220 St-Cyprien.
Tel: 53.29.50.01
Open April 17–October 16
Dbl rm F260–F280

This imposing hotel, run by the charming Madame Bonnet, stands beside the road on a tranquil section of the Dordogne. More than half the bedrooms, all with en-suite bathrooms, have river views. However, in summer, when the road can be busy, some regular clients prefer rooms at the rear which look out towards the castle and countryside behind. The restaurant's creeper-shaded terrace, overlooking the river, seats 50 for breakfast and lunch only. Six inside tables also enjoy water views. Classic Périgordine dishes dominate the menus, but Madame Bonnet also appreciates the need for lighter, low-calorie dishes. Guests are asked to dine in the restaurant. Last orders: lunch 1.30pm; dinner 8.30pm. Set menus from F120; à la carte around F200.

River swimming, fishing, canoes and kayaks for hire in village, boat trips along Dordogne to St-Vincent

BEYNAC-ET-CAZENAC

📷 2/17 ▭ £

Hostellerie Maleville, Beynac-et-Cazenac, 24220 St-Cyprien.   Tel: 53.29.50.06
Closed two weeks in November and Monday October–Easter
Dbl rm F200

This modern restaurant, built in traditional style using local stone, is wedged between the riverbank and the road which passes behind. The airy first-floor dining-room has floor-to-ceiling glass doors on two sides to maximize the river views. In fine weather, these doors are pulled back. Meals are also served on the terrace and there are tables for drinks on the grassy riverbank. Good, reasonably priced Périgordine cuisine. Snacks, drinks and ice-creams served 10am–9pm. Last orders: lunch 2pm; dinner 9.30pm. Set menus from F79; à la carte around F150.

Boat trips along the Dordogne depart outside, swimming from riverside beach, fishing, canoes and kayaks for hire

BIARRITZ

🏨 🍽 <u>103/158</u> 🛏 ££££

Hôtel du Palais, 1 Avenue de l'Impératrice, 64200 Biarritz.
Tel: 59.24.09.40
Open all year
Dbl rm F1350–F2250

Originally built as a summer residence for Napoleon III, but
rebuilt on similar lines at the turn of the century after a fire,
this is one of the few hotels where guests can experience the
grace and elegance of a bygone age. But while it is a reminder
of Biarritz's grand Edwardian heyday, no expense has been
spared to modernize it to meet today's standards of pampered
luxury. Rooms are spacious and contain beautiful period
furniture and those with terraces are worth paying up for.
Most of the tables in the two restaurants, La Rotonde and La
Grande Siècle, have expansive views across the bay, and the
service is as discreetly attentive as you would expect. Last
orders: lunch 3.30pm; dinner 10.30pm. Set menus are available from F290; à la carte around F400.
Heated seawater pool, sandy beach with lifeguards; surf-boards and
windsurfers for hire; tennis courts and golf 500m

BIARRITZ

🏨 🍽 <u>31/31</u> 🛏 £££

Carlina Hôtel, Boulevard de Galles, 64200 Biarritz.
Tel: 59.24.42.14
Open June 1–September 30; restaurant closed Tuesday in
June and September
Dbl rm F500–F900

This modern seaside hotel, set into the cliffs of the Cote des
Basques, stands at the end of a cul-de-sac so there is no noise
from passing traffic. Bedrooms are small but well appointed,
with balconies; some have annexes for children's beds. The
restaurant serves generous portions of well-prepared regional

dishes, especially seafood. Last orders: lunch 2.30pm; dinner 11pm. Set menus from F80; à la carte around F230.
Safe sandy beach across road

BIARRITZ

🏨 ⏐◯⏐ 21/49 ▭ ££

Hôtel Windsor, Grand Plage, 63200 Biarritz.
Tel: 59.24.08.52
Closed for two months in winter
Dbl rm F250–F700

A reasonably priced and centrally located hotel, the family-run Windsor sits across the road from the promenade and the beach. It is a good place to stay if you are travelling with children as many of the comfortable rooms are designed for families of four. The building dates from the turn of the century but rooms are furnished in a tasteful modern style and many of those with sea views have doors opening on to small balconies. Best views are from rooms on the second floor up which have fine views over the beach and the Hôtel du Palais. Views from the restaurant are obscured by parked cars. Set menus from F100; à la carte around F200.

BIARRITZ

🏨 ⏐◯⏐ 9/26 ▭ ££

Les Flots Bleus, 41 Perspective de la Côte Basque, 64200 Biarritz.   Tel: 59.24.10.03
Open all year
Dbl rm F232–F475

Located at the top of Biarritz's corniche road in the direction of St-Jean-de-Luz, this unassuming hotel and restaurant has a marvellous view over the ocean and the coastline running south to the Spanish Pyrenees. Far preferable to the run-of-the-mill seaside hotels along the beach, it is a great favourite with French holidaymakers and discerning Brits, so book early for summer. Bedrooms are arranged in two properties: those in the main hotel are simply furnished but agreeable and sea-view rooms have balconies. Next door, there are studios comprising a bedroom, sitting room and equipped kitchenette which are rented by the night. Their decor is rather faded but they are large and convenient, especially if you have a young family. The restaurant is extremely popular with locals and we found the home cooking both delicious and very good value. The fish soup is superb, and don't leave without a slice of *Gateau Basque*. Eight tables have views over the sea. Last orders: 1.30pm; dinner 9.30pm. Set menus from F80; à la carte around F150.

BIARRITZ

🍷 🍽 £

Le Corsaire, Port des Pecheurs, 64200 Biarritz.
Tel: 59.24.63.72
Closed December–mid-February and Monday

This bustling *tapas* bar and café is in the heart of Biarritz's fishing port. Open from 10am until the early hours of the morning, it is always full of fishermen and locals, as well as tourists looking for somewhere cheap and authentically French. Fresh coffee, beer, wine and light snacks are available all day.

BIARRITZ

🍷 🍽 £

Le Miremont, 1 Place Clémenceau, 64200 Biarritz.
Tel: 59.24.01.38
Open all year

This beautiful *salon de thé* is a reminder of 19th-century Biarritz. Take a morning coffee or chocolate and enjoy splendid views of the casino and sea through the huge picture windows. The panorama from the upstairs salon, its white-and-gold mouldings recently renovated, is even better. Salads and quiches are available at lunchtimes, and mouth-watering ice-cream sundaes all day. You will also find it difficult to leave without buying a box of homemade chocolates. Open 9am–7.30pm.

BIARRITZ

⬚🍷 ✉ £

Dodin, Grande Plage, 64200 Biarritz.   Tel: 59.24.16.37
Open April–October

This Biarritz institution is *the* place to go for a beachside breakfast, afternoon tea or late-night drink after your post-prandial promenade. All the pastries, tarts and ice-creams are homemade as it is owned by Dodin, makers of the best chocolates and *patisserie* along this coast, who also own the Miramont. Pizzas, quiches, sandwiches and salads are also served for lunch and dinner. From its large terrace bordering the beach there are fabulous views along the bay in both directions. Open 10am–1am.

BIDARRAY

🏠 🍴 14/17 ✉ £

Hôtel du Pont d'Enfer, Bidarray, 64780 Osses.
Tel: 59.37.70.88
Closed January–February 28
Dbl rm F135–F270

This charming hotel run by Madame Gagnant is a friendly, informal place. The best views of the river Nive are from three comfortable rooms (Nos. 14, 16, and 18) in the annexe, which have balconies overhanging the water. In the main building, room No. 20 has excellent views from its terrace. In summer, meals are served on a terrace overlooking the verdant riverbanks. Regional Basque cooking including the traditional *merlu koskeza*, hake with asparagus, peas and red peppers served on a bed of garlic. Last orders: lunch 1.30pm; dinner 8.30pm. Set menus from F88; à la carte around F140.

Fishing, pleasant country walks

BIDART

IOI ⊟ £

Blue Cargo, Plage d'Ilbarritz, 64210 Bidart.
Tel: 59.23.54.87
Closed January 7–mid–February, Sunday evening and Monday

A very friendly restaurant with a pub-like interior, it stands alone on top of a grassy dune and is reached along a potholed lane off the main coast road. In the 19th-century, these were kitchens of hill-top Ilbarritz Castle, linked to it by a long tunnel, as the baron who owned it could not bear the smell of cooking in his home. The restaurant is run by the genial, easy-going Monsieur Cazayous, who speaks fluent English, and is popular with locals, especially in the evenings. The day's specials are chalked up on a blackboard and vary according to what's good in the market. Expect simple traditional home cooking. Half the tables have sea views and, between April–end October, wooden trestle tables are set out on a large outdoor terrace. In season, there is also a bar–brasserie down on the beach serving simple grilled dishes and salads all afternoon. Last orders: lunch 2.30pm; dinner 11pm. No set menus; à la carte around F70 (lunch); F130 (dinner).

Superb sandy beach with lifeguard in season

BILLY

IOI ⊟ £

Auberge du Pont, Route de Marcenat, Billy, 03260 St-Germain-des-Fosses.   Tel: 70.43.50.09

Closed January; Monday evening and Tuesday

This purpose-built restaurant is set back from the road on the banks of the river Allier in Billy, a medieval village just north of Vichy. Although none of the tables in the restaurant has a view of the river, in fine weather, guests can dine on a terrace overlooking an arched bridge and the Allier as it winds away down the valley. The young owners have successfully created a warm and friendly ambience and provide an interesting menu which is inspired by North African cuisine. Last orders: lunch 1.30pm; dinner 9.30pm. Snacks and ice-creams available from 10am. Set menus from F88; à la carte around F120. *Fishing; sightseeing and pleasant walks in Billy; swimming pool 3km*

BISCAROSSE PLAGE

🏨 |○| 32/34 ▭ ££

Hôtel de la Plage, 2 Avenue de la Plage, Biscarosse Plage, 40600 Biscarosse.   Tel: 58.78.26.69
Open April 1–September 30
Dbl rm F325–F440

Situated on a bluff above a wide, sandy beach stretching as far as the eye can see, this is a good base for a relaxing family bucket-and-spade holiday. Bedrooms are functional, but pleasantly decorated. A particularly attractive semi-circular bar sits right beside the beach, as does the restaurant. Seafood is a speciality. Last orders: lunch 2pm; dinner 11pm. Set menus from F95; à la carte around F150.
Sandy beach (lifeguards on duty); riding, tennis and golf nearby; excursions to Landes forests and lakes

BLAYE

🏨 |○| 14/21 ▭ ££

La Citadelle, Place d'Armes, 33390 Blaye.
Tel: 57.42.17.10

Open all year
Dbl rm F325–F350

Magnificently situated above the fortifications built by Vauban in 1689 to repel the invading English, this hotel makes latter-day British visitors feel very much at home. The decor may be unimaginative, but the bedrooms are clean and comfortable, seven with balconies. From the swimming-pool terrace, there is a marvellous view over the Gironde estuary. Nearly all the restaurant's tables have water views. Regional cuisine including the house speciality, *lamproie*, an eel-like fish much appreciated by the Plantagenets. Last orders: lunch 2pm; dinner 9.30pm. Set menus from F120; à la carte around F240.
Hotel swimming pool, fishing, tennis, riding 5km

BORDEAUX

|○| ⊟ ££

Aliénor, Embarcadère (Pier) No. 7, Quai Louis XVIII, 33000 Bordeaux.   Tel: 56.51.27.90
Open all year

Like the *bateaux mouches* on the Seine, the Aliénor takes 250 diners along the Garonne for lunch and dinner. Routes vary from city tours, with an interesting commentary on the port and its history, from Richard II to the present, to longer cruises downstream to Blaye or along the Dordogne to Libourne. Good regional cooking. Lunch cruise F140; dinner cruise F110. Departures at 11am (stopping either at Blayes or Carillac), noon (non-stop), and 8.30pm. Cruises last between three and seven hours.

BOUSSENS

🏠 |○| 6/12 ⊟ £

Hôtel du Lac, 7 Promenade du Lac, Boussens, 31360 St-Martory.   Tel: 61.90.01.85

Hotel and restaurant closed Friday and Saturday nights
November–April
Dbl rm F180–F280

Just off the main Toulouse–Tarbes trunk road, this is a good
place to stop for lunch or even overnight. Accommodation is
basic – six rooms have en-suite bathrooms – but the restaurant and its large terrace have pleasant views over an artificial
lake. Owners, Hubert and Marie-Alice Soulie, are very
friendly and the restaurant is a great favourite with locals.
Good regional cooking including breast of duck with honey
and Toulouse *cassoulet*. Last orders: lunch 2pm; dinner
9.30pm. Set menus from F75; à la carte around F175.
*Fishing, pleasant lakeside walks, tennis; riding 3km; sailing and
windsurfing 7km*

BOUZIC

◻ ▱ £

Chez Sylvestre, Bouzic, 24250 Domme.   Tel: 53.28.41.01
Open all year
Dbl rm F120–F140

It is worth making a detour to visit this small restaurant
situated beside a bubbling stream in the Dordogne valley,
to sample Madame Sylvestre's excellent cooking. Her family
has been in the restaurant business for three generations and
dinner is based on whatever her husband brings back from
the daily market in Sarlat. It is best to reserve at least a day
ahead so Madame Sylvestre can prepare some of her delicious
speciality dishes, which are only available if ordered in
advance, as everything is homemade. She is happy to explain the choice on the telephone, but in French only. These
include *confit de canard en croûte* (a duck speciality) and *ris de
veau aux truffes et aux morilles* (calf sweetbreads with truffles
and mushrooms), served as main courses, together with a
starter, salad, cheese board and homemade pudding. If you
simply turn up you will only be offered the limited menu of

the day. As it is rather off the beaten track, there are six simple bedrooms which share bathroom facilities. Last orders: lunch 1pm; dinner 8.30pm. Speciality meals F130–F200.

BOUZIES

🏨 🍴 <u>25/39</u> 🛏 ££

Les Falaises, Bouziès, 46330 Cabrerets.   Tel: 65.31.26.83
Closed November–March
Dbl rm F226–F285

This pleasant, modern hotel takes its name from the steep cliffs flanking the river Lot. Bedrooms are comfortable and tastefully furnished, all with en-suite bathrooms. Most enjoy delightful views over a peaceful stretch of river towards the honey-coloured cliffs on the far bank. Ideal for active family holidays, the hotel contains a playground, games room and heated swimming pool. Family suites and rooms for the disabled are available. In summer, meals are served on the poolside terrace overlooking attractive lawns which lead down to the water's edge. One of the homemade regional specialities is a delicious *pastis* gateau. Last orders: lunch 2pm; dinner 9pm. Set menus from F73 (children F45); à la carte around F150.
Hotel provides free bicycles, rowing boats and canoes; river-boat excursions to St-Cirq, Lapopie and Cahors; tennis courts

BOUZIGUES

🏨 🍴 <u>26/32</u> 🛏 ££

Motel Côte Bleue, Bouzigues, 34140 Mèze.
Tel: hotel 67.78.31.42; restaurant 67.78.30.87
Open all year; restaurant closed January 6 for a month, Tuesday evening and Wednesday
Dbl rm F300

Motel is a misnomer for this attractive two-storey hotel overlooking the beautiful inland lagoon of the Etang du

Thau. Bedrooms are spacious and nicely decorated in pastels; most have balconies or terraces. Bouzigues is famous as a centre for oyster and mussel cultivation, and guests are sometimes invited out to view the extensive shellfish beds in the lagoon. In a warehouse next door, fishermen clean and sort the shellfish. Built out into the lake, the restaurant's terrace looks across to the fishing village of Bouzigues and is an attractive spot to enjoy appetizing shellfish dishes prepared by Monsieur Jacquinot and his eight sous-chefs. Last orders: lunch 2.15pm; dinner 9.45pm. Set menus from F148 (F180 at weekends); à la carte around F350.

Beach with windsurfing and sailing; boats to mussel and oyster beds from Mèze

BRANTOME

Moulin de l'Abbaye, 1 Route de Bourdeilles, 24310
Brantôme.   Tel: 53.05.80.22
Closed November 1–May 1; restaurant closed
Monday lunch
Dbl rm F700–F950

The owner of the Moulin de l'Abbaye, Régis Bulot, is the president of the prestigious Relais et Châteaux hotel group so the high quality of the decor, food and service comes as no surprise. Originally a 15th-century mill, the hotel has been beautifully restored and its water-wheel still turns. Bedrooms have been tastefully decorated, seven looking out over the weir, the old town bridge and the imposing abbey. Monsieur Bulot has recently renovated a 13th-century house on the opposite bank, to provide nine further bedrooms, three with river views. The restaurant is highly acclaimed and has a delightful shady terrace overlooking the Dronne. Last orders: lunch 2.30pm; dinner 10.30pm. Set menus from F195; à la carte around F380.

Fishing, canoe and kayak hire nearby

BRANTOME

⌨ ▭ £

Au Fil de l'Eau, 21 Quai Bertin, 24310 Brantôme.
Tel: 53.05.73.65
Closed November–Easter

As its name indicates, this small café, with room for about 30 customers inside, is at the water's edge. Weather permitting, there is room for many more tables, shaded by attractive parasols, on the grassy riverbank. The café is owned by Monsieur Bulot, owner of the Moulin de l'Abbaye, and the hotel's acclaimed chef is in charge of the menu. You can choose between two *plats du jour* or settle for a simple salad or hot savoury flan. Open 11am–10pm.

BRANTOME

🏢 🍴 **8/19** ▭ ££

Hôtel Chabrol, 57 Rue Gambetta, 24310 Brantôme.
Tel: 53.05.70.15
Closed November 15–December 10 and two weeks in February; restaurant closed Sunday evening and Monday October–June
Dbl rm F280–F400

This is a pleasant, traditional hotel on the banks of the river Dronne in the heart of Brantôme, the so-called Venice of Périgord. The decor is somewhat old-fashioned but the bedrooms are comfortable. A major attraction is its restaurant, Les Frères Charbonnel, which sweeps around a wide curve on the river affording lovely views through large windows. The restaurant serves generous portions of traditional Périgordine cuisine. Last orders: lunch 2pm; dinner 9pm. Set menus from F130; à la carte around F250.
Romanesque bell tower and 15th-century abbey

BRANTOME

🏚 🍴 <u>10/10</u> 🍽 ££

Hostellerie Les Griffons, Le Pont, Bourdeilles, 24310
Brantôme.   Tel: 53.03.75.61
Closed October 1–Easter; restaurant closed Tuesday lunch
Easter–mid-June
Dbl rm F390
Brantôme 9km

The stark exterior of this 16th-century house belies the
elegance of its country house interior. Lace bedspreads and
fine antique furniture soften the natural stone walls and
beamed ceilings. All the rooms look out over the Dronne
as do most tables in the restaurant whose decor is typically
French – plain walls, white table cloths and high-backed
chairs. Traditional regional cuisine includes many local specialities. All dishes are freshly prepared from market produce.
Last orders: lunch 2pm; dinner 9pm. Set menus from F150; à
la carte around F250.
Fishing, river swimming, tennis courts, riding 2km

BROUSSE-LE-CHATEAU

🏚 🍴 <u>12/14</u> 🍽 £

Le Relays du Château, Brousse-le-Château, 12480
Broquiès.   Tel: 65.99.40.15
Closed December 20–January 20; restaurant closed Friday
evening and Saturday lunch October–April
Dbl rm F150–F180

Spectacularly situated in the heart of medieval Brousse-le-
Château where the river Alrance flows into the Tarn, this
simple hotel has a pretty view across the river to an ancient
castle. Sybile and Philippe Senegas speak good English and
have many British guests who appreciate their warm welcome. Bedrooms are simply but tastefully decorated and by
this summer all rooms should have attached shower and WC.

The restaurant serves regional cuisine and, although tables have no river views, its café has an outdoor terrace overlooking the river. Last orders: lunch 2pm; dinner 9pm. Set menus from F60; à la carte around F85.
Trout fishing in the Tarn; canoes and kayaks for hire 10km

LE BUGUE

🏨 🍽 24/53 🛏 ££

Royal-Vézère, Place de l'Hôtel de Ville, 24260 Le Bugue.
Tel: 53.07.20.01
Closed October 1–May 1; restaurant closed Monday lunch and Tuesday lunch
Dbl rm F420–F500

Designed for those in search of a smart, well-equipped international-style hotel rather than a traditional family-run establishment, this pleasant, modern hotel sits on the banks of the river Vézère. Buffet breakfasts are served on its rooftop poolside terrace, which enjoys excellent river views. The restaurant, L'Albuca, also has an outdoor waterside terrace seating 50 diners. Last orders: lunch 2pm; dinner 9pm. Set menus from F130; à la carte around F300.
Heated swimming pool, fishing, canoe hire, nearby tennis and golf

BUSSEAU-SUR-CREUSE

🏨 🍽 3/7 🛏 £

Hôtel du Viaduc, Busseau-sur-Creuse, 23150 Ahun.
Tel: 55.62.40.62
Closed January; restaurant closed Sunday evening
Dbl rm F220

Monsieur Le Mestre extends a warm welcome to his guests, who include many regular British visitors. The spacious bedrooms are simply but attractively furnished, five with

well-equipped bathrooms. Window tables in the restaurant have spectacular views over the Creuse valley and an impressive iron viaduct which influenced the young Gustave Eiffel. Guests are free to wander around the attractive, south-facing gardens which lead down to the river. The food is appetizing and beautifully presented. Last orders: lunch 2pm; dinner 9.30pm. Set menus from F68 (weekdays), F98 (weekends); à la carte around F250.
Fishing; pleasant walks; son-et-lumière in Château de Villemonteix 20km

CAHORS

▥ ⑪ 23/32 ▭ ₤₤₤

Château de Mercuès, Mercuès, 46090 Cahors.
Tel: 65.20.00.01
Closed November 11–April 1
Dbl rm F600–F1870
Mercuès 3km

This beautiful 13th-century chateau, perched high above the river Lot just outside Cahors, offers the height of luxury. Bedrooms are vast, stylish and opulently furnished, with marble bathrooms. The round tower rooms are much sought after. In the Chambre de la Tour, the ceiling can be raised, at the touch of a button, to reveal the wooden supports of the turret. The Chambre de l'Evèque has a sundial carved into the wooden floor. The restaurant is housed in the old courtyard with the original stone well as its centrepiece. Its service and cuisine enjoy a good local reputation. There are river views from four tables. Last orders: lunch 2pm; dinner 9.30pm. Set menus from F195; à la carte around F320.
Lovely swimming pool and terrace, tennis courts, extensive grounds which include a 90-acre vineyard; canoes and kayaks for hire 8km; historic Cahors and Lot valley vineyards nearby

CAHORS

🏨 🍽 14/23 ▭ £

Hôtel Les Chalets, Vers, 46090 Cahors.   Tel: 65.31.40.83
Closed January 14–March 1; restaurant closed Wednesday
and Friday evening November–Easter
Cahors 15km
Dbl rm F190–F250

This simple hotel stands on the banks of the river Vers beside
the 19th-century Pont de Vers and overlooks a calm natural
pool and waterfall. The seven rooms in the original building
are modest and rustic but all have attached shower and WC.
A new annexe on the other side of the bridge contains a
further 16 neat, pleasant rooms, all with well-equipped
bathrooms. Imaginative use of hanging baskets with flowers
brightens up public areas, which include a waterside dining
terrace. The menu features some interesting traditional dishes
as well as paella and *cassoulet*. Last orders: lunch 2.30pm;
dinner 9.30pm. Set menus from F70; à la carte around F150.
*Fishing in the Lot and the Vers; nature trails and interesting walks
(booklets of routes available in hotel); remains of Roman aqueduct in
Vers; historic Cahors*

CAHORS

🍽 ▭ ££

Les Deux Saisons, Laroque des Arcs, 46090 Cahors.
Tel: 65.35.30.58
Closed January or February and Sunday evening and
Monday (July and August Monday lunch only)
On D653 to Figeac, Cahors 5km

Reached through the rather shabby lobby of the Hôtel Beau
Rivage, this airy restaurant, decorated in fashionable pastels,
enjoys panoramic views over the river Lot. Enclosed by
floor-to-ceiling sliding doors, pulled back in summer to
create an open-air terrace, all tables look out on leafy gardens and the wide, slow-moving river. In summer, grilled

dishes are also served at tables set out in the riverbank garden. A pontoon allowed direct access for boats cruising the Lot. *Nouvelle cuisine*. Last orders: lunch 2pm; dinner 9.30pm. Set menus from F98; à la carte around F230.

CAMBES

IOI ▭ ££

Auberge André, Le Grand Port, 33880 Cambes.
Tel: 56.21.31.08
Closed 3 weeks in November, Tuesday evening and Wednesday mid–September–mid–June

The interior of this traditional restaurant, arranged on two levels, has lots of rustic charm. However, tables on the large pontoon outside have the best views over the wide river Garonne. It is advisable to book or arrive early for a pontoon table in summer. The menu is varied and imaginative, featuring regional dishes based around fresh seasonal produce. Last orders: lunch 2.30pm; dinner 10.15pm. Set menus from F95 (lunch), F145 (dinner); à la carte around F140.

CARENNAC

🏨 IOI **8/16** ▭ ££

Hostellerie Fénelon, Carennac, 46110 Vayrac.
Tel: 65.38.67.67
Hotel and restaurant closed January 10–March 10 and Friday–Saturday lunch October–Easter
Dbl rm F260

Named after the Bishop of Fénelon, whose bust stands outside Carennac's 12th-century church, this modern hotel has been built and decorated in traditional style. It backs on to the river with pretty views over its leafy banks, Calypso Island and a small canal built to supply Carennac's water. Bedrooms are comfortable and well appointed, all with recently re-fitted en-suite bathrooms. Four tables in the restaurant look out over the river. Its regional cooking and wines are popular with locals and tourists alike. During July and August guests are asked to dine in the restaurant. Last orders: lunch 2pm; dinner 9pm. Set menus from F80; à la carte around F250.

Swimming pool; delightful village of traditional Quercy houses; fishing; canoes and kayaks for hire; other watersports at leisure centre in Vayrac 8km; boat trips through Padirac limestone caves 8km

CARENNAC

🏨 |○| 11/13 ▭ £

Hotel des Touristes, Carennac, 46110 Vayrac.
Tel: 65.38.47.07
Open May 1–September 30
Dbl rm F110–F180

Madame Brilliant's simple, family-run hotel offers excellent value and a warm welcome, and has many regular guests. Bedrooms are comfortable, nicely decorated and well maintained; eight with en-suite bathrooms. Four rooms open on to a shared terrace, and room No. 5 has a private balcony. Window tables in the bright, airy restaurant have views across the garden to the river, and there are sliding doors opening on to a terrace for drinks in summer. Traditional home cooking including quiches, omelettes and steaks. Last orders: lunch 2pm; dinner 9pm. Set menus from F65 (children F20); à la carte around F90.

CASTELNAUDARY

🏨 17/33 ▭ £

Hôtel du Canal, 2 Avenue Arnaut Vidal, 11400
Castelnaudary.   Tel: 68.94.05.05
Open all year
Dbl rm F240–F260
From Castelnaudary follow signs to Mazères

Built on the banks of the Canal du Midi, this new hotel is within walking distance of the town centre. All the bedrooms are well equipped and comfortable and quiet, thanks to the addition of soundproofing and double glazing. Bedrooms at the back overlook the tow path and the canal. The owners are considering opening a restaurant but until then guests will have to go elsewhere to taste the culinary delight of Castelnaudary: the *cassoulet*, a French family favourite usually made from shoulder of pork, conserve of goose and sausage and *lingot* beans cooked together for several hours.

Canal walks; boat trips; municipal tennis courts and pool opposite, August Fête de Castelnaudary with concerts, theatre and dance performances

CASTRES

🏛 🍽 **18/40** 🛏 £

Grand Hôtel, Rue de la Libération, 81100 Castres.
Tel: 63.59.00.30
Closed December 15–January 15; restaurant closed
Friday evening and Saturday
Dbl rm F120–F270

Castres, built on the profits of the wool trade, is reminiscent of Venice, its impressive mansions designed to be approached by boat from the river Agout. This elegant hotel rises from the stone river wall in the centre of the town, its cool interior a welcome respite from the bustle in the streets. Bedrooms are comfortably furnished, all with en-suite bathrooms. Room No. 23 has a precarious balcony overhanging the water. The restaurant's shuttered windows look directly on to the Agout. Last orders: lunch 2pm; dinner 9pm. Set menus from F80; à la carte around F150.

Boat trips on the Agout from Castres to Gourjade, Goya museum, 17th-century St-Benoit cathedral, street market four days a week

CASTRES

IOI ⊟ ££

La Caravelle, 150 Avenue de Roquecourbe, 81100
Castres.   Tel: 63.59.27.72
Open June 15–September 15; closed Friday evening
and Saturday
Castres 1km

A marble staircase leads down to a large dining-room where
five sets of shuttered doors open on to a lamp-lit terrace
overlooking the river Agout. Surrounded by willows and
flowers, this is a peaceful relaxing spot for lunch or dinner.
Traditional regional cuisine such as duck *confit* and *cassoulet*.
Last orders: lunch 2.30pm; dinner 9.30pm. Set menus from
F80; à la carte around F200.

CAYRES

▒ IOI 8/10 ⊟ £

Chalet du Lac, Lac du Bouchet, 43510 Cayres.
Tel: 71.57.30.22
Hotel closed November 1–April 1; restaurant closed
January and Tuesday October–May
Dbl rm F200–F250

This simple hotel is the only building on a volcanic crater lake
high in the wooded Devès hills. It provides a peaceful escape
from the world. Bedrooms are homely, with locally made
furniture and woollen curtains and bedcovers; seven have en-
suite bathrooms. The restaurant has expansive views over the
royal-blue lake, especially from its enclosed terrace. The
huge lava-stone fireplace maintains a roaring fire on cool
days. Regional home cooking, notably delicious cold meats,
frogs' legs, lake trout. Café–bar open 8am–11pm. Last orders:
lunch 2pm; dinner 9pm. Set menus from F90; à la carte
around F120.
*Pedalos for hire; trout, perch and carp fishing; lake swimming;
woodland walks*

LA CELLE-DUNOISE

🏠 🍽 5/7 🛏 £

Auberge de Pecheurs, La Celle-Dunoise, 23800
Dun-le-Palestel.   Tel: 55.89.02.45
Open all year
Dbl rm F110–F150

This pretty ivy-covered hotel sits on the the banks of the river
Creuse in the heart of a pretty Limousin village, popular with
French holidaymakers. Bedrooms are comfortable but simply
furnished, four with en-suite bathrooms. Exceptionally
friendly staff create a convivial atmosphere, especially in
the restaurant where most diners enjoy river views. Good
regional fare. Last orders: lunch 2pm; dinner 10pm. Set
menus from F50; à la carte around F100.
*Fishing, supervised river swimming, canoes, kayaks and bicycles for
hire, marked footpaths, tennis and riding nearby*

CERBERE

🏠 🍽 20/20 🛏 £

La Vigie, Route Espagne, 66290 Cerbère.
Tel: 68.88.41.84
Open mid-March–end October
Dbl rm F230–F270

Perched on a clifftop near the small fishing port of Cerbère,
this is a convenient place to break a journey to Spain – the
border lies just a few miles away. The hotel is set back from
the busy N117, and all the clean, simply furnished bedrooms
face the sea so guests are not disturbed by excess traffic noise.
Some rooms have private balconies, and all have en-suite
bathrooms. The restaurant provides simple, wholesome fare
with fish dominating the menu. In fine weather, meals are
served on a shaded terrace overhanging the cliff. Last orders:
lunch 1.30pm; dinner 10pm. Set menus from F90; à la carte
around F150.

*Steps down to pebble beach below hotel, scuba-diving from Cerbère,
sailing and windsurfing at Banyuls*

CHAMPAGNAC-DE-BELAIR

🏨 🍽 12/14 🛏 £££

Moulin du Roc, 24530 Champagnac–de–Belair.
Tel: 53.54.80.36
Open all year; restaurant closed Tuesday and
Wednesday lunch
Dbl rm F400–F650

Delightfully situated on the banks of the river Dronne, this
17th-century walnut-crushing mill has been converted into a
pleasant hotel and restaurant, presided over by Madame
Gardillou whose cooking has won many accolades. Many
of the mill's original features have been retained, and the
spacious, country-style bedrooms are very comfortable. Pots
of begonias and geraniums decorate the waterside garden
which, pleasantly shaded by tall trees and attractive parasols, is a thoroughly relaxing and scenic venue for lunch.
Last orders: lunch 2pm; dinner 9.30pm. Set menus from
F200; à la carte around F300.
Private swimming pool and tennis court; fishing

CHASTEAUX

🍽 🛏 £

Le Couzage, Port Couzage, Chasteaux, 19600 Larche.
Tel: 55.85.33.51
Closed January, February, and Wednesday
mid-September–mid-June

Set in rolling countryside near Brive, this attractive modern
restaurant overlooks the Lac du Causse. Decorated with
stained-glass windows at the rear, it is a good place for a
long, leisurely meal. There are fine lake views from window
tables and, in summer, meals are served on an outdoor

terrace. Traditional Périgordine cuisine. Service is friendly and discreetly attentive. Last orders: lunch 2pm; dinner 9pm. Set menus from F75 (children F35); à la carte around F180. *Fishing; lake swimming; windsurfers and rowing boats for hire; water-skiing; pleasant lakeside walks*

CHATEAUNEUF-LES-BAINS

IOI 🍴 £

Au Rendez-Vous des Pecheurs, Châteauneuf-les-Bains, 63390 St-Gervais-d'Auvergne.　Tel: 73.86.67.89
Closed November 1–April 1

As its name suggests, this simple restaurant is popular with fishermen and locals, especially on Sundays. Four tables enjoy good views of the river Sioule rushing through a wooded valley. Regional cooking, especially fresh trout or *friture* (small fry) caught in the river. Last orders: lunch 2pm; dinner 9.30pm. Set menus from F50; à la carte around F70. *Trout fishing; canoes and kayaks for hire 2km; hikes and walks in the gorges*

LE CHATENET-EN-DOGNON

🏠 IOI 11/15 🍴 ££

Le Chalet du Lac, Pont du Dognon,
Le Chatenet-en-Dognon, 87400 St-Léonard-de-Noblat.
Tel: 55.57.10.53
Open all year; restaurant closed Sunday evening
Dbl rm F280–F350

This attractive chalet-style hotel stands alone on a wooded hillside overlooking a large tranquil lake. The interior is elegant, and Madame Schaub provides a warm welcome. Bedrooms, each decorated in a different style, are comfortable and well equipped. The restaurant serves fresh market produce, especially high-quality Limousin beef. There are good lake views from five tables. Last orders: lunch 1.30pm;

dinner 9.30pm. Set menus from F90; à la carte around F175.
*Fishing, lake swimming, water-skiing and pedalos for hire; nearby
riding and tennis*

CHOUVIGNY

🏨 ⏺ 📶 🛏 £

Les Gorges de Chouvigny, Chouvigny, 03450 Ebreuil.
Tel: 70.90.42.11
Closed December and January
Dbl rm F180–F190
Take the Vichy exit from the A71; follow signposts to
Ebreuil then Gorges de Chouvigny and hotel is on D915
through gorge

Situated on the wooded banks of the river Sioule, this small
hotel is cheerful and welcoming. Its young and enthusiastic
owners, Sylvie and Eric Fleury, have redecorated the bedrooms with floral fabrics and attractive furniture and all have
attached shower and WC. The restaurant and its outdoor
terrace are particularly attractive and there are lovely river
views from the terrace. Varied and appetizing menus. Open
for meals from noon to 9pm. Set menus from F85; à la carte
around F120
*Fishing (category A river; permits sold by hotel), river swimming
100m; canoes and kayaks for hire 7km; walks and sightseeing along
Sioule gorges*

CHOUVIGNY

⏺ 🏊 🛏 £

Les Roches, Gorges de Chouvigny, 63560 Menat.
Tel: 73.85.51.49
Closed November 1–January 15
Dbl rm F130
See entry above for directions

On the banks of the river Sioule just before it enters the Chouvigny gorges, this small, well-maintained establishment has a pretty conservatory-style restaurant just feet from the river. It serves regional home cooking with specialities including homemade terrines, casserole of duck livers with mushrooms, and baked trout. The main building, on the opposite side of the road, contains another dining-room and five simple, comfortable bedrooms which glimpse the river through trees. Only one has an en-suite bathroom, the rest have showers. Last orders: lunch 2.30pm; dinner 9.30pm. Set menus from F109 (children F48); à la carte around F130.

Trout fishing (licence needed); river swimming; canoes, kayaks and rafts for hire 2km; walks along the gorges and to Château de Chouvigny 2km

CIBOURE

🏠 7/20 ▭ ££

La Caravelle, Boulevard Pierre Benoit, 64500 Ciboure.
Tel: 59.47.18.05
Open all year
Dbl rm F230–F400

Across the bay from St-Jean-de-Luz, Ciboure is much quieter and just as pretty with narrow streets lined with red-shuttered Basque-style houses. This small modern hotel stands on the seafront and from seven rooms there are lovely views of the bay across the entrance to the fishing harbour. The modest-sized bedrooms have been recently renovated by the owners, Elizabeth Devancoux and her sister, with pretty floral wallpapers and matching curtains and new bathrooms. Three rooms share a glassed-in verandah and a further two have small balconies. Room no. 20 has the best sea views. Breakfast only.

All watersports; very good scuba diving; safe sandy beach for children at Socoa 1km away; boat and fishing trips depart from harbour

CLERGOUX

🏠 ○ **9/18** ⊟ £

Hôtel du Lac, Etang Prévôt, 19320 Clergoux.
Tel: 55.27.77.60
Hotel closed November–end March; restaurant closed
lunchtime in winter
Dbl rm F160–F220
Tulle 10km west

The only building on the shores of one of the purest freshwater lakes in France, this solid 1940s hotel is a favourite
haunt of anglers. There are six bedrooms in the main house
and a further 12 in a more modern annexe alongside. All offer
basic accommodation, some with lino floors and solid country furniture, but all have attached bathrooms. Those in the
annexe have more open views over the deep blue waters of
the lake and its forested shoreline. The genial owner–chef,
Monsieur Dumas, cooks delicious Périgourdine cuisine and
has attracted a loyal local following. Specialities include *confit
de canard*, pike in *beurre blanc*, and trout mousse. In winter,
meals are served in the panelled dining room where window
tables glimpse the lake through trees but, as soon as summer
arrives, tables are set out beneath trees at the water's edge for
meals and afternoon refreshments. Great value for escapists.
Last orders: lunch 2.30pm; dinner 9.30pm. Set menus from
F95; à la carte around F180.
*Swimming from lakeside beaches; excellent pike and trout fishing;
rowing boats for hire (motorboats forbidden); lovely walks along
lakeshore and to Sédières Castle.*

COLLIAS

○ ⊟ £

L'Enclos, Bord du Gardon, 30210 Collias.
Tel: 66.22.88.40
Closed December 1–March 1 and Tuesday

Set in wild and spectacular scenery, this restaurant and café–bar sits above the river Gardon just before it enters dramatic and scenic gorges. Barbara and Pierre Chamboredon's good humour and informal hospitality make it a very popular venue with locals. Simple appetizing hot or cold dishes include Provencal *brochettes*, snails, steak and chips, trout *meunière* and large salads. Open 10am–midnight for snacks. Last orders for meals: lunch 2pm; dinner 9pm. Set menus from F65.

Good river swimming from pebble beaches; canoes and kayaks for hire; fishing; delightful walks

COLLIOURE

🏚 🍴 <u>23/23</u> 🛏 £££

Relais des 3 Mas, Route de Port Vendres, 66190 Collioure. Tel: 68.82.05.07
Open all year
Dbl rm F345–F765

This is a very smart hotel tucked away on the edge of Collioure, a busy but delightful fishing port which inspired a string of famous artists including Picasso, Matisse and Dufy. Occupying several carefully restored old buildings, the hotel has made imaginative use of these associations, naming bedrooms after painters and decorating them to reflect the mood of each painter's work. Some rooms have private terraces, and all enjoy lovely views across to the old harbour and church of Collioure. The restaurant, La Balette, is in a new building and all the tables have harbour views. There is also a pleasant terrace for meals in fine weather. The menu is varied and specialities of the house include smoked meat and lobster. Last orders: lunch 2pm; dinner 10pm. Set menus from F165; à la carte around F280.

Heated swimming pool; small sandy beach; sailing in catamarans and Catalan fishing boat trips from Collioure to Argelès; windsurfing, scuba-diving and water-skiing in Collioure; golf and tennis courts in St-Cyprien; mountain bikes for hire; large programme of cultural activities and fiestas in summer

COLLIOURE

🏨 🍴 11/21 🛏 ₤₤

Hostellerie des Templiers, Quai de l'Amirauté, 66190
Collioure.   Tel: 68.98.31.10
Closed January; restaurant closed Sunday evening and
Monday October–June 1
Dbl rm F295–F365

In the heart of old Collioure, this charming harbour-front
hotel doubles as an art gallery. Jo Pous owns an impressive
collection of 2,000 paintings and drawings displayed on
every available wall, illustrating the popularity of Collioure
with artists over the last century. Bedrooms contain unusual Catalan furniture and most have new bathrooms.
Second- and third-floor rooms have balconies and enjoy
the best views of the harbour and the fortified chateau.
The bar, built to resemble a fishing boat, is popular with
the locals. None of the restaurant's tables have water views,
but there is a pleasant outdoor terrace. Specialities include
fish patés, paella and Catalan fish soup. Last orders: lunch
2pm; dinner 10.30pm. Set menus from F98; à la carte
around F200.

COLLIOURE

🏨 16/16 🛏 ₤

Les Caranques, Route de Port Vendres, 66190 Collioure.
Tel: 68.82.06.68
Open Easter–October 10
Dbl rm F170–F285
Signposted from N114

Terraced into the cliffs, this small hotel has a peaceful setting
and enjoys beautiful views over a bay towards the old
harbour. Small winding paths, lined with flowering shrubs,
link the terraces and lead down to a small pebble beach.
Modestly priced for such a popular resort, bedrooms are
clean but plainly furnished, 14 with attached shower and

WC. Open June–September, its simple restaurant, which has similar bay views, serves dinner for residents. Half-board, obligatory June 15–September 30, costs F295 per person.

COLLIOURE

IOI ⊟ ££

L'Ecume, Route de Port Vendres, 66190 Collioure.
Tel: 68.82.02.27
Closed January 1–mid-February, and Wednesday except mid-June–mid-September

Occupying a series of terraces built into the cliffs at different levels, this popular restaurant provides a romantic setting for dinner under the stars. The view over Collioure village and the mountains beyond is magnificent and, in the evenings, the chateau and the old port are floodlit. Guests can linger over coffee and *digestifs* until 2am. Oyster soup, sea bream in fennel sauce, red mullet in puff pastry, and mussel flan with shallots are popular choices.
Last orders: lunch 2pm; dinner 10.30pm. Set menus from F90; à la carte around F180.

COLY

🏠 10/10 ⊟ £££

Manoir d'Hautegente, Coly, 24120
Terrasson-la-Villedieu.   Tel: 53.51.68.03
Open Easter–November 11
Dbl rm F470–F750
Near Le Lardin 5km on D62

This beautiful creeper-covered manor has been the Hamelin family home for more than 300 years. Many guests become family friends, returning year after year. Courteous hospitality is assured and Monsieur Hamelin is always in great demand to take the children fishing and karting. All ten bedrooms are elegantly furnished in a rather English country style with chintz fabrics and antiques. All look out on a pond which originally provided water power for a forge and later a mill. Madame Hamelin's cooking ranges from classic French dishes to simple family favourites, using fresh market produce. She even managed to cater for a vegetarian family for three weeks which must be a miracle in France. In the evenings a fire is lit in one of the drawing rooms so that guests can enjoy coffee and a vintage armagnac by the fireside. Dinner only; picnic hampers prepared on request. Half-board is obligatory July–September and costs F490–F670 a person. Last orders for dinner 8.30pm. Set menus from F180; à la carte around F270.

Fly fishing on private stretch of category A river for guests, swimming pool in grounds, tennis courts nearby

COULANDON

🏚 🍴 3/25 ⊟ ££

Le Chalet, Coulandon, 03000 Moulins.   Tel: 70.44.50.08
Closed November 15–January 31
Dbl rm F310–F380
A71 exit Montmarault 30 minutes away

This delightful family-run hotel has an exceptionally quiet location in the heart of the Bourbonnais. Simply furnished bedrooms are decorated in pretty floral wallpapers and contain old family furniture; ten have en-suite bathrooms. At the bottom of the garden is a small tree-shaded lake – a peaceful vista for guests dining on the outdoor terrace. The restaurant is only open for dinner and serves a selection of regional dishes and wines at reasonable prices. Last orders 9pm. Set menus from F80; à la carte around F160.

Carp fishing in lake; pleasant country walks; Moulins, the old Boubonnais capital on the banks of the river Allier, has good museums and an attractive cathedral

CROZANT

🏨 🍽 7/10 ✉ £

Hôtel du Lac, Pont de Crozant, Crozant, 23160
St-Sebastian.   Tel: 55.89.81.96
Open May 1–September 30; restaurant closed Tuesday
May 1–June 30 and September
Dbl rm F190–F270

Guests are made to feel very much at home in this small
modern hotel set on the river Creuse where it opens out into
a long narrow lake. Bedrooms are sparsely but adequately
furnished, comfortable and spotlessly clean; four have en-
suite bathrooms. The hotel provides an inexpensive base for
exploring Limousin's glorious countryside. The restaurant
serves good hearty regional dishes, all tables enjoying river
views. Last orders: lunch 1.30pm; dinner (for residents only)
8pm. Set menus from F60; no à la carte.
*On Lake Eguzon sailing boats and windsurfers for hire 7km; hotel
has boat for lake excursions; water-skiing; lake swimming from
beaches 8km; riding 10km*

DOMME

🏨 🍽 8/10 ▦ ££

Hotel de l'Esplanade, 24250 Domme.   Tel: 53.28.31.41
Closed mid–November–mid–February; restaurant closed
Monday October–April
Dbl rm F300–F550

Guests can survey the Dordogne meandering over a fertile
plain from the Esplanade's terrace, just as sentinels did during
the Hundred Years' War, when Domme was a French-held
Bastide town. Bedrooms are tastefully decorated, many
furnished with antiques. Those with water views are in the
main hotel building. Monsieur Gillard's inventive interpretations of traditional Périgordine dishes have earned him
culinary accolades, and he has one of the region's best

cellars, specializing in wines from Bergerac and Cahors vineyards. Five restaurant tables have views of the river, several hundred feet below, and there is a shady terrace for breakfast and drinks. Last orders: lunch 2pm; dinner 9.30pm. Set menus from F150; à la carte around F350.
River swimming, canoes for hire

ENCAUSSE-LES-THERMES

🏨 🍽️ 10/10 🛏️ £

Aux Marronniers, Encausse-les-Thermes, 31160 Aspet.
Tel: 61.89.17.12
Closed January; restaurant closed Sunday evening and
Monday October–May 15
Dbl rm F120–F145

This small hotel on the banks of the Job, an excellent trout fishing river, is hospitably run by Michel and Christiane Estrampes. Bedrooms, housed in a riverside annexe, are basic but very clean; bathroom facilities are shared. Guests can eat breakfast on a long balcony overlooking the garden and river. The restaurant serves traditional regional cuisine and nearly all tables have river views. In summer, meals are also served on a flower-decked riverside terrace. Off-season, advance booking is required for dinner. Last orders: lunch 2pm; dinner 9.30pm. Set menus from F70; Sunday lunch F120.
Trout fishing is the only activity in this tiny village

ENTRAYGUES

🏨 🍽️ 18/25 🛏️ £

Hôtel de la Truyère, 60 Avenue du Pont de Truyère,
12140 Entraygues.   Tel: 65.44.51.10
Closed December 1–April 1; restaurant closed Monday
Dbl rm F180–F230

A lovely hotel on the banks of the river Truyère beside a listed medieval bridge, it is a five-minute walk from the

centre of Entraygues, so-called because it is at the point where the rivers Lot and Truyère meet. Gérard Gaudel and his mother offer guests a warm welcome. Bedrooms are modern and tastefully decorated, all with attached bathrooms. There is a lift and also a bedroom specially equipped for disabled visitors. Book well ahead for a summer visit. The restaurant specializes in regional cuisine with menus based on seasonal produce. Most tables enjoy river views and the outdoor terrace is open all day for refreshments. Last orders: lunch 1.30pm; dinner 8.30pm. Set menus from F65; à la carte around F180.
Rafting, canoe and kayak instruction and hire; tennis and riding nearby

ESTERENCUBY

🏨 🍴 6/20 ▭ £

Hôtel des Sources de la Nive, Estérencuby, 64220
St-Jean-Pied-de-Port.   Tel: 59.37.10.50
Closed January
Dbl rm F180
Esterencuby 4km

The foothills of the Pyrenees form the impressive backdrop to this simple country hotel in the heart of the French Basque country. Traditional country-style decor with richly polished old furniture gives public areas a homely rustic charm. Accommodation is basic but clean and tidy and most of the rooms have en-suite bathrooms. Although only six bedrooms look out over the Nive, all have peaceful country views. The river tumbles past the conservatory-style dining-room which serves traditional country fare. Last orders: lunch 1.30pm; dinner 8.30pm. Set menus from F50; à la carte around F120.
Trout fishing; good walking country

ESTERENCUBY

🏠 IOI 9/17 ☰ £

L'Auberge Etchegoyen, Esterencuby, 64220
St-Jean-Pied-de-Port.   Tel: 59.37.09.77
Closed January; restaurant closed Wednesday
November–Easter
Dbl rm F140–F160

The drive alongside the river Nive, from St-Jean-Pied-de-
Port to its source near the Spanish border, is magnificent and
reminiscent of Cumbria. Standing at the confluence of two
small rivers, this unpretentious, traditional hotel offers simple
but comfortable bedrooms, most with attached shower and
WC. The restaurant serves fresh local produce; only window
tables have river views. Last orders: lunch 2pm; dinner 9pm.
Set menus from F65; à la carte around F110.

EYMOUTIERS

IOI ☰ ££

Le Pré L'Anneau, Chemin du Pré L'Anault, 87120
Eymoutiers.   Tel: 55.69.12.77
Closed November 11–December 20; Sunday evening
and Monday

In a pretty location on the banks of the river Vienne – the
restaurant's well-tended gardens lead down to the water's
edge. From the outdoor dining terrace there is a lovely view
over the weir, a bridge and an 18th-century mansion on the
other side of the river. The elegant but informal dining-room
serves traditional regional dishes such as smoked goose,
salmon and trout. Friendly, enthusiastic staff are happy to
explain the menu in English. Last orders: lunch 1.30pm,
dinner 8.30pm. Set menus from F90; à la carte around F150.

LES-EYZIES-DE-TAYAC

🏨 🍽 20/20 ▭ ££

Moulin de la Beune, 24620 Les-Eyzies-de-Tayac.
Tel: hotel 53.06.94.33; restaurant 'Le Vieux Moulin'
53.06.93.39
Hotel closed November–Easter; restaurant closed
Tuesday lunch
Dbl rm F260–F350

The river Beune splits into countless little streams all around
this old mill, which nestles under a bridge in the middle of Les
Eyzies near a busy road junction. The mill has been carefully
restored and the wheel still turns lazily in the dining-room.
Bedrooms are nicely furnished, all with views over one or
other of the streams. One brook is stocked with trout for the
table. Unusually for France, Georges Soulié appreciates the
need for an occasional rest from rich Périgordine cuisine and
offers the choice of a low-calorie menu. However, bison,
which features in the prehistoric Lascaux cave paintings, is
always on the menu – but now it comes from Canada. Last
orders: lunch 2.30pm; dinner 9.30pm. Set menus from F85; à
la carte around F220.
*Trout fishing, nearby Lascaux cave paintings, interesting walks to
limestone cliffs riddled with caves*

GAN

🍽 ▭ £

Le Tucq, Route de Laruns, 64290 Gan.   Tel: 59.21.61.26
Closed October and Monday evening, Tuesday and
Wednesday
Pau 8km

Set in beautiful countryside on the banks of the small, fast-
flowing river Nez. Visitors will be pleasantly surprised by the
varied and inexpensive menus which feature some unusual
combinations, such as sole with *chanterelle* mushrooms and *foie*

gras with apple. There is a good selection of local and Bordeaux wines. The waterside terrace caters for 60 diners. Last orders: lunch 2pm; dinner 9.30pm. Set menus from F60; à la carte around F120.

GENERARGUES

🏨 |O| 22/34 🛏 ££

Les 3 Barbus, Générargues, 30140 Anduze.
Tel: 66.61.72.12
Hotel and restaurant closed January 1–March 10, Sunday and Monday nights October–end December
Dbl rm F280–F520

Perched high above the wooded gorge of the Vallée des Camisards, with spectacular views over the river Gardon de Mialet towards the Cévennes. Some of the comfortable bedrooms have balconies overlooking a curve of the gorge. Most of the restaurant's tables look down over the river far below and, in summer, there is a shaded terrace with a barbecue. The menu includes traditional regional dishes and more refined *nouvelle cuisine*; plenty of game in season. Last orders: lunch 1.30pm; dinner 9.30pm. Set menus from F120 (lunch), F180 (dinner); à la carte around F320.
Hotel swimming pool; trout fishing; pebble beach below hotel for river swimming; Cévennes steam train rides; riding

GIMEL-LES-CASCADES

🏨 |O| 3/9 🛏 ££

Hostellerie de la Vallée, Gimel-les-Cascades, 19800 Corrèze.   Tel: 55.21.40.60
Closed November–March
Dbl rm F220–F300

Set in one of the most picturesque spots in Limousin, this pleasant hotel looks out over spectacular waterfalls and forested mountains. Madame Calis is justifiably enthusiastic about this delightful village and happy to talk at length, in fluent English, about the local attractions. The bedrooms are simply but tastefully decorated; all have en-suite bathrooms. The pretty restaurant and outdoor terrace look out over a series of cascades tumbling 400ft into the gorge. Gimel boasts a zero pollution rating, and visitors are encouraged to drink the local tap water instead of bottled imports! Last orders: lunch 2.30pm; dinner 9.30pm. Set menus from F95; à la carte around F150.

Trout fishing; swimming in caves; watersports and boats for hire on lake 3km; bird and deer reserves in forest

GOUDARGUES

🏨 🍽 <u>16/50</u> 🛏 £

Hôtel de Commerce, 30630 Goudargues.
Tel: 66.82.20.68
Closed October 20–end November
Dbl rm F155–F240

This charming canalside hostelry has been run by the Coste family for more than 60 years. Bedrooms are simple but comfortable and most have en-suite bathrooms. The water-side terrace is a delightful spot for lunch or dinner. Swans and ducks glide along the canal, which is shaded by plane trees and crossed by wrought-iron bridges. The menus offer a good choice of regional dishes including freshwater fish, calf sweetbreads and duck. A good base for exploring the Cèze valley and the Ardèche Gorges. Excursions can be arranged through the hotel. Last orders: lunch 2pm; dinner 9.30pm. Set menus from F105; à la carte around F135.

Fishing and swimming in river Cèze; canoes and kayaks for hire

GOUDARGUES

🍽 🛏 ££

Le Plan d'Eau, 30630 Goudargues.   Tel: 66.82.27.50

Closed January

This converted olive-oil mill stands beside a pretty duck pond on the edge of the village. The waterside terrace is open for meals and drinks in fine weather. Chef Elaine Cantin serves seafood and traditional dishes of the Gers region, including homemade patés, duck in green pepper and grilled pork in a spicy sauce. Crêpes, ice-creams and drinks are served from 10am–midnight. Last orders: lunch 2pm; dinner 10pm. Set menus from F100; à la carte around F140. Reservations advised.

LA GRANDE MOTTE

🏨 🍽 117/135 🛏 £££

Altea Hôtel, 140 Rue du Port, 34280 La Grande Motte.
Tel: 67.56.90.81
Closed December 1–February 28
Dbl rm F715

La Grande Motte is a bizarre, purpose-built resort, designed by French architect Jean Balludur in the 1970s. A mixture of pyramid shapes, many of its buildings reflect a nautical theme. This member of the Altea hotel group, which sits in the heart of the yacht marina, is no exception. The comfortable, well-equipped bedrooms have sliding doors which lead on to balconies shaded by facades designed to resemble portholes. The pleasant restaurant opens on to a quayside terrace. Fresh fish and seafood are specialities. Last orders: lunch 2.30pm; dinner 10pm. Set menus from F95; à la carte around F175.
Hotel swimming pool, large, safe, sandy beaches with all watersports, deep-sea tuna fishing and boat trips; nearby 18-hole golf course, tennis courts and riding on Camargue horses

LA GRANDE MOTTE

🏨 20/20 🛏 £££

Hôtel Azur, Presqu'ile du Port, 34280 La Grande Motte.

Tel: 67.56.56.00
Closed December 1–January 4
Dbl rm F495–F650; family apartments F695–F900

This small friendly hotel, run by the Guillemain family, stands on its own at the edge of the marina and is almost entirely surrounded by water. First-floor bedrooms with balconies enjoy the best sea views, but ground-floor rooms have the advantage of direct access to the swimming pool. Rooms are comfortably furnished in a hotch-potch of styles. English is spoken by the owners and most of the staff, who will be happy to explain what goes on in La Grande Motte and where to eat and drink. No restaurant. Private parking – a rarity in this resort.

LA GRANDE MOTTE

IOI ▭ £££

Alexandre, Esplanade de la Capitainerie, 34280
La Grande Motte.   Tel: 67.56.63.63
Closed January 6–February 12; Sunday evening and
Monday October–May

This busy first-floor restaurant, run by genial brothers, Dany and Michel Alexandre, has a good reputation. The sunny hexagonal dining-room has a splendid view over the marina and out to sea. Both *nouvelle cuisine* and traditional regional dishes are served. The emphasis is on fish and seafood and good use is made of fresh herbs and spices. Last orders: lunch 2pm; dinner 10pm. Set menus from F185 (children F75); à la carte F185.

LE GRAU-DU-ROI

▥ IOI 14/21 ▭ £££

Le Spinaker, Port-Camargue, 30240 Le Grau-du-Roi.
Tel: 66.53.36.37

Hotel closed January 8–February 15; restaurant closed
Sunday evening and Monday September 15–May 1
Dbl rm F390–F680

This modern hotel sits on a quay built out into the water,
completely surrounded by an impressive array of pleasure
craft. It has its own moorings at the end of the garden which
make it a popular venue for yachtsmen. A good base for a
long or a short stay, the hotel is comfortable, peaceful and
extremely well run by the genial Cazals family. All the
bedrooms are on the ground floor and either look out over
the marina or have terraces by the swimming pool. There are
good views of the marina from the first-floor restaurant, and
meals are also served on the pool terrace, which is shaded by
palm trees. Monsieur Cazals is well known for his culinary
skills. The adventurous menu includes unusual and inventive
combinations such as poached salmon with pistachio sauce.
Last orders: lunch 1.30pm; dinner 9.30pm. Set menus from
F245; à la carte around F300.
*Sandy beach 5 minutes' drive; all watersports, including scuba-
diving; boat trips along coast and up Canal du Midi; Camargue
National Park can be toured on foot, by horseback or four-wheel-
drive jeep*

GRENADE-SUR-L'ADOUR

⌂ 6/11 ⊨ £££

Pain Adour et Fantaisie, 7 Place des Tilleuls, 40270
Grenade-sur-L'Adour.   Tel: 58.45.18.80
Restaurant closed Sunday evening and Monday
(Monday lunch only during July and August)
Dbl rm F480–F780

Already well-known as a restaurant, there are now 11 rooms
in the restored half-timbered house next door, six with
balconies on which guests can enjoy breakfast overlooking
the river Adour. In the summer, meals and drinks are served
on a terrace adjoining the dining-room; both have delightful

river views. Didier Oudill's culinary skills have earned this restaurant critical acclaim. Last orders: lunch 2.30pm; dinner 10.30pm. Set menus from F170; à la carte around F310.
Hotel arranges fishing, rafting and four-wheel-drive tours. Rugby fans can make a pilgrimage to Notre Dame de Rugby, a small oratory in Larrivière, where there is a stained-glass window of Christ about to throw a rugger ball to the players below

GRUISSAN

IOI ▭ ££

L'Estagnol, Bord de l'Etang, Gruissan Village, 11430 Gruissan.   Tel: 68.49.01.27
Closed Monday lunch all year and evenings, except Saturday, October–March

This appealing restaurant near a ruined fortress in the old village, overlooks a shallow lagoon. Both the food and the owners are popular with locals and fishermen, who can be seen mending their nets and painting their boats just outside. In fine weather, meals are served on a small roadside terrace. Fresh fish and seafood are the order of the day and the menu has been translated into English. Last orders: lunch 2pm; dinner 11.30pm. Set menus from F88 (lunch), F120 (dinner); à la carte around F200.
Sandy beach and watersports 2km; boat and deep-sea fishing trips from port

GUETHARY

IOI ▭ £

Txamara, Chemin du Port, 64210 Guethary.
Tel: 59.26.53.54
Closed December 1–Easter

The curious name of this restaurant is the Basque word for crab. A small, simple establishment beside the sea wall, it overlooks the fishermen sorting out their nets on the jetty.

The best seats for a summer lunch or dinner are on the upstairs terrace, which has panoramic views over the coastline between Biarritz and St-Jean-de-Luz. The food is freshly prepared, well presented and good value. Crab is, of course, a speciality. Last orders: lunch 2.30pm; dinner 10.30pm. No set menus; à la carte around F100. Open all day for drinks and snacks.

GUJAN-MESTRAS

IOI ▭ ₤₤

Les Viviers, Port de Larros, 33470 Gujan-Mestras.
Tel: 56.66.01.04
Closed two weeks in November
Signposted on D650

This unpretentious restaurant, housed above an oyster-packing business, is off the beaten track but well worth the effort of finding. Trays of oysters lie in the water alongside the jetties and, depending on the time of day and season, packers may be at work downstairs. There are two dining-rooms; the first-floor one is the smarter of the two and has good views across the jetties. In fine weather, tables are set out on a quayside terrace. Seafood dominates the menu, but there is a limited selection of meat dishes. Last orders: lunch 2pm; dinner 9.30pm. Set menu F120; à la carte around F200.
Oyster fair in second week of August

HOSSEGOR

▦ IOI <u>10/14</u> ▭ ₤₤

Hôtel de la Plage, Place des Landais, Hossegor.
Tel: 58.43.50.12
Closed January–mid–February; restaurant closed
Wednesday out of season
Dbl rm F220–F280

This old-fashioned post-war hotel stands on the tiny central square of Hossegor facing the open sea. It is a typical French seaside hotel, popular with families, and staff are very friendly. The rooms could do with a facelift but are spotlessly clean, reasonably spacious, and most have expansive views along the coast. All sea-view rooms have balconies which you can sit out on. The restaurant occupies a glassed-in verandah directly overlooking the wide sandy beach and, in summer, there is an open-air terrace for meals and drinks. Regional cooking with an emphasis on fish and seafood. Last orders: lunch 2pm; dinner 10pm. Set menus from F70; à la carte around F150.

Beach with lifeguards in season; sail-board and bicycle hire

HOSSEGOR

🏠 6/9 🛏 £

Les Huitrières du Lac, 1187 Avenue du Touring Club, 40150 Hossegor.   Tel: 58.43.51.48
Closed December 1–March 1; restaurant closed Tuesday evening and Wednesday except mid-June–end September
Dbl rm F230–F260

Set beside a seawater lake surrounded by pine forests, the restaurant cultivates its own oysters for the table, keeping them in trays below the terrace until consumed. Nearly all the tables enjoy views over the lake and a canal leading through to the sea. Excellent fresh fish and seafood as well as game and other local specialities. Bedrooms are comfortable and pleasantly furnished, all with en-suite bathrooms. Last orders: lunch 2pm; dinner 10pm. Set menus from F85 (weekdays), F135 (weekend); à la carte around F230.

Pedalos and sailing boats for hire, water-skiing, lake swimming from beach 200m, bicycle trails through forest

ISSOIRE

🍽 🛏 £

Auberge du Pont d'Orbeil, Le Pont d'Orbeil, 63500 Issoire.   Tel: 73.89.32.58

Lunch only; closed August and weekends
A71 exit Issoire 3km

This simple auberge has been a restaurant since the end of the last century, when fishermen would sell their day's catch or even have it cooked for them. Despite its proximity to the autoroute, it is a peaceful spot, with seven tables in the pretty dining-room overlooking the river Allier. Open for breakfast, drinks and snacks 8am–9pm. Because of its popularity, it is necessary to book a table for lunch, which is served noon–2.30pm. Set menus from F58.

LACANAU

▥ Ⅰ○Ⅰ 25/30 ▭ ££

L'Oyat, Front de Mer des Allées Ortal, Lacanau-Océan, 33680 Lacanau.   Tel: 56.03.11.11
Closed October 15–April 15
Dbl rm F360

Oyat translates as marram grass, and this modern hotel in the small seaside town of Lacanau-Ocean is set among marram grass-covered sand-dunes. Bedrooms are small but well appointed, all with en-suite bathrooms. Because international surfing championships are held at the resort in mid-August, it is advisable to confirm bookings for this period in advance. The restaurant is renowned for its seafood, but non-residents may not be able to dine here from mid-June to mid-September as L'Oyat operates a compulsory half-board policy during these two months costing F390 per person per night. Last orders: lunch 2pm; dinner 10pm. Set menus from F80; à la carte around F150.
Fine sandy beach; sailing boats, sail-boards and pedalos for hire and water-skiing at Le Moutchic on Lacanau lake; eel and perch fishing

Above: La Chaine d'Or, on the banks of the Seine: Les Andelys. (The hotel is on the extreme left of the picture.)

Right: Domaine du Château de Rochevilaine perches on a promontory: Muzillac.

Below: Le Cheval Blanc offers pretty harbour views: Honfleur.

View from the terrace of Relais de Gué de Selle: Evron.

Auberge du Moulin-Bureau, overlooking the Indre: La Châtre.

Domaine de Beauvois, a lakeside chateau with 15th-century tower: Luynes.

The 16th-century loggia at Château de la Verrerie: Aubigny-sur-Nère.

Left: Altea Hôtel, on the river Tarn: Albi.

Above: Hôtel des Sources de la Nive, in the foothills of the Pyrenees: Esterencuby.

Below: Hôtel du Palais, the former summer residence of Napolean III: Biarritz.

Many guests at the Manoir d'Hautegente become family friends: Coly.

A la Belle Gasconne, a 14th-century mill: Poudenas.

Opposite: Château de la Caze, built on a ledge in the Tarn gorge: Ste-Enimie.

Left: Hostellerie du Moulin, dating from the 12th century: Flagy.

Above: L'Epuisette, fine views across the bay: Marseille.

Below: Château Vault-de-Lugny, ringed by a moat: Avallon.

Les Roches Blanches overlooks the bay: Cassis.

Hostellerie Le Château, at the source of the river Sorgue: Fontaine-de-Vaucluse.

LACAVE

🏠 ÏOÏ 6/13 🛏 ££££

Château de la Treyne, Lacave, 46200 Souillac.
Tel: 65.32.66.66
Closed November 15–Easter
Dbl rm F900–F1800

An exclusive retreat in the heart of the Dordogne valley, this fairytale castle stands alone on a rocky crag directly above the river. Bedrooms are beautifully furnished, each in a different period style and bear names such as Louis XV, Henri IV, Gothic and Empire. Six bedrooms and the rear terrace, used for dining in fine weather, enjoy spectacular views over the river. It is difficult to imagine a more romantic setting for a candle-lit dinner. Traditional Périgordine cooking. Last orders: lunch 2.30pm; dinner 9.30pm. Set menus from F180 (lunch) and F280 (dinner); à la carte around F300.
Heated swimming pool and tennis court in 300-acre grounds, fishing, canoes and kayaks for hire 2km, riding 2km

LACAVE

🏠 ÏOÏ 13/13 🛏 ££

Le Pont d'Ouysse, Lacave, 46200 Souillac.
Tel: 65.37.87.04
Closed November 11–March 1; restaurant closed
Monday (Monday lunch only June–September)
Dbl rm F350–F450

This pretty, family-run hotel sits in a delightful garden beneath a cliff crowned by Belcastel castle. It is a lovely peaceful place away from any road and there are splendid views over the clear waters of the river Ouysse. The rooms are spacious and immaculately kept. Its restaurant is renowned in the area for Monsieur Chambon's appetizing menus, which offer regional favourites and *nouvelle cuisine* dishes. There are no river views from the dining-room, but

there's a wonderful tree-shaded terrace for meals in summer. Ask for a table with a river view there. Refreshments are served to passers-by from 8am to 10pm. Last orders: lunch 2pm; dinner 9pm. Set menus from F150; à la carte around F300.
Secluded heated pool on riverbank, fishing, lovely walks along marked footpaths. In Souillac, 8 km away, canoes and kayaks for hire, tennis courts, golf course, July jazz festival and August mime festival

LALINDE

🏠 |◯| ⛊ 🛏 ♨

Hôtel du Château, 1 Rue de Verdun, 24150 Lalinde.
Tel: 53.61.01.82
Closed December 1–February 28; restaurant closed
Friday (lunch only July and August)
Dbl rm F180–F280

On the river's edge, this small 19th-century chateau is wrapped around a 13th-century fortress. Quietly situated just off the town's one-way system, six of its eight pleasantly furnished bedrooms look out over a shallow section of the river, popular with fishermen. All have en-suite bathrooms. There are two dining-rooms, one with river views from window tables. Its delightful riverside terrace seats 40 and Monsieur Gensou serves all the local Périgordine specialities and plenty of fresh fish. He will cater for vegetarians (who have included George Harrison). Last orders: lunch 1.45pm; dinner 9pm. Set menus from F140; à la carte around F270.
Outdoor pool on terrace, boat trips to wine cellars, canoe hire 2km

LANGEAC

🏠 |◯| ⛊ 🛏 £

Auberge de L'Ile d'Amour, Route de Saugues, 43300 Langeac.   Tel: 71.77.00.11.

Closed three weeks in January; restaurant closed Sunday
evening and Monday October–Easter
Dbl rm F140–F150

On a tranquil wooded stretch of river Allier, the six clean,
simply furnished bedrooms occupy a modern annexe beside
the river. The restaurant has expansive river views, and meals
and drinks are served on a large terracotta-tiled waterside
terrace in summer. Good regional cooking using fresh local
produce such as river salmon and wild mushrooms. Last
orders: lunch 2pm; dinner 9.30pm. Set menus from F85; à
la carte around F200.
Trout and salmon fishing; canoes and kayaks for hire; river swim-
ming, tennis and children's playground 200m, horse and cart rides in
Allier gorges; excellent walking country

LEON

🏠 IOI <u>9/15</u> 🛏 £

Hôtel du Lac, Bord du Lac, 40550 Léon.   Tel: 58.48.73.11
Open Easter–September 30
Dbl rm F145–F210

In the heart of the pine forests and sand-dunes of the Landes
region, this pleasant small hotel sits on the banks of a recreational lake. Nine of the simply furnished bedrooms enjoy
lake views, as does the restaurant, which serves good regional
dishes including oysters, *foie gras*, duck *confit* and a delicious
Landes *pastis* cake. Last orders: lunch 1.30pm; dinner
8.45pm. Set menus from F65; à la carte around F150.
Pike and perch fishing; swimming; sail-boards, pedalos and canoes
for hire; boat excursions along canal, with its unusual sub-tropical
vegetation

LEUCATE

🏠 IOI <u>22/32</u> 🛏 £

Hôtel de la Plage, La Franqui, 11370 Leucate Plage.
Tel: 68.45.70.23

Open May 1–October 1; restaurant open June–September
Dbl rm F240

Situated near the end of a cul-de-sac around from Cap
Leucate, this pleasant family-run hotel has an excellent view
of the sea, although there is a car park between it and the
beach. Bedrooms, all recently carpeted and decorated with
floral wallpaper, are comfortable if simply furnished, and
have sliding doors leading out to balconies. The spacious
restaurant has similarly good sea views and specializes in
fresh seafood. There are ten tables on an outdoor terrace.
Last orders: lunch 2.30pm; dinner 10pm. Set menus from
F59; à la carte around F130.
*Undeveloped 11km sandy beach with windsurfing, sand-yachting,
scuba-diving and spear-fishing, riding by night on beach*

LOURDES

🏨 ΙΟΙ 25/50 🛏 £

Hôtel de Provence, 50 Avenue Peyramale, 65100
Lourdes.   Tel: 62.94.20.57
Closed November 1–Easter
Dbl rm F220

At the quieter end of the Avenue Peyramale, this is one of the
few hotels in Lourdes to enjoy a river view that is not marred
by the clutter of tacky souvenir shops. The bedrooms are
spacious and simply furnished, all with en-suite bathrooms,
and half have views over the river Pau crossed by the
Peyramale bridge. No rooms are specially equipped for the
disabled, but there is a lift and bathrooms are large enough for
wheelchairs. The ground-floor restaurant has an oblique
view over the river and offers reasonably priced but unadventurous menus, including low-calorie and vegetarian
dishes. Last orders: lunch 1pm; dinner 8pm. Set menus from
F57; no à la carte.
*Guided tours of sanctuaries and places associated with St Bernadette,
impressive wax museum, medieval Lourdes fort; riding around Lac
de Lourdes 2km*

LOURDES

{O} ⊟ ££

L'Ardiden, 48 Avenue Peyramale, 65100 Lourdes.
Tel: 62.94.30.55
Closed January; Monday and evenings Tuesday–Thursday
in winter

Reminiscent of a smart Parisian brasserie, this large establishment in a quiet part of Lourdes comprises a first-floor
restaurant and a ground-floor brasserie as well as a bar and
pizzeria. Opened a year ago, it is a particularly atmospheric
venue in the evenings. Regional and classic dishes are served
in both the brasserie and the restaurant, but the latter has
better views over the river Pau. There is also a first-floor
covered terrace outside the restaurant where meals are served
in fine weather. Bar open 9am–2am; brasserie and restaurant
open noon–midnight. Set menus from F60; à la carte around
F170.
Lourdes historic sights 5 minutes on foot

LOURES-BAROUSSE

▦ {O} 4/10 ⊟ £

Hostellerie de l'Ourse, Antichan, 65370 Loures-Barousse.
Tel: 62.99.25.02
Closed three weeks in January; restaurant closed Sunday
evening and Monday October–March
Dbl rm F105

This simple hostelry, dating back two centuries, is set in
stunning Pyrenean scenery on the banks of one of France's
premier trout-fishing rivers, the Ourse. Just half an hour from
the border with Spain, Spanish influence is apparent
throughout. Expect simply furnished bedrooms with shared
bathroom facilities. The extensive menu, which is also good
value, includes Spanish specialities such as paella, zarzuela and
gaspacho with Garenne rabbit. Owner Jean Fernandez is a

great storyteller and often entertains guests in the evenings with his amusing anecdotes on local life. Last orders: lunch 1.30pm; dinner 9.30pm. Set menus from F69; à la carte around F125.

Trout fishing (national championships in June); canoes and kayaks for hire 5km; rock-climbing in Troubat 1km; riding 5km

LOURES-BAROUSSE

🏠 ⅠⓄⅠ 5/12 ▭ £

Le Moulin d'Aveux, Aveux, 65370 Loures-Barousse.
Tel: 62.99.20.68
Closed November 15–Easter; restaurant closed Sunday lunch mid-November–mid-April
Dbl rm F100–F270

The gardens of this cleverly converted 18th-century flour mill border the river Ourse. Having opened it as a hotel in 1980, the Chomy family prides itself on offering traditional hospitality and a warm welcome. Decor is tasteful, rustic and well maintained, and all but two rooms have attached bathrooms. The original mill stone serves as a coffee table in the courtyard and the open wood fire in the restaurant enhances the cosy, restful atmosphere. There's a pleasant riverbank terrace for meals and drinks. Hearty regional country cooking; set menus offer limited choice. Last orders: lunch 2.30pm; dinner 10pm. Set menus from F84; à la carte around F160.

LUNAS

ⅠⓄⅠ ▭ ££

Château de Lunas, 34650 Lunas.   Tel: 67.23.87.99
Open all year at weekends only; daily June 15–September 15

Lunas is an interesting medieval village and this 17th-century chateau is a good place to stop for a simple lunch while exploring southern Languedoc. In a picturesque setting

overlooking the river Gravezon, around 12 inside tables
have river views, but it is far nicer to sit outside on the
paved terrace. Simple traditional cooking – trout, steaks
and salads – and Italian pizza and pasta dishes. Last orders:
lunch 2pm; dinner 11pm. Set menus from F89; à la carte
around F100.

*Fishing, canoes and pedalos for hire in front of restaurant; interesting
riverside walks to trout farm and ruined castle; riding arranged from
restaurant*

MADIERES

🏠 🍽 6/10 🛏 £££

Château de Madières, Madières, 34190 Ganges.
Tel: 67.73.84.03
Closed November 15–Easter
Dbl rm F480–F810
On D25 18km SW of Ganges, direction Lodève

Painstakingly restored from the ruins of a 14th-century
fortress, this chateau–hotel is perched high above the gorges
of the river Vis. Many original features have been retained –
including the vaulted ceilings and carved stone fireplaces. A
peaceful base for exploring the valley of the Hérault and the
Tarn gorges, guests are invited to make themselves at home.
Bedrooms are spacious and comfortable, each decorated in a
different style, and facilities include a gym and heated swimming pool. Owner Madame Brucy cooks good regional fare,
served in a vaulted dining-room. Seven tables enjoy panoramic views through tall, arched windows down over the
valley of the Vis. Breakfast and drinks are served on a terrace
overlooking the river, and in summer you can have lunch
and dinner in the courtyard. Last orders: lunch 2.30pm;
dinner 9pm. Set menus from F170; à la carte around F250.

*Trout fishing, river swimming, canoes and kayaks for hire in
Ganges, famous circular canyon, Cirque de Navacelles, 15km*

MARSEILLAN

🏨 13/15 🛏 ££

Hôtel du Château du Port, 9 Quai de la Résistance,
34340 Marseillan.   Tel: 67.77.65.65
Open March 15–November 15
Dbl rm F270–F460

A good touring base away from the crowded beaches, this
solid 19th-century quayside building was originally designed
for a wealthy wine merchant who wanted to supervise the
loading and unloading of his wine barrels. Many original
features still remain, including the stone staircases, fireplaces
and ornate plaster mouldings. Bedrooms are generally large
and decorated with pretty fabrics. The attic rooms are smaller, but they enjoy splendid views of the fishing port and
marina. No restaurant.
*Marseillan, a pretty town with a covered market place, is on the
Etang de Thau, where oysters and mussels are cultivated; hotel
motorboats and bicycles for hire*

MEYRONNE

🏨 🍴 8/19 🛏 ££

La Terrasse, Meyronne, 46200 Souillac.   Tel: 65.32.21.60
Closed November 15–March 15
Dbl rm F220–F350

This creeper-covered manor in the small village of Meyronne dates back to the 16th century. Built of warm honey-
coloured stone, it stands on a cliff above the Dordogne and
has been turned into a lovely small hotel. It is enthusiastically
run by the genial Monsieur Liébus, who in restoring the
building has been careful to retain its historic character.
Bedrooms are designer rustic and very comfortable. The
stone-arched cellar dining-room is an atmospheric place
for dinner but in summer most guests prefer to eat in the
terrace dining-room which has lovely views down over the

river from both indoor and outdoor tables. The regional cooking has a good local reputation. Last orders: lunch 2pm; dinner 9.30pm. Set menus from F65; à la carte around F160.
Hotel pool and river swimming, canoe and kayak rental, riding

MIMIZAN

🛏 5̲/̲7̲ 🛏 £££

Au Bon Coin du Lac, 34 Avenue du Lac, 40200 Mimizan.   Tel: 58.09.01.55
Closed February, Sunday evening and Monday except June 15–September 15
Dbl rm F480–F580

This attractive restaurant, in the heart of the Landes, is beautifully situated on the Aureilhan lake. The elegant dining-room and its shady terrace overlook the lake, which is edged with pine trees and busy with boats. Jean-Pierre Caule's cooking is highly acclaimed, with specialities including a baked seafood casserole, langoustine and salmon terrine, and *paupiettes* of duck. Bedrooms are tastefully decorated. Last orders: lunch 2pm; dinner 10pm. Set menus from F150 (weekdays), F280 (weekend); à la carte around F300.
Lake swimming; sailing boats, windsurfing, rowing boats and pedalos for hire

MOISSAC

🏨 🍽 7̲/̲1̲2̲ 🛏 £

Le Pont Napoléon, 2 Allées Montebello, 82200 Moissac.
Tel: 63.04.01.55
Hotel and restaurant closed January, Sunday and Monday nights in winter
Dbl rm F180–F290

This family-run hotel, in the centre of historic Moissac, overlooks the river Tarn. Although traffic enters the town

via the Napoléon bridge, the volume is low and the hotel
reasonably quiet. The comfortable bedrooms are double-
glazed, and all have en-suite bathrooms. In summer, meals
and drinks are served on a small terrace overlooking the
narrow Allées Montebello and the Tarn. Monsieur Peyre
cooks a wide variety of traditional regional dishes using fresh
local duck, goose and salmon. Last orders: lunch 2pm; dinner
9.15pm. Set menus from F63 (weekdays), F82 (Sunday); à la
carte around F200.
*A water-taxi takes visitors to watersports centre at St-Nicholas-de-la-
Grave for sailing, canoeing and windsurfing at the confluence of Tarn
and Garonne; July jazz festival in Montauban*

LE MONT-DORE

🏠 🍽 5/11 🛏 £

Auberge du Lac de Guéry, 63240 Le Mont-Dore.
Tel: 73.65.02.76
Closed November 1–December 15
Dbl rm F200
Le Mont-Dore lies 8km south

In a tranquil location high in the Auvergne mountains, this
small turn-of-the-century inn stands alone on the shores of a
lake. It is an appealing retreat for anglers, walkers and nature-
lovers and has a cosy rustic charm. Bedrooms are small and
simply but comfortably furnished. All have en-suite bathrooms. Downstairs, a fire blazes in the huge, stone fireplace
on cool days, and all the dining room's 12 tables enjoy
splendid lake views. There is also a summer terrace for
drinks. Simple country cooking, especially local salmon
and trout. Last orders: lunch 2.30pm; dinner 9pm. Set
menus from F70; à la carte around F130.
*Trout and carp fishing; windsurfing (bring your own board); moun-
tain bikes for hire; beautiful mountain walking (nearby Puy de Sancy
highest point in central France with skiing in winter); thermal spa
town of Le Mont-Dore*

MONTGEARD

IOI ▭ ££

La Ferme de Champreux, Lac de la Thézauque,
Montgéard, 31560 Nailloux.   Tel: 61.81.33.13
Closed mid-January–February 28 and Monday
A61 exit Villefranche 15 minutes

On the shores of a small recreational lake, this pleasant
restaurant started as a farmhouse. Extended several times in
recent years, its large seating capacity, spanning four dining-
rooms, is a testament to the success of its good regional
cooking and peaceful countryside location. Tables inside
do not have lake views, but there is a large canopied dining
terrace with unobstructed water views. Last orders: lunch
2.30pm; dinner 10.30pm. Set menus from F85; à la carte
around F150.
Pedalos for hire, fishing

MONTIGNAC

🏛 IOI 4/14 ▭ £

Hôtel Le Périgord, Place Tourny, 24290 Montignac.
Tel: 53.51.80.38
Closed December 1–February 28; restaurant closed Sunday
evening and Monday lunch September–November
Dbl rm F120–F170

This is a typical country-town hotel on the banks of the river
Vèzere and a nice spot for lunch after visiting Lascaux II,
where facsimiles of the original prehistoric cave paintings are
displayed. There is ample car parking beside the large dining-
room and its waterside terrace. Accommodation is basic but
clean; five rooms have en-suite bathrooms. Open for snacks
and drinks 7.30am–10.30pm. Last orders: lunch 2pm; dinner
9pm. Set menus from F69; à la carte around F140. Drop in to
book for lunch before visiting Lascaux.

MONTPELLIER

IOI 🍴 £

Brasserie St-Germain, Place de l'Europe, Antigone, 34000
Montpellier.   Tel: 67.22.27.98
Open all year
Montpellier centre 10 minutes away

On the banks of the river Lez in the impressive modern
Antigone quartier, designed by Ricardo Boffil, this lively
Art Nouveau-style brasserie is a pleasant place for lunch.
Its delightful summer terrace, shaded by white parasols,
looks out over the riverside esplanade with its fountains
and manicured gardens. Traditional dishes, including *foie
gras* and breast of duck, feature alongside more modern
variations such as leek terrine flavoured with truffles. Last
orders: lunch 2pm; dinner 11pm. Open all day for drinks and
ice-creams. Set menus from F59 (lunch), F100 (dinner); à la
carte around F150.
*Interesting walks around Montpellier, ancient capital of Bas Lan-
guedoc*

MONTPELLIER

IOI 🍴 £££

La Réserve Rimbaud, 820 Avenue de St-Maur,
Quartier des Aubes, 34000 Montpellier.   Tel: 67.72.52.53
Closed mid-January–mid-February, Sunday evening and
Monday

Built in the 1870s, this was originally a country restaurant
with open-air dancing, frequented by Montpellier's bour-
geoisie who would stroll along the promenade or row up and
down the river. Although residential buildings have now
crept up around it, the restaurant and its romantic summer
terrace, overlooking the calm river and floodlit gardens
opposite, can still conjure up the past. After lunch, rowing
boats are available for diners to cross the river for a stroll in the

park. Its traditional regional cuisine is highly regarded by the locals. Last orders: lunch 2pm; dinner 9.45pm. Set menus from F190; à la carte around F250.

NAGES

🏨 🍽 16/22 🛏 £

Hôtel L'Escapade, Lac du Laouzas, Nages, 81320 Murat-sur-Vèbre.   Tel: 63.37.40.51
Open all year
Dbl rm F210

Run by the Cavailles family for 25 years, what used to be a simple, old-fashioned inn has been extended to include a comfortable new bedroom annexe on the lake shore. In the heart of the mountainous Lacaune National Park, both bedrooms and dining-room enjoy peaceful lake vistas. Traditional country cooking with limited menu choice. Last orders: lunch 1pm; dinner 9pm. Set menus from F80; à la carte around F120.
Lake swimming; fishing; sail-boards, pedalos and canoes for hire in summer; tennis courts nearby; excellent country for walking

NAJAC

🏨 🍽 17/39 🛏 £

Belle Rive, Le Roc de Pont, 12270 Najac.
Tel: 65.29.73.90
Closed mid-November–mid-April
Dbl rm F240–F280

This pleasant hotel, run by a friendly and energetic couple, Carole and Jacques Mazières, sits above the river Aveyron and below the ruined fortress of Najac. The comfortable modern bedrooms are tastefully furnished, and all have en-suite bathrooms. The hotel is ideal for those looking for an active holiday in a peaceful verdant setting. Organized fishing and walking holidays can be arranged with the owners.

Monsieur Mazières is renowned in the area for his delicious regional cooking, and his *magret de canard aux morilles* won the 1990 Prix Nationale des Logis de France. The large dining terrace overlooks the river. Last orders: lunch 2pm; dinner 9pm. Set menus from F78; à la carte around F150.
Heated swimming pool and tennis court; canoes and kayaks for hire; pony-riding 1km, four-wheel-drive jeep excursions organized from hotel

NEUVIC

🏨 🍽 <u>15/15</u> 💳 ££

Hôtel du Lac, 19160 Neuvic.   Tel: 55.95.81.43
Open Easter–September 30
Dbl rm F260–F280

A relatively modern building in an idyllic setting on the shores of a lake, this hotel is run by a friendly English couple, Sally and John Watson. The pretty bedrooms, all with en-suite bathrooms and balconies, have lake vistas, which are especially romantic in the early morning as the mist clears. The large, well-furnished bar and restaurant have similar expansive views. Be sure to reserve window tables ahead in season. The French chef cooks innovative versions of traditional regional dishes. There is a canopied terrace for meals and drinks in good weather. Last orders: lunch 1.30pm; dinner 9.30pm. Set menus from F120; à la carte around F170.
Neuvic is a lively resort in the summer, offering plenty of activities including windsurfing, sailing and water-skiing, lake swimming from beach, fishing, new 9-hole golf course; hotel tennis courts

OLONZAC

🍽 💳 £

Auberge de l'Escale du Canal, Ecluse d'Ognon, 34210 Olonzac.   Tel: 68.91.24.41
Closed mid-November–Easter
Signposted from junction of D124 and D11

This popular restaurant overlooking the Canal du Midi is set beside a busy lock, and has a terrace shaded by plane trees. Popular with both locals and foreign barge travellers, it provides good traditional home cooking in a relaxed atmosphere. An attractive spot for lunch while exploring the Canal du Midi or the Corbières and Minervois vineyards. Last orders: lunch 2.30pm ; dinner 11pm. Set menus from F70; à la carte around F120.

Canal fishing; pleasant tow-path walks

PALAVAS-LES-FLOTS

🍽 🛏 £££

La Marine, 1 Quai Paul Cinq, 34250 Palavas-les-Flots.
Tel: 67.68.00.05
Open all year

A model of a bearded mariner, pipe in hand, guards the door of this elegant seafood restaurant. Inside, there is a feeling of dining on a cruise ship: sunlight pours through the large windows enhancing the effect of the cane seating and pastel decor. In summer, the sliding doors that enclose the covered terrace are removed to create an open-air patio overlooking the quay and brightly painted fishing boats. Specialities include *bouillabaisse* and baked salmon. Lobster and crawfish are kept alive in a tank. Because of its proximity to Montpellier it can become very crowded at weekends. Last orders: lunch 2.30pm; dinner 11pm. Set menus from F98; à la carte around F250.

Deep-sea fishing trips including night fishing can be booked outside restaurant; sailing school; sandy beach 50m

PARAZA

🍽 🛏 £

Le Coup de Foudre, Paraza, 11200 Lézignan-Corbières.
Tel: 68.43.21.45

Open April 1–October 31
On D67 on north side of canal

The name of this small, convivial restaurant, opened last year, translates as 'love at first sight'. The airy, conservatory-style dining-room and its partly-covered wooden terrace look out over a peaceful stretch of the Canal du Midi and the Corbières hills. There is live music and dining by candle-light on summer evenings. Specialities include meat fondue, grilled kebabs, and raw fish salad. In summer, meals and drinks are served from 11am until the early hours. Last orders off-season: lunch 2pm, dinner 10pm. No set menus; à la carte around F130.
Children's playground, fishing by permit

PERIGUEUX

IOI ▭ £££

Aux Berges de l'Isle, 2 Rue Pierre Magne, 24000 Périgueux.   Tel: 53.09.51.50
Closed Saturday lunch all year and Sundays in winter

Tucked alongside the bridge which carries the Roman road over the river Isle, this well-appointed restaurant has room for 25 diners; ask for a window table. There are also four tables out on the terrace which have a view of the pinnacles and domes of St-Front Cathedral reflected in the water below. The menu changes daily, depending on what chef Claude Milhac buys in the market. Last orders: lunch 2.30pm; dinner 9.30pm. Set menus from F135; à la carte around F250.

PESSAC-SUR-DORDOGNE

IOI ▭ ££

Le Belvédère, Juillac, Pessac-sur-Dordogne, 33890 Gensac.   Tel: 57.47.40.33
Closed October, Tuesday evening and Wednesday except during July and August

A few hundred feet above a bend in the Dordogne, the Belvédère's terrace enjoys commanding views over the river as it winds through fields of maize and neat rows of vines. Only two inside tables have river views, but meals are also served on the terrace when the weather permits. Well-prepared regional dishes based around oysters, game and fish. Children have their own *petit gourmand* menu for F35. Good wine list. Last orders: lunch 2.30pm; dinner 9.30pm. Set menus from F125; à la carte around F300.

PEYRAT-LE-CHATEAU

🏨 IОI 21/21 ▭ ££

La Caravelle, Lac de Vassivière, 87470 Peyrat-le-Château.
Tel: 55.69.40.97
Closed January 1–March 15
Dbl rm F290–F300

This modern hotel stands right on the shore of a large and rather beautiful lake in the Limousin. Its bedrooms, decorated in different styles, may not be to everyone's taste but they are well furnished and very comfortable. Best of all, most of them have private balconies overlooking the lake. Heavy curtains and tapestries give the restaurant a warm ambience, and most tables enjoy lake views. In summer, meals and drinks are also served on a pleasant lakeside terrace. Much of the food served is local home-grown produce and the restaurant has a good reputation. Last orders: lunch 2pm; dinner 9pm. Set menus from F150; à la carte around F200. *Watersports centre has sailing boats and windsurfers for hire, water-skiing, lake swimming from beaches, fishing, tennis courts, riding*

PEYRELEAU

🏨 IОI 38/38 ▭ ££

Grand Hôtel de la Muse et du Rozier, La Muse,
12720 Peyreleau.   Tel: 65.62.60.01

Closed December 1–March 1
Dbl rm F360–F550

This beautiful architect–designed hotel stands alone on the banks of the Tarn just before the start of its famous gorges. A perfect spot for a romantic getaway, its spacious bedrooms are beautifully decorated in different styles, some with terraces and glassed–in balconies. All enjoy superb views of a peaceful, wooded stretch of the Tarn. There are three handsome dining–rooms, but in good weather everyone chooses to eat on the large terrace directly overlooking the river – which is illuminated at night. Some regional favourites are served, as well as light *nouvelle cuisine* dishes based on fresh seasonal produce. Wines from Cahors, Gaillac and Fronton-nais. Popular for off–season conferences which tend to take over and spoil the atmosphere so check when booking. Last orders: lunch 2pm; dinner 9.30pm. Set menus from F155; à la carte around F250.

Steps down from hotel terrace for river swimming and canoe trips; rafting 8km; boat trips through Tarn gorges from La Malène; fishing; hotel tennis courts; riding nearby

LES PLANTIERS

IOI ▭ ₤₤

La Sariette, 30122 Les Plantiers.   Tel: 66.83.92.71
Closed January 6–February 28; Thursday
October–mid–May

Set in a wooded river valley, this is a pleasant tranquil spot for lunch while exploring the Cévennes hills. Owner–chef Philippe Labatut cooks traditional Cévenol specialities with many dishes featuring chestnuts and wild mushrooms. In fine weather, meals are served on a shaded open–air terrace built out over the river. Open 9am–10.30pm for breakfast, crêpes, ice–creams and drinks. Last orders for meals: lunch 2pm; dinner 9pm. Set menus from F78 (children F38); à la carte around F150.

Pedalos (free for clients), river swimming, trout fishing, marked footpaths

POILHES

IOI ▭ ₤₤₤

La Tour Sarrasine, Boulevard Paul Riquet, Poilhes, 34310 Capestang.   Tel: 67.93.41.31
Closed January 10–February 15; Sunday evening and Monday except during July and August
A9 exit Beziers West 15 minutes

One of the more gastronomic stops on the Canal du Midi, this former forge has been converted into an attractive restaurant with a good reputation locally. Most of the nine inside tables have canal views and, in summer, a handful of tables are set up on the pavement outside. Owner–chef Monsieur Frontier uses only fresh local produce for his imaginative meat and fish dishes. Last orders: lunch 1.30pm; dinner 9.30pm. Set menus F100 (weekday lunch) and F165; à la carte around F250.

PONT-DE-LARN

🏚 IOI **3/9** ▭ ₤₤

Château de Montlédier, Route d'Anglès, 81660 Pont-de-Larn.   Tel: 63.61.20.54
Closed January; restaurant closed Sunday evening except during July and August
Dbl rm F420–F570

From its isolated position high above the river Arn, this 13th-century fortified chateau enjoys spectacular views of the river as it flows through a deep, wooded gorge. It is an intimate and imaginatively converted chateau–hotel with rooms named after local dignitaries of the past. The spacious bedrooms are handsomely decorated in baronial style; room Raymond IV enjoys the best river views. The cellar bar

was once the stables, and the restaurant occupies the old kitchens. Last orders: lunch 2pm; dinner 9.30pm. Set menus from F95; à la carte around F150.
Hotel swimming pool; 2km walk to waterfalls and gorge; watersports at Castres 17km

PONT-D'HERAULT

Château du Rey, Le Rey, Pont-d'Hérault, 30570 Valleraugue.   Tel: 67.82.40.06
Hotel closed November 15–April 15; restaurant closed January and February only
Dbl rm F298–F370

This ancient castle, parts of which date from the 13th century, is flanked by the river Arre on one side and a small stream on the other which join to flow into the scenic river Hérault a mile downsteam. The hotel's appeal lies in its peaceful woodland setting and the old-fashioned hospitality of owners Marcel and Marie-Jacqueline Cazalis de Fondouce. Rooms are filled with antique family furniture and bric-a-brac. All the homely bedrooms have en-suite bathrooms, and rooms 1 and 2 have bathrooms in round turrets. Although river views are obscured by tall horse-chestnut trees, the sound of rushing water is ever present. The restaurant, in a 13th-century sheep-fold beside the river, serves traditional French cuisine with many Cévenol favourites. In summer, meals are served on a small terrace which enjoys the sound, rather than the sight, of the river. Last orders: lunch 2pm; dinner 9pm. Set menus from F150; à la carte around F250.
Trout-fishing for guests, river swimming, marked footpaths through wild, wooded mountain scenery, convenient base for visiting Tarn gorges, Cévennes National Park and Alès

PONT-DU-CHATEAU

🍴 🛏 ££

Auberge du Pont, 70 Ave de Doctor Besserve, 63430
Pont-du-Château.   Tel: 73.83.00.36
Open all year; closed Wednesday
A72 exit 1, 5km

Once a river port for commercial barges using the Allier,
Pont-du-Château is now a peaceful village. The roadside
Auberge du Pont has a plain, rather off-putting, exterior
but the interior is attractively furnished with fresh flowers
on the tables. Nine tables enjoy good river views, as does the
tree-shaded garden terrace. Good, simple, country cooking –
especially salmon and trout. Last orders: lunch 2pm; dinner
9.30pm. Bar open 9am–9pm for drinks and snacks. Set
menus from F84; à la carte around F120.
Salmon fishing; canoes and kayaks for hire nearby; riverside walks

PONTEMPEYRAT

🏰 🍴 **16/24** 🛏 ££

Hôtel Mistou, Pontempeyrat, 43500
Craponne-sur-Arzon.   Tel: 77.50.62.46
Closed November 4–Easter; restaurant closed weekday
lunch out of season
Dbl rm F250–F460
Turn right off D498 between Craponne and
Usson-en-Forez

Off the beaten track, and in the heart of the forests of the Haute
Loire, this converted 18th-century mill stands in a park on the
banks of the river Ance. The mill still provides electricity for
the entire building. The hotel is popular as a romantic retreat,
and Bernard and Jacqueline Roux provide a warm welcome.
The comfortable bedrooms, some in a separate chalet-style
annexe, have recently been re-decorated in fashionable pastels. The restaurant's two dining-rooms are equally elegant,

with tables on the enclosed verandah enjoying the best river views. The menus are imaginative; only fresh local produce is used, especially freshwater fish. Last orders: lunch 1.30pm; dinner 9.15pm. Set menus from F135; à la carte around F220. *Trout fishing (licences from Craponne); beautiful forest walks*

PORT-DE-GAGNAC

🏠 🍽 <u>12/12</u> 🛏 £

Hostellerie Belle-Rive, Port-de-Gagnac, 46130 Bretenoux.   Tel: 65.38.50.04
Closed December and January
Dbl rm F210–F250
Signposted from D940 at Beaulieu and Bretenoux

This 18th-century mansion, complete with turrets, stands in a hamlet on the north bank of the Cère river, a tributary of the Dordogne, and is separated from it by a narrow road which is rarely busy. It is run by the hospitable Madame Dumont and her family and has the feeling of an old country inn. Rooms are very comfortable in an old-fashioned way. Those on the first floor and in the turret have more character than those on the more modern second floor. All have lovely views across a wide stretch of river in a pastoral landscape. The dining-room is decorated in an appealing rustic style and, in summer, meals are also served on a roadside terrace. The home cooking is excellent with menus including Périgourdine specialities and tasty country fare such as chicken in a cream and wild mushroom sauce. Last orders: lunch 1.30pm; dinner 9.30pm. Set menus from F50; à la carte around F120.
Riverbank walks, trout fishing with licence, Fête de Gagnac takes place on Sunday after August 15 and lasts three days

PORT-VENDRES

🍽 🛏 ££

La Côte Vermeille, Quai du Fanal, 66660 Port-Vendres. Tel: 68.82.05.71

Closed November 11–December 22

This simple restaurant overlooks fishing trawlers in port and often their crews can be seen checking and repairing their nets on the quayside. The building and its decor are plain, but the fish and seafood are beautifully presented and always fresh and perfectly cooked. Last orders: lunch 2pm; dinner 9.45pm. Set menus from F98; à la carte around F180.

POUDENAS

🏨 🍴 **5/6** 🛏 £££

A La Belle Gasconne, Poudenas, 47170 Mezin.
Tel: 53.65.71.58
Hotel and restaurant closed December 1–15 and
January 1–15 and Sunday and Monday nights
May–August
Dbl rm F490–F530

This 14th-century mill on the river Gélise has been beautifully restored, and is as much a family home as a hotel. Marie-Claude Gracia, who was born in the village, and her husband, Richard, enjoy telling guests about Aquitaine's history and attractions. The bedrooms are beautifully appointed and look out on to the mill-stream which flows around the building and over a weir. The cooking is superb, featuring regional delicacies and a very special chocolate gateau for diners who know how to pace themselves. Reserve ahead in summer as restaurant is small. Last orders: lunch 2.30pm; dinner 10pm. Set menus from F165; à la carte around F225.
Canoes for residents, fishing, tennis courts, hotel pool

PUY-L'EVEQUE

🏨 🍴 **14/15** 🛏 £

Hôtel Bellevue, Place de la Truffière, 46700
Puy-l'Evêque.   Tel: 65.21.30.70

Closed November 15–April 1
Dbl rm F149–F234

Not for those who suffer from vertigo, this friendly hotel has been built into a steep rock face above the river Lot. Bedrooms are starkly furnished, but clean and well kept. Only three have full en-suite bathrooms, but nearly all have French windows opening on to small balconies with panoramic views down over the river. One of the hotel's major attractions is its terrace restaurant, enclosed by glass off-season, which gives diners the feeling of being suspended high over the river. There is also a smaller terrace, with similar spectacular views, for coffee and drinks. The cooking is regional and attractively presented. Last orders: lunch 2pm; dinner 9pm. Set menus from F87; à la carte around F150.
Outdoor swimming pool, canoes and kayaks for hire, 1km; fishing, golf and riding; visits to local vineyards and china factory can be arranged through hotel

PUY-L'EVEQUE

🏨 |O| **5/15** ⊟ ♀♀

La Source Bleue, Touzac, 46700 Puy-l'Evêque.
Tel: 65.36.52.01
Closed November 15–April 1; restaurant closed Tuesday to non-residents
Dbl rm F320–F410
Puy-l'Evêque 6km

Taking its name from the natural spring and the deep-blue pool on the property, this charming hotel stands in pretty grounds on the banks of the river Lot. It comprises three old mill buildings that have been tastefully converted with great attention to detail, successfully combining original features with modern comforts which include a sauna and gym. The restaurant, which overlooks the spring, serves good regional cooking. There is no need to worry about understanding the menu; Madame Bouyou comes from Wales and is most helpful and hospitable. Last orders: lunch 1.30pm; dinner 9pm. Set menus are available from F95; à la carte around F150.

Secluded pool in grounds and river swimming, bamboo forest, boat rides along Lot 50m, canoe and kayak hire 500m, fishing, walks along St James of Compostela pilgrimage route

PYLA-SUR-MER

🏬 ⦿ 10/15 ▭ ££

La Corniche, Pilat Plage, 33115 Pyla-sur-Mer.
Tel: 56.22.72.11
Closed November 1–March 31
Dbl rm F220–F470
Arcachon 8km

This small seaside hotel stands at the northern end of the curious Dune du Pyla, a 300-foot-high sand-dune, bereft of vegetation, which stretches for a mile along the coast. Bedrooms are comfortable, most with balconies and en-suite bathrooms, although those with the best views have only washbasins and bidets. Its restaurant serves mostly seafood and has good views over the encroaching dune and the sea. There is also a terrace for drinks. Last orders: lunch 2pm; dinner 10pm. Set menus are available from F85; à la carte around F170.

Steps lead down to sandy beach with lifeguards; sailing-boat hire and windsurfing in Arcachon basin, 2km

REMOULINS

🏬 ⦿ 6/11 ▭ ££

Le Moulin de Roy, Avenue du Pont-du-Gard, 30210 Remoulins.   Tel: 66.37.27.28
Open all year
Dbl rm F240–F280

This former mill, parts of which date back to the 11th century used to crush olives and grapes. Now a comfortable hotel, it stands beside the river Gardon, a 15-minute walk from the Pont-du-Gard aqueduct built in 19BC by the Romans. Bedrooms are comfortable and well equipped, all with en-suite bathrooms. Guests can relax on lounge-beds arranged on the grassy banks of the river. Simple meals, mostly grilled meats and fish, are served in a new restaurant. Last orders: lunch 2.30pm; dinner 10pm. Set menus from F52; à la carte around F100. *River swimming at cascades, fishing, canoes and kayaks for hire at Pont-du-Gard, good base for excursions to Nimes and Avignon*

REMOULINS

🏨 IOI 12/14 🛏 ££

Hôtel du Vieux Moulin, Pont-du-Gard, Rive Gauche, 30210 Remoulins.   Tel: 66.37.14.35
Closed mid-November–mid-March
Dbl rm F330–F495

This former flour mill sits beside the river Gardon overlooking a small pebble beach and the magnificent Roman aqueduct. A peaceful and romantic spot in the evenings, after the tour coaches have gone, guests can dine on the tree-shaded terrace looking out over the illuminated aqueduct. Some inside tables enjoy partial views of the aqueduct through a huge semi-circular window. Bedrooms are comfortable with exposed beams and Provencal furniture. Imaginative, traditional cuisine. Last orders: lunch 2pm; dinner 9pm. Set menus from F160; à la carte around F250.
Private pebble beach at water's edge for river swimming, fishing, canoes and kayaks for hire

LA ROCHE L'ABEILLE

🏨 IOI 8/9 🛏 £££

Moulin de la Gorce, La Roche l'Abeille, 87800 Nexon. Tel: 55.00.70.66

Closed January, Sunday evening and Monday
September 15–April 1
Dbl rm F350–F650
Near St Yrieix-la-Perche

Set amid the rolling farmlands of Limousin, this 16th-century
mill has been converted into an appealing hotel and restaurant. The elegant bedrooms, each decorated in a different
style, have been furnished with tapestries and antiques. Most
overlook the mill-stream, but three have views of a large
mill-pond. The restaurant is beautifully arranged and ideal for
a romantic dinner. Several window tables have views of the
water. Classic French cuisine based on fresh seasonal produce. Last orders: lunch 1.30pm; dinner 9pm. Set menus
from F160; à la carte around F400.
*Fishing (free for residents), pedalos for hire and windsurfing at Lac
Arfeuille 8km, tennis court in the village, riding at St-Yrieix 10km*

LA ROQUE-GAGEAC

🏨 🍴 12/17 🛏 £

La Belle Etoile, La Roque-Gageac, 24250 Domme.
Tel: 53.29.51.44
Open Easter–October 15
Dbl rm F130–F300

Sheltered beneath craggy cliffs, this charming old hotel is one
of a cluster of honey-coloured stone houses on the banks of
the Dordogne. The bedrooms are nicely furnished in traditional country style and all have en-suite bathrooms. Window tables in the pretty dining-room enjoy lovely views over
the river, as do tables on the edge of the vine-covered first-
floor terrace. Father and son team, Guy and Régis Ongaro,
dream up imaginative fish dishes as well as rich Périgordine
specialities. Last orders: lunch 2.30pm; dinner 9.30pm. Set
menus from F100; à la carte around F200.
*Fishing, boat trips to Beynac, canoes and kayaks for hire, river
swimming and village tennis court*

LA ROQUE-SUR-CEZE

🍽 ⊟ £

Mas du Bélier, La Roque-sur-Cèze, 30200
Bagnols-sur-Cèze.   Tel: 66.82.78.73
Open Easter–September 30 and Wednesday except during
July and August

Originally a hunting lodge belonging to La Roque's chateau,
this simple restaurant looks across the river to a beautifully
preserved medieval village. The cane-covered terrace, decorated with terracotta pots of geraniums and hanging lanterns,
overlooks an arched Romanesque bridge over the Cèze.
Traditional regional fare. Last orders: lunch 2pm; dinner
10pm. Set menus from F68; à la carte around F120.
Swimming and riding at Cascades du Sautadet 1km

ST-AMBROIX

🍽 ⊟ £

Le Moulin du Roc Tombé, Le Moulinet, 30500
St-Ambroix.   Tel: 66.24.32.03
Open June 15–September 15

Cut into the rock face, this former corn mill appears to be
built on water. A steep flight of stone steps leads down to an
outdoor dining terrace built out over the old mill-race. A
good place for a family lunch in summer, there are pedalos
and aqua-cycles for children to mess around in. It is also a
popular place for swimming as the stone weir filters the water
into a very clear pool as well as providing a natural diving
platform. There is also a pebble beach on the opposite bank.
Grilled meats, pizzas and salads are the order of the day. Open
10am–midnight for ice-creams and drinks. Last orders: lunch
1.30pm; dinner 10pm. Set menu F65.
Rowing boats, canoes and kayaks for hire in St-Ambroix 3km;
Ardèche gorges, Alès and the Cèze valley a 30-minute drive away

ST-ANTONIN-NOBLE-VAL

🏠 🍽 12/18 🛏 £

Hôtel des Thermes, Place des Moines, 82140
St-Antonin-Noble-Val.   Tel: 63.30.61.08
Open all year
Dbl rm F180

Charmed by the beauty of its setting, the founders of this
Gallo-Roman spa resort named it Noble-Val. The medieval
core of the town rises above the right bank of the river facing
a vertical cliff, and the hotel, named after a natural spring near
its entrance, has unobstructed views over a wide, calm stretch
of the river Aveyron. It has been recently renovated so
bedrooms are modern and comfortable, all with new en-
suite bathrooms. The large restaurant has magnificent views
over the picturesque and verdant river valley. Weather
permitting, meals and drinks are also served on a waterside
terrace. Traditional regional cooking. Last orders: lunch
2pm; dinner 10.30pm. Set menus from F65; à la carte
around F110.
Fishing, canoe and kayak hire, winter river-rafting in Najac 8km,
marked walking paths, good base for exploring Aveyron gorges

ST-AULAYE-DE-BREUILH

🍷 🛏 £

Café Pierre, St-Aulaye-de-Breuilh, 24230 Vélines.
Tel: 53.58.27.01
Open all year; closed Monday and Tuesday out of season

Londoner Peter Apsley acquired a former bakery in this tiny
medieval village and has opened a pleasant café on the banks
of the Dordogne. Views from the ground floor are partly
obscured by a stone wall, but there's a terrace on the first floor
with splendid river views. Simple meals – steaks, omelettes
and sandwiches – are served from noon–10.30pm and the bar
is open until the last customer decides to leave, which can be
as late as 2am in summer.

ST-CYPRIEN

🏨 🍽 <u>22/22</u> 🛏 £££

L'Ile de la Lagune, 66750 St-Cyprien Sud.
Tel: 68.21.01.02
Closed January 5–February 15; restaurant closed
Sunday evening and Monday except June–September
Dbl rm F700–F800

Situated on a small landscaped island in the middle of a lagoon,
this is an extremely comfortable modern hotel. Bedrooms
have designer furniture, specially made for the hotel, and
are separated from a sitting area by a large archway. All have
private balconies. There are also villas to rent by the week. The
dining area is light and airy, although in summer guests generally take meals on the outdoor terrace which looks out over
the lagoon. Last orders: lunch 2pm; dinner 9.30pm. Set menus
area available from F160; à la carte around F250.
*Hotel swimming pool, lagoon windsurfing from small beach, com-
plimentary motorboat to La Lagune (see below) whose sporting
facilities are available to residents*

ST-CYPRIEN

🏨 🍽 <u>36/36</u> 🛏 ££

La Lagune, 66750 St-Cyprien.   Tel: 68.21.24.24
Open May 1–October 15
Dbl rm F310

Flanked by a wide sandy beach on one side and a lagoon on
the other, this modern, low-rise hotel has something of a club
atmosphere, with guests informed of the week's events and
activities at a welcome meeting. Spacious bedrooms are
comfortable and well equipped, all with private terraces.
The complex also includes privately owned apartments that
share the hotel's facilities. There are several dining-rooms
and terraces offering traditional French cuisine as well as

international buffets and a pizzeria. Half-board obligatory in July and August; F350 a person. Last orders: lunch 2pm; dinner 9.30pm. Set menus from F120; à la carte around F180. *Two swimming pools (with lessons and exercise sessions), windsurfing and tennis tuition, pedalos and jet-skis for hire, deep-sea fishing and sailing trips from port, nearby 18-hole golf and riding*

ST-ETIENNE-DE-BAIGORRY

🏨 🍽 12/25 🛏 £££

Hôtel Arcé, 64430 St-Etienne-de-Baigorry.
Tel: 59.37.40.14
Closed November 15–March 15
Dbl rm F525–F650

This typical Basquaise house, set amid magnificent mountain scenery, is a real gem setting. It backs on to the river Nive–des–Aldudes framed against the impressive backdrop of the Pyrenees. The Arcé family provides a friendly welcome and real value for money. Rooms are decorated in a tasteful country way. The restaurant has a very good reputation. There are three menus based around regional specialities and trout straight from the river, as well as à la carte treats such as *tournedos Navarrais* and sole with wild mushrooms. In summer, meals are served on a tree-shaded terrace on the riverbank. Last orders: lunch 1.45pm; dinner 8.30pm. Set menus from F100; à la carte around F250. Reservations advised.
Heated pool and tennis court across bridge in gardens, fishing (permit needed), riding 10km, excursions to Bidarray caves

ST-ETIENNE-DE-FURSAC

🏨 🍽 4/12 🛏 ££

Hôtel Nougier, 23290 St-Etienne-de-Fursac.
Tel: 55.63.60.56

Closed December 1–February 28, Sunday and
Monday nights except during July and August
Dbl rm F300

In the centre of a pretty Limousin town, this stylish yet
homely hotel stands in gardens on the banks of the river
Gartempe. Bedrooms are spotlessly clean, tastefully decorated and compact without being pokey. The staff are
charming and discreetly attentive. The restaurant has no
view of the river, but drinks are served in the waterside
garden. Inventive cuisine based on fresh local produce. Last
orders: lunch 2pm; dinner 9.30pm. Set menus from F98; à la
carte around F220.

*Trout fishing, beautiful walks through a verdant hilly landscape
crossed by many small rivers*

ST-FOY-LA-GRANDE

IOI ▭ £

La Terrasse, 3 Rue de la Rouquette, Port St-Foy, 33220
St-Foy-la-Grande.　Tel: 53.24.72.60
Open all year; closed Monday

This simple restaurant backs on to the Dordogne, its shaded
terrace suspended above the water. There are fine views
across the river to the old town of St-Foy-la-Grande from
the ten terrace tables and window tables inside. It is a friendly,
family-run place: the genial Monsieur Liteau does the cooking and opens the wine, while his wife supervises in the
dining-room. Expect good home cooking at very reasonable prices: *confits*, fish, grills, *coq au vin*, and beef and lamb
dishes. Last orders: lunch 1.45pm; dinner 9.30pm. Set menus
from F60 (weekdays), F100 weekends; à la carte around
F130.

Walks along riverside promenade in St-Foy-la-Grande

ST-FOY-LA-GRANDE

IOI ▭ ££

Le Moulin de la Carretterie, 332200 St-Foy-la-Grande.
Tel: 57.46.39.70
Closed for several months in winter, Sunday evening
and Monday except June–September
Turn north off RN89 opposite hypermarket 1km east of
St-Foy; restaurant is on right 1km further along

This ancient mill stands beside a small river on a quiet country
lane. It has recently been completely renovated and its tiny
dining-room – there are only 25 covers – has a glass wall
making the most of the water view. There is also a glass panel
in the floor so you can see the water flowing beneath your
feet. In summer, meals are served on a wooden deck overhanging the river. The welcome is warm and friendly and the
restaurant, which has only been open for a year or so, is very
popular with locals. Daniel Marcillac's cooking is delicious
with specialities including grilled langoustines, steak with
wild mushrooms or *foie gras*, and salmon in an orange butter
sauce. Last orders: lunch 1.30pm; dinner 9.30pm. Reservations essential. Set menus from F100; à la carte around F200.

ST-GEORGES

▥ IOI 10/22 ▭ £

Le Bout du Monde, St-Georges, 15100 St-Flour.
Tel: 71.60.15.84
Open all year
Dbl rm F100–F200

This welcoming hotel at the entrance to the Lander gorges is
run by three generations of the Albisson family. A decade ago
it was their farmhouse, and they still raise ducks and chickens
and grow vegetables for the restaurant. As its name suggests, it
is off the tourist trail. Bedrooms are charmingly old-fashioned with lace curtains and thick eiderdowns; only six have

en-suite bathrooms. There are pleasant country views over lawns to the river. The restaurant, which has no river view, specializes in hearty Auvergne cooking, with dishes such as pork hash with prunes, bacon casserole with spinach and tripe. Last orders: lunch 2pm; dinner 9pm. Café–bar open from 7am for breakfast, drinks and sandwiches, which can be eaten on a terrace overlooking the river. Set menus from F50; à la carte around F70.

Trout and pike fishing, lovely walking country, village cattle fair every weekend in summer, medieval St-Flour 5km

ST-GENIEZ-D'OLT

⌨ 🛏 £

Café du Pont, 2 Place du Marché, 12130 St-Geniez-d'Olt.
Tel: 65.70.40.07
Open all year; closed Monday October–May

This simple café–bar may not be pretty but its terrace is suspended over the river Lot. With folk music playing in the background, its good-humoured owners serve coffee, beers and many local wines and spirits including strawberry, prune and pear liqueurs, as well as croissants and sandwiches. Open 7am–1am.

ST-GILLES

🏠 5/21 🛏 ££

Hôtel Héraclée, 30 Quai du Canal, Port de Plaisance,
30800 St-Gilles.   Tel: 66.87.44.10
Closed February
Dbl rm F250–F320

In a quiet street bordering the Rhône canal on the north side of the Camargue, this small, new hotel has comfortable, well equipped bedrooms. Only five look out over the canal, which is busy with pleasure boats and barges and two of these have private terraces. Breakfast only. A reasonably priced base for those who are touring the region.

Boat trips down canal to Aigues-Mortes and the Camargue via Le Petit Rhone depart from in front of hotel, bicycles, canoes and kayaks for hire, tennis, riding and golf nearby

STE-ENIMIE

🏠 🍽 **17/19** 💳 £££

Château de la Caze, 48210 Ste-Enimie.   Tel: 66.48.51.01
Open May 1–November 1; restaurant closed Tuesday
Dbl rm F550–F850
On D907 between Ste-Enimie and La Malène

This beautiful 15th-century castle stands on a limestone ledge beneath the rugged cliffs of the spectacular Tarn gorges. Great care has been taken to preserve a sense of the castle's history by exposing stonework and furnishing it in baronial style. Bedrooms are named after people associated with the castle's history. Some have stone-vaulted ceilings and four-poster beds swathed in tapestry hangings, others have round bathrooms in the narrow, circular towers with their arrow-slit windows. There are 13 bedrooms in the chateau and six apartments in an equally historic farmhouse next door. Nearly all have views over the rushing waters of the Tarn. The restaurant occupies the old chapel but, in summer, meals are also served on a terrace from which diners glimpse the river. Traditional, regional cooking, including a menu of Lozère specialities. Last orders: lunch 2pm; dinner 9.30pm. Set menus from F150–F300; no à la carte. Non-residents must reserve in advance.

Fishing (permits from Ste-Enimie), river swimming, canoes and kayaks for hire, excellent base for touring Tarn gorges on foot or by car

STE-ENIMIE

🏨 🍽 8/12 🛏 ££

Manoir de Montesquiou, La Malène, 48210 Ste-Enimie.
Tel: 66.48.51.12
Open Easter–October 15
Dbl rm F350–F470; suites F640

At the foot of a rocky escarpment just a stone's throw from
the river Tarn, this 15th-century chateau stands in the middle
of the tiny village of La Malène, an atmospheric base for
exploring the Tarn gorges. Bedrooms are comfortable and
some are furnished with four-posters and heavy old antique
pieces. Rooms on the top floor have the best river views. The
homely restaurant, which has no view of the river, serves
reasonably priced regional dishes. Guests are asked to dine in
the hotel. Last orders: lunch 2pm; dinner 9pm. Set menus
from F155; à la carte around F240.
*Fishing, river swimming, canoe and kayak rental, boat trips through
gorges*

STE-ENIMIE

🍽 4/4 🛏 £

Restaurant des Deux Sources, 48210 Ste-Enimie.
Tel: 66.48.53.87
Closed November 11–Easter and Thursday except
during July and August
Dbl rm F175–F200

Nestling beneath the ancient arched bridge that links the two
halves of Ste-Enimie, the dining-room occupies a glass-sided
verandah that sits above the river Tarn. On summer evenings, it is turned into an open-air terrace, the riverbank is
floodlit, and the view through the tall trees to the fast-flowing
river makes this an attractive spot for dinner. It is popular

with locals who like to linger after dinner sipping nut, pear
and peach liqueurs. Traditional regional cooking. Four simple bedrooms, all with en-suite bathrooms, were recently
added. Last orders: lunch 2pm; dinner 10pm. Set menus from
F75; à la carte around F120.

STE-MARIE-DE-GOSSE

⊨ 3/3 ⊞ £

Marchannau, 40390 Ste-Marie-de-Gosse.
Tel: 59.56.35.71
Closed over Christmas
Dbl rm F200
Turn off N117 at Ste-Marie and follow riverside road
for 2km

Michel Fevrier and his wife moved here 12 years ago from
Paris and have since opened their home to guests who are
assured of a warm, friendly welcome. A former hunting
lodge, its interior is tastefully rustic with bare stone walls
and beamed ceilings. The three bedrooms are very large
and furnished with some family antiques; all have attached
bath or shower rooms. There are lovely views over a wide,
peaceful rural stretch of the river Adour from the rooms and
the front terrace where breakfast is served in fine weather. A
quiet narrow lane separates the house from the riverbank.
Tow-path walks along Adour as far as Bayonne

STE-MARIE-DE-GOSSE

IOI ⊞ ££

Auberge Piet, Chemin de Halage, 40390
Ste-Marie-de-Gosse.   Tel: 59.56.32.08
Open all year
4km from N117

Philippe Laugareil speaks fluent English and loves to chat with English clients about the Landes region. His restaurant occupies a former farm cottage dating back to 1704 which stands at the end of a quiet lane overlooking the confluence of the Adour and the Gave. The dining-room is a smart rustic affair with beamed ceiling, flagstone floor and a large working fireplace. Tables are elegantly arranged with crisp white linen and fine glassware. Only one inside table has a river view but from May–end October you can enjoy a meal or a drink at one of seven tables on the shaded deck of a former river barge, moored in front of the restaurant. The cooking is excellent and based on fresh market produce. Menus include many dishes traditional to the Landes region. Last orders: lunch 2pm; dinner 10pm. Set menus from F70; à la carte around F150.

LES SALELLES

◎ ¼ ▭ ££

La Lauze, Les Salelles, 48230 Chanac.   Tel: 66.48.21.80
Closed October 1–Easter; Tuesday–Thursday
Easter–April 30
Dbl rm F270–F390

This delightful farmhouse restaurant occupies a former Roquefort cheese dairy on the grassy banks of the river Lot. Its owners, the Augouy family, are great anglophiles and keen to share their local knowledge. Directly overlooking a peaceful stretch of the river's upper reaches, this is one of the few good restaurants in the area, using only the best market produce to create interesting, appetizing dishes. In summer, lunch is often served in the garden overlooking a weir. There are four comfortable bedrooms above the restaurant. Last orders: lunch 2.30pm; dinner 10pm. Set menus from F100 (weekday lunch), F150 (dinner); à la carte around F220.
Fly-fishing (permits from Chanac), river swimming, marked footpaths (owners are enthusiastic walkers), riding centre nearby

SALLES-LA-SOURCE

IOI ⊠ £

Auberge du Créneau, Pont-les-Bains, Salles-la-Source,
12330 Marcillac-Vallon.   Tel: 65.71.74.21
Closed November and Friday evening

Very peacefully situated in a tiny village near Rodez, this
simple waterside restaurant has great charm. Weather permitting, meals and drinks are served on a terrace straddling
the river. Open from 8.30am–10pm, it is popular with locals
rather than tourists and serves dishes such as *foie gras* and
homemade quiches, as well as ice-creams, coffees and beer.
Set menus from F55.

SAUVETERRE-DE-BEARN

🏠 IOI **8/14** ▭ £

Hostellerie du Château, 64390 Sauveterre-de-Béarn.
Tel: 59.38.52.10
Closed January–mid-February
Dbl rm F120–F180

Situated high on a cliff above the river Gave d'Oloron in the
medieval walled town of Sauveterre, this used to be the
residence of the local Marquis and has retained a certain
faded splendour. A grand staircase and wide creaky corridors
lead to the bedrooms which look as if they have not been
renovated for many decades. You will sleep well in the
massive beds, but these are basic rooms so do not expect
frills. Only five rooms have attached bathrooms. Although
eight bedrooms have views over the river, a ruined castle and
the Pyrenees, Nos 1–3 have the best water views. The
restaurant has no river view but, in fine weather, you can
enjoy drinks and pastries on a splendid terrace built out over
the river cliff. The regional cooking includes homemade *foie
gras*, chicken Basque-style, and *piperade*, an omelette with

tomatoes and peppers. Last orders: lunch 1.30pm; dinner 9pm. Set menus from F80; à la carte around F150.
Lovely riverside walks, canoes for hire, salmon fishing (with permit), river swimming

SETE

🏨]O] <u>17/52</u> 🛏 ££

Le Grand Hôtel, 17 Quai de Lattre de Tassigny, 34200 Sète.   Tel: hotel 67.74.71.77; restaurant 67.46.12.10
Open all year
Dbl rm F355–F475
This 19th-century canal-side hotel lives up to its name. A red carpet ushers guests through the entrance lobby and into an attractive internal courtyard, which has been elegantly furnished with easy chairs and exotic plants. Bedrooms are comfortably furnished, some with air-conditioning and soundproofing. A good base for exploring Sète, a lively and picturesque port criss-crossed by canals, and the nearby Etang de Thau. Its new restaurant, La Rotonde, also looks out on to the canal and serves freshly-caught fish and seafood. Last orders: lunch 2.30pm; dinner 10pm. Set menus from F95 (lunch), F145 (dinner); à la carte around F200.
Boat trips (one glass-bottomed) to oyster farms and through the canals and lagoon, sea-jousting competitions every Sunday June–September, large sandy beaches nearby

SETE

]O] 🛏 ££

La Palangrotte, 1 Rampe Paul Valéry, Quai de la Marine, 34200 Sète.   Tel: 67.74.80.35
Closed January, Sunday evening and Monday except July–September

A well-established and popular restaurant in the heart of the port. The dining-rooms are arranged on two floors in an elegant building above the wharf where the fishing boats moor. During the summer, the portside windows are removed to create a delightful open-air terrace. The talented owner–chef, Alain Gemignani, comes from a family of Italian émigrés and loves pasta, which he incorporates into his predominantly seafood dishes. Last orders: lunch 2pm; dinner 10pm. Set menus on offer from F130; à la carte around F275.

SIORAC-EN-PERIGORD

🏨 ⏏ **18/18** 🛏 £

Hotel L'Escale, Siorac-en-Périgord, 24170 Belvès.
Tel: 53.31.60.23
Open Easter–October 15
Dbl rm F200–F250

The building may be unprepossessing and the decor unadventurous, but the views over the river are excellent. Bedrooms are homely and well-maintained and all have en-suite bathrooms and river views. The attractive lounge, with parquet floor and beamed ceiling, has a large, open fire which is lit on cool days. Meals and drinks are served on two large first-floor terraces which look out over the slow-moving river. Well-regarded Périgordine cuisine. Half-board preferred June 15–September 15; F210–F245 per person. Last orders: lunch 2.30pm; dinner 10pm. Set menus from F62; à la carte around F200.
Small beach for river bathing, fishing, canoes for hire, tennis courts and riding nearby

SOUILLAC

⏏ 🛏 £

L'Ajoupa, Le Port, 46200 Souillac.   Tel: 65.37.07.34
Open all year

This attractive modern grill and bar overlooks the Dordogne in Souillac. It is a lively place in summer as there is a swimming pool, baby pool, Jacuzzi and games room on the riverbank terrace. It will appeal especially to families on a hot summer's day and serves excellent homemade ice-cream, a large range of beers, pizzas and mixed grills. All the tables in the dining-room and on the terrace have river views. Open 9am–2am. Set menus from F65.

Souillac is a pretty town with a 12th-century abbey and two museums; canoes for hire; riverbank walks

SOUSTONS

🏨 ❘○❘ 16/27 ▭ ££

Le Pavillon Landais, 26 Avenue du Lac, 40140 Soustons.
Tel: 58.41.14.49
Closed January; restaurant closed Sunday evening and
Monday out of season
Dbl rm F270–F450

This lovely white-washed hotel with its wooden balconies and tiled roofs is beautifully situated on the banks of the freshwater Lac de Soustons. The original villa-style building, called the *ancien pavillon*, dates back to the 1930s and contains eight large rooms with antique furniture and large old-fashioned bathrooms, some with balconies. Room No 1 has a four-poster. In the new wing, built two years ago, the light, airy rooms open either on to lakeside terraces or balconies large enough to sit out on. One room is suitable for disabled guests. Public rooms are elegantly decorated in wine red and creamy white. Half the restaurant's tables overlook the lake and from May–September meals and drinks are also served on a terrace. Good Landaise cooking with the emphasis on fish. Last orders: lunch 2.30pm; dinner 10pm. Set menus from F150; à la carte around F250.

Watersports centre 500m, carp fishing, hotel has swimming pool and tennis court

SOUSTONS

IOI 🛏 ££

Le Lac d'Azur, Azur, 40140 Soustons.   Tel: 58.48.10.15
Closed on weekdays November 11–Easter

This small half-timbered restaurant stands at the northern end
of the Lac de Soustons. It is run by two brothers, Jean and
Alain Freche, and given its popularity it is advisable to book.
Whenever the weather permits, meals are served on an open-
air terrace under the pine trees. Good regional fare; duck is a
firm favourite. Last orders: lunch 2pm; dinner 10pm. Set
menus are available from F56; à la carte around F150.
Lake swimming, sail-boards available for hire nearby

TARASCON-SUR-ARIEGE

🏨 IOI **15/30** 🛏 £

Hostellerie de la Poste, 16 Avenue Victor Pilhes, 09400
Tarascon-sur-Ariège.   Tel: 61.05.60.41
Open all year
Dbl rm F200–F280

In search of a cure for his failing health, Napoleon III spent
time at this simple hotel, just an hour from the Spanish
border. A friendly traditional establishment, it offers a wide
range of accommodation (single occupancy is half-price)
but even the simplest rooms are clean and comfortable, and
most have en-suite bathrooms. However, rooms on the
road side can be noisy so ask for a room overlooking the
garden and the river Ariège as these are quieter and have
small balconies. Public areas are rustic in style with stone
walls, dark wood and beamed ceilings. In the dining-room,
an open fire makes for warm, cosy evenings in the depths
of winter while, in summer, meals and drinks are also
served on a tree-shaded waterside terrace with views to
the Pyrenees beyond. Good regional cooking including

cassoulet and *La Parillade*, a selection of home-cured meats. Last orders: lunch 1.30pm; dinner 10pm. Set menus from F63; à la carte around F140.

Heated indoor pool and tennis courts 500m, trout-fishing; canoes, kayaks and mountain bikes for hire; hotel can arrange Pyrenean tours by jeep at weekends

TARGET

⊨ 5/5 ⊟ £££

Château de Boussac, Target, 03140 Chantelle.
Tel: 70.40.63.20
Closed November 30–April 1
Dbl rm F580
On D42 10km N of Chantelle

Set in beautiful wooded grounds, this captivating chateau is surrounded by a moat and faces a small lake. Its owners, the Marquis and Marquise de Longueil, whose family has lived here since the mid-17th century, enjoy having guests in their home and will advise on touring itineraries and some of the hidden attractions of the Auvergne. Arranged around a central courtyard, the rooms are full of character and furnished with beautiful 18th-century family antiques and portraits. Guests join the owners for dinner *en famille* at one large dining table. The Marquis breeds Charolais cattle, some of which find their way to the table. Dinner, served on advance request, costs F210–F310, including aperitif, wine and brandy.

The Marquis advises on forest walks and will book restaurants for lunch; good base for touring the Auvergne chateaux

LE TEMPLE-SUR-LOT

🏚 🍴 6/10 ⊟ ££

Hostellerie du Plantié, Le Temple-sur-Lot, 47110 Ste-Livrade-sur-Lot.   Tel: 53.84.37.48

Open all year
Dbl rm F340–F360

On his return from working with the Hilton group in the
United States and Bermuda, Monsieur Jalibat and his Cana-
dian wife bought an old apple orchard with a long river
frontage on the Lot. The farmhouse and barns have since
been converted to provide ten comfortable, tastefully decorated bedrooms. One is fully equipped for disabled visitors
and there are ramps in all the public areas. The restaurant
occupies an old barn, but there is also a waterside dining
terrace in summer. International and regional dishes based on
fresh seasonal produce. Last orders: lunch 2pm; dinner
9.30pm. Set menus are available from F80; à la carte around
F200.
*Private swimming pool, fishing, tennis court; sail-boards, canoes and
kayaks for hire at watersports centre 400m*

THIERS

Chez la Mère Dépalle, RN 89, Pont-de-Dore,
63300 Thiers.   Tel: 73.80.10.05
Closed December 2–31; restaurant closed Saturday and
Sunday evening November–April
Dbl rm F240–F270
A72 exit 2 Thiers 3km

This recently renovated hotel has been run by the Giraud
family for five generations. Bedrooms are clean and simply
furnished, all with new en-suite bathrooms. The congenial
restaurant and its terrace, which has been built out over the
water, both enjoy good views over the river Dore. Well
frequented by locals, the terrace is open for refreshments
7am–10pm. Menus are based around fresh market produce. Specialities include freshwater fish and gourmet

salads. Last orders: lunch 2pm, dinner 9pm. Set menus from
F95; à la carte around F200.
Fishing, pedalos for hire; river swimming and watersports at Iloa 5km

THOURON

◙ 4/4 ▭ ££

La Pomme de Pin, La Tricherie, Thouron, 87140 Naniat.
Tel: 55.53.43.43
Closed January, Monday and Tuesday lunch
Dbl rm F240–F290

This inn is reached via a road that crosses some beautiful
countryside reminiscent of Impressionist paintings and stands
on the banks of a large lake, the Etang de Tricherie. The four
spacious bedrooms are tastefully and elegantly furnished, all
with en-suite bathrooms. Monsieur Mounier oversees
everything himself and makes guests feel very much at
home. The restaurant has no lake view, but serves good
traditional French cooking including homemade *foie gras*.
Last orders: lunch 1pm; dinner 9.30pm. Set menus from
F100; à la carte around F200.
Fishing, lake swimming, water-skiing and sailing 8km

TOULOUSE

▥ 17/20 ▭ ££

Hôtel des Beaux Arts, 1 Place du Pont Neuf, 31000
Toulouse.   Tel: 61.23.40.50
Open all year
Dbl rm F330–F560

Located in the heart of old Toulouse, this pleasant hotel is
separated from the river Garonne by a narrow street.
Although the hotel's facade is 19th-century, inside the decor
is ultra-modern and minimalist. The immaculately kept
bedrooms are tastefully decorated in a black, grey and white

colour scheme with interesting examples of modern art on the walls. Most rooms have excellent views out over the river and its ancient bridges. The Pont Neuf is usually busy with traffic but all the rooms are double-glazed. No restaurant, but breakfast can be sent up to rooms.

An excellent base for exploring the centre of Toulouse on foot

TOULOUSE

|O| ⊟ ££

La Jonque de Yang-Tsé, Canal du Midi, Boulevard Griffoul-Dorval, 31400 Toulouse.   Tel: 61.20.74.74
Open all year; closed Monday lunch

This old river barge once used for transporting grain has been converted into a sophisticated and authentic Chinese restaurant with the help of Asian architects. The deck, which is covered by a pagoda-style roof and lit by hanging lanterns, is a delightful shady spot for lunch or dinner overlooking the canal. The table settings are exactly as they would be in China and a small army of Chinese chefs prepares everything on board. Last orders: lunch 2pm; dinner 10.30pm. Set menus from F109 (lunch) and F196 (dinner).

USTARITZ

▥ |O| 6/9 ⊟ ££

La Patoula, 64480 Ustaritz.   Tel: 59.93.00.56
Closed January 10–February 15; restaurant closed Sunday evening and Monday except June 15–September 15
Dbl rm F300–F430

A haven of peace disturbed only by the chimes of the church clock by day, this large pink house stands on the banks of the river Nive. The interior is bright and airy, and tasteful period furniture contrasts well with the plain, white-washed walls and tiled floors. Pierre and Anne-Marie Guilhem are justifiably proud of their restaurant, which serves beautifully presented fresh seasonal produce, especially fish and game. The plane-tree-shaded waterside terrace seats 50 and is delightful for lunch or dinner in the summer. Last orders: lunch 2pm; dinner 10pm. Set menus from F130; à la carte around F250.

Fishing (permit needed), tennis courts nearby, four golf courses within 15km

UZERCHE

🏨 🍽 **15/19** 🛏 £

Hotel Ambroise, Avenue de Paris, 19140 Uzerche.
Tel: 55.73.28.60
Closed November and Monday out of season
Dbl rm F120–F250

This homely modern hotel lies at the foot of medieval Uzerche overlooking the Vézére. It is a friendly place, run by the amiable Madame Brossard. Bedrooms have recently been tastefully renovated and those with river views have the added advantage of facing away from the N20, so are fairly quiet. You can play croquet or sit in easy chairs on the riverside lawn. The dining-room sits high above the river and opens on to a terrace where meals are served April–October. Traditional regional cooking; specialities include cêpes, mushroom omelettes and black pudding with apple. Last orders: lunch 2pm; dinner 9pm. Set menus from F75; à la carte around F150.

Walks along river and through Uzerche's walled old town, canoes and kayaks for hire

VENERQUE

🍽 🛏 £

La Plage, 31120 Venerque.   Tel: 61.08.50.12
Closed January, September, Sunday evening, Monday evening and Tuesday

The charm of this restaurant lies in its simplicity and authenticity. Popular with local families, it is described by Madame Carol as a 'family affair' and her substantial home cooking is served in an old, ivy-covered building on the banks of the river Ariège. In good weather, tables and chairs are set out on a waterside terrace next to a beach. Open 9am–11pm for snacks and drinks. Last orders: lunch served all afternoon; dinner 9pm. Set menus F70 and F100; no à la carte.
Trout-fishing, river swimming from beach, canoes and kayaks for hire in village

VICHY

IOI 🖭 £

Le Bungalow, 1 Quai d'Allier, 03900 Vichy.
Tel: 70.98.51.93
Open all year
In Vichy follow signs to Le Lac and yacht club

The owners of this large restaurant and piano–bar beside the river Allier have created the impression of being transported to a jungle. Its riotous greenery, toy parrots, bamboo chairs and exotic tablecloths are a far cry from the traditional French bistro. Obviously successful, it has a convivial atmosphere as well as lovely views over a calm, wide stretch of river. In fine weather, clients can also dine on a waterside terrace shaded by an enormous poplar. Snacks and drinks are served in the afternoons, when it doubles up as a tea room. Fish and seafood are the house specialities; live lobster tank. Last orders: lunch 2pm, although light meals served all afternoon; dinner 11pm . Set menus from F105; à la carte around F150. Reservations advised at weekends.
Fishing; water-skiing; canoes, kayaks and wind-surfers for hire at sailing club; Vichy's thermal spas and casino

VIEILLE TOULOUSE

🏨 6/12 🛏 ££

Hotel de la Flanerie, Route de Lacroix-Falgarde, 31320
Vieille Toulouse.   Tel: 61.73.39.12
Closed December 23–January 5
Dbl rm F390–F520

A warm welcome is assured at this elegant country house
hotel, a 15-minute drive south of Toulouse. Popular with
French actors and musicians – the visitors' book is worth
perusing. The spacious bedrooms are richly decorated in
different styles and are immaculately maintained, although
only eight have attached bathrooms. Half of them have
lovely views over the river Garonne. There is a reading-
room, and a salon which leads out to a terrace for breakfast
(served until 11am) and drinks. No dining-room, but the
genial owners recommend several restaurants nearby.
Outdoor swimming pool, fishing, walks in the 50-acre nature reserve
1km; water-skiing, canoeing 3km; 18-hole golf nearby

VIEUX MAREUIL

🏨 🍴 6/11 🛏 ££

Auberge de L'Etang Bleu, Vieux Mareuil, 24340 Mareuil.
Tel: 53.60.92.63
Hotel and restaurant closed January 15–April 1, Sunday
and Monday nights October–Easter, Monday only
Easter–end May
Dbl rm F320–F360

The interior of this otherwise plain building is reminiscent of
a hunting lodge, with stags' heads decorating the oak-
beamed entrance hall, and a bar hung with tapestries and
copper pots. Bedrooms are cheerful, and those overlooking
the lake have small balconies. The majority of guests are
British and the restaurant is popular with the British living

in the area. During school summer holidays, the park and the facilities around the small lake are open to the public, but otherwise the grounds are for guests only. The restaurant and terrace, where Perigordine dishes are served, have lake views. Half-board is obligatory in July and August; F350 per person. Last orders: lunch 2pm; dinner 9.30pm. Set menus from F75; à la carte around F220.

Lake swimming from beach (water is treated), fishing, pedalos for hire, pleasant walks around lake and peaceful woodlands

VIGNEC

🏨 🍽 <u>11/21</u> 🛏 ££

Motel de la Neste, Vignec, 65170 St-Lary–Soulan.
Tel: 62.39.42.79
Closed May and October 1–December 15
Dbl rm F230–F270

This modern chalet-style mountain hotel, a member of the French fishing association's Relais St-Pierre, stands on the banks of a category A trout river, the Neste d'Aure, in a charming Pyrenean village. The bedrooms have beautiful views over the river valley, which is framed by high mountain peaks. Water views from the restaurant are somewhat oblique. Traditional, regional cooking. A popular base for winter sports with 80km of piste in the immediate vicinity. Half-board compulsory July 1–September 10; F245 per person. Last orders: lunch 2pm; dinner 9pm. Set menus from F65; à la carte around F120.

Fishing (permits sold in town); canoes, kayaks, rafts and mountain bikes for hire in St-Lary-Soulan (2km), famous for its modern, natural spring bath therapy

VILLEFORT

🏨 🍽 <u>10/10</u> 🛏 ££

Hotel du Lac, 48800 Villefort.   Tel: 66.46.81.20

Closed November 30–March 15
Dbl rm F220–F320
Take D906 to Lac de Villefort; hotel on left after dam

This attractive modern hotel stands on its own beside a scenic reservoir in the gorges of the river Altier. On the borders of the Cevennes National Park, it is very much off the beaten track and reached along twisting mountain roads. Bedrooms are very simply furnished (four with en-suite bathrooms), but they are clean and have good lake views. Guests are warmly welcomed and made to feel at home by Madame Severan. There are panoramic lake views from window tables in the restaurant, which serves simple appetizing home cooking. Last orders: lunch 2pm; dinner 9pm. Set menus from F90; à la carte around F110.

Trout fishing with permit; lake swimming; sailing boats, sail-boards and pedalos for hire; water-skiing; good marked walking trails

VILLEFRANCHE-DE-PANAT

🏨 🍽 13/25 🛏 £

Hostellerie du Lac, 12430 Villefranche-de-Panat.
Tel: 65.46.58.07
Open all year
Dbl rm F170–F260

On the shores of the attractive Villefranche-de-Panat reservoir, this pleasant hotel is run by helpful and friendly staff. The simple, comfortably furnished bedrooms are clean and well-maintained, all with en-suite bathrooms. Those overlooking the lake have panoramic views over the countryside. In summer, pizzas, grilled meats and drinks are served on a large lakeside terrace. Full meals are served in the dining-room, where a roasting spit is set over a roaring fire. Regional cooking with menus varying with the seasons and including a rather unusual wild boar casserole. Last orders: lunch 2.30pm; dinner 10.30pm. Set menus from F65; à la carte around F120.

*Fishing in lake and streams; private lakeshore area for swimming;
sail-boards, canoes and kayaks for hire (1km); tennis courts and
riding nearby*

VILLEFRANCHE-DE-ROUERGUE

🏨 🍽 <u>13/30</u> 🛏 ££

L'Univers, 2 Place de la République, 12200
Villefranche-de-Rouergue.   Tel: 65.45.15.63
Open all year; restaurant closed two weeks in March,
one week in June and November 23–December 8
Dbl rm F185–F330

This traditional town-centre hotel on the banks of the river
Aveyron faces away from a busy road bridge. Inside it has a
homely if somewhat cluttered appearance. Bedrooms are
comfortable, all with en-suite bathrooms. The first-floor
restaurant has a good reputation for traditional regional
cooking and the portions are more than generous. Diners
at window tables have splendid views over the river but the
noise of traffic is ever-present. Last orders: lunch 2pm; dinner
9pm. Set menus are available from F70; à la carte F150.
*Villefranche is a characterful Bastide town with a medieval quarter
and typically French squares and cafés; a good base for exploring the
Aveyron gorges and the valley of the river Lot*

VILLENEUVE-LES-AVIGNON

🏨 🍽 <u>10/20</u> 🛏 ££

Le Vieux Moulin, Rue du Vieux Moulin, 30400
Villeneuve-lès-Avignon.   Tel: 90.25.00.26
Closed November 15–March 15; restaurant is open for
dinner Tuesday–Saturday only
Dbl rm F280–F400

This 17th-century flour mill sits on the banks of the Rhone
with moorings for those arriving by boat. Tastefully converted and full of rustic charm, it has heavy beamed ceilings

and arched doorways. Bedrooms are comfortable, most with en-suite bathrooms, and many with outstanding views across the river to Avignon on the opposite bank. In the top bedroom, guests can relax in the bath and admire the silhouette of the Palais des Papes through the window. In the restaurant, built out over the river, all the tables have expansive views, and there is a small outdoor terrace for meals, snacks and drinks in good weather. Good Provençal cooking, which is a rarity in this area nowadays. Half-board is obligatory but a dine-around card gives guests a choice of 25 restaurants. Last orders: lunch 1.30pm; dinner 9.30pm (later June–September). Set menus are available from F115; à la carte around F140.

Boat trips along Rhone depart from pontoon next door; hotel organizes excursions to an island and beach on Rhone 5km away, and dinner cruises to Avignon at 7.30pm in summer

VILLENEUVE-LES-BEZIERS

IOI ⊟ ££

L'Ecluse, 34420 Villeneuve-lès-Béziers.   Tel: 67.62.11.02
Open all year; closed Wednesday evening except
June 15–September 15
On N112; A9 exit Beziers 3km

This restaurant's attractive covered dining terrace is on the canal bank and diners can enjoy the sight of barges chugging past down the Canal du Midi. Indoor tables have no water views so this is a fair-weather stop only. Good, well-presented regional dishes and all the food is freshly prepared on site. Last orders: lunch 2.30pm; dinner 10pm. Set menus from F97; à la carte around F150.

Pleasant walks along the tow-path shaded by plane trees

VILLENEUVE-SUR-LOT

IOI 🖛 ££

Aux Berges du Lot, 3 Rue de l'Hotel de Ville, 47300
Villeneuve-sur-Lot.   Tel: 53.70.84.41
Closed two weeks in November; Sunday evening and
Monday except June 15–September 15

Alongside the town hall, this lovely restaurant is almost
hidden beneath its verdant terrace. The restaurant occupies
a 17th-century building, which was once the town's police
station, and has a good reputation. Only the six terrace tables
have views over the river Lot. Classical and regional cuisine
with the emphasis on fresh fish. Slimmers will be unable to
resist the delicious puddings. Last orders: lunch 1.30pm;
dinner 9.30pm. Set menus are available from F69 (weekday
lunch), F98 (dinner); à la carte around F200.

Eastern France

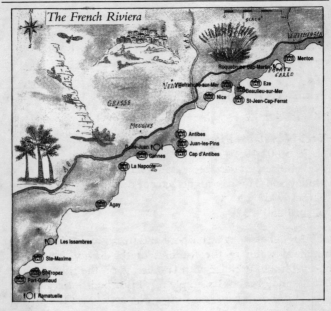

AGAY

 |O| <u>41/47</u> ▭ £££

Le Sol e Mar, Le Dramont, Agay, 83700 St-Raphael.
Tel: 94.95.25.60
Open Easter–October 15
Dbl rm F460–F610

This seaside hotel stands in its own grounds, on a relatively secluded part of the coast, with the N98 running behind it. Nearly all the well-equipped bedrooms, many of which have been recently renovated, have small balconies with views of the Iles d'Or and the Gulf of St-Tropez in the distance. Its large terrace-restaurant, which has a retractable roof, occupies the top floor of the building. Nearly all diners enjoy excellent seascape panoramas. Fish and seafood dominate the menus, especially grilled red mullet, sea bass, mussels and *bouillabaisse*. Half-board is obligatory during July and August and costs F390–F510 per person. Last orders: lunch 2.15pm;

dinner 9.15pm. Set menus are available from F138; à la carte around F300.
Private cove with shingle beach, private moorings, two seawater swimming pools, sail-boards for hire nearby

LAKE AIGUEBELETTE

📷 |O| 12/12 🛏 ££

Hôtel Novalaise Plage, 73470 Novalaise.
Tel: 79.36.02.19
Hotel and restaurant closed early October–April 1,
Monday and Tuesday nights except during July and
August
Dbl rm F250–F320

Lake Aiguebelette is an unspoilt and surprisingly un-touristy stretch of water in the foothills of the Savoy Alps. This modern hotel, popular with families, is on the shore beside a small sandy beach. Its simply furnished bedrooms are well cared for and all have balconies. The restaurant has a large second-floor terrace with splendid views over the lake, and serves traditional French cuisine including lake fish. Last orders: lunch 2pm; dinner 9.30pm. Set menus from F85; à la carte around F200.
Beach for lake swimming; pedalos, electric boats, sail-boards and canoes for hire nearby; children's playground; tennis courts and riding nearby

LAKE AIGUEBELETTE

|O| 🛏 ££

Restaurant Aitis, Aiguebelette-le-Lac, 73610
Lépin-le-Lac.   Tel: 79.36.03.27
Closed December 15–February 1 and Wednesday
October–May

In a verdant and tranquil setting at the foot of the Montagne de l'Epine, this air-conditioned restaurant is built out over the water. All the tables have good views across the lake and, in summer, meals and drinks are also served on a large terrace shaded by trees. Menus offer a wide choice of dishes including fish freshly caught from the lake. Last orders: lunch 2.30pm; dinner 10.30pm. Set menus from F100; à la carte around F160.

Lake swimming and fishing

AIGUINES

🏠 IOI 6/13 🛏 £

Altitude 823, Aiguines, 83630 Aups.   Tel: 94.70.21.09
Closed November 15–March 15; restaurant closed
Friday October–May
Dbl rm F150–F250

This modest hotel and restaurant looks out over the strikingly blue waters of the Lac de Ste-Croix. Bedrooms are simply furnished but cosy; only two have en-suite bathrooms. Its restaurant serves traditional Provençal dishes, and there is a small terrace, shaded by trees, for meals and drinks in summer. Last orders: lunch 2.30pm; dinner 9.30pm. Set menus from F80; à la carte around F140.

Fishing (permits sold at lakeside); pedalos, wind-surfers, sailing boats and kayaks for hire; nearby Grand Canyon du Verdon

AIGUINES

IOI 🛏 ££

Restaurant Les Cavaliers, Falaise des Cavaliers, Aiguines, 83630 Aups.   Tel: 94.76.91.31
Closed October 15–May 1 and Wednesday
September 15–October 15
On D71; Aiguines 15km

On the edge of the Cavaliers cliff, this recently renovated restaurant looks down on the river as it winds through the Crand Canyon du Verdon, 1000ft below. It is advisable to arrive early or book ahead to secure a window table. There is also a separate café with a terrace where snacks, drinks and ice-creams are served 8am–8pm. Last orders: lunch 2pm; dinner 8.30pm. Set menus from F100 (lunch), F120 (dinner); à la carte around F180.

AIRE-SUR-LA-LYS

🏠 ⏺ 22/27 ▭ ££

Hostellerie des Trois Mousquetaires, Château du Fort de la Redoute, 62120 Aire-sur-la-Lys.   Tel: 21.39.01.11
Closed December 22–January 15; restaurant closed
Sunday evening and Monday
Dbl rm F240–F500

This 19th-century chateau was originally a fort in the time of the military engineer Vauban. Now it is surrounded by the remains of a moat which drains into a river and a lake where black swans cruise. You can expect a warm welcome from the owners, the Venet family, who run the hotel themselves. Public rooms have highly polished parquet floors, Hungarian oak panelling and ornate gilt mirrors. Bedrooms, which include 15 in a new extension, are elegantly furnished in period style and the bathrooms have all been recently reno-vated. The dining-room looks out over manicured lawns to the river and, in summer, coffee, drinks and pastries are served on its banks. Inventive menus, based around fresh seasonal produce, are translated into English. Last orders: lunch 2.30pm; dinner 9.30pm. Set menus from F101; à la carte around F290.
Country walks, riding and tennis nearby

ALBERTVILLE

⏺ ▭ £££

Chez Uginet, 8 Place Charles-Albert, 73200 Albertville.
Tel: 79.32.00.50
Closed June 24–July 5, November 12–20 and Wednesday
Near the Pont des Adoubes

This restaurant is small, intimate and very French. Extremely popular with locals as well as visitors breaking their journey between Geneva and the Savoy Alps, it serves delicious Savoyarde cuisine. The food is beautifully presented and menus are based around fresh seasonal produce and may include hare and venison. Most diners have views of the fast-flowing river Arly through large windows and, in summer, meals are served on a waterside terrace. Last orders: lunch 1.30pm; dinner 9.30pm. Set menus from F110; à la carte around F250.

ALTHEN-DES-PALUDS

🏠 🍽 18/27 🛏 £££

Hostellerie du Moulin de la Roque, Route de la Roque, Althen-des-Paluds, 84210 Pernes-les-Fontaines.
Tel: 90.62.14.62
Open May 1–October 31
Dbl rm F500–F1200

A haven of tranquillity, comfort and good taste, this former watermill straddles a mill-race flowing from the river Sorgue. Bedrooms are spacious and simply but luxuriously furnished, three with private terraces. The elegant dining-room, which looks out over the gardens, the pool and the river, serves a mixture of traditional Provençal and modern dishes. Last orders: lunch 2.30pm; dinner 9.30pm. Set menus from F200; à la carte around F300.
In hotel grounds: trout fishing, outdoor swimming pool and tennis court; nearby Carpentras truffle market; July Choregies festival in Orange

AMIENS

🍽 🛏 ££

Le Pré Porus, 95 Rue Voyelle, 80000 Amiens.
Tel: 22.46.25.03
Closed February 15 for a month and Tuesday

A five-minute drive from the city centre, this popular restaurant sits on a small island flanked by the river Somme and a canal. It has a relaxed, convivial air, especially at weekends when it is popular with local families. All inside tables have river views and there is a large shady waterside terrace for meals and drinks in summer. Last orders: lunch 2.30pm; dinner 10.30pm. Set menus from F95; à la carte around F200. *Rowing boats for hire*

LAKE ANNECY

🏠 🍽 14/32 ▭ £££

L'Abbaye de Talloires, Talloires, 74290 Veyrier-du-Lac.
Tel: 50.60.77.33
Closed December 15–March 1; restaurant closed Sunday evening and Monday lunch October 15–April 30
Dbl rm F600–F1065

The abbey buildings of this 17th-century Benedictine monastery have been sensitively converted to create a quietly luxurious hotel surrounded by landscaped lakeside gardens. The cloister is lined with beautiful antiques and bedrooms, in what were once the monks' cells, are soberly but handsomely furnished. Guests are assured of a warm welcome and discreetly attentive service from its owners, the Tiffenat family. Few of the restaurant's tables have water views but, in the summer, cold buffet lunches and dinner are served on a terrace overlooking the lake. Last orders: lunch 2.30pm, dinner 9.30pm. Set menus from F160 (lunch), F250 (dinner); à la carte around F350.

LAKE ANNECY

🏠 🍽 28/35 ▭ £££

Le Cottage, Talloires, 74290 Veyrier-du-Lac.
Tel: 50.60.71.10

Closed mid–October–April 15
Dbl rm F600–F1100

Of the several four-star waterside hotels in Talloires, Le Cottage is the smallest and most reasonably priced. With its pitched roof and wooden balconies it is more a chalet than a cottage. Bedrooms are spacious and decorated in pastels; 18 with balconies overlooking the pretty lakeside gardens. The traditionally furnished dining-room is lit by candelabra. Last orders: lunch 1.45pm; dinner 9.30pm. Set menus from F180; à la carte around F300.

LAKE ANNECY

🏨 🍽 25/34 💳 ££££

Auberge du Père Bise, Route du Port, Talloires, 74290 Veyrier-du-Lac.   Tel: 50.60.72.01
Closed November 15–February 15; restaurant closed Tuesday lunch
Dbl rm F1000–F2500

This chalet-style inn stands amid terraced gardens on the water's edge in the exclusive and painstakingly preserved lakeside village of Talloires. Bedrooms are spacious and handsomely furnished, many with balconies which overlook the lake. The restaurant is considered to be one of the finest in France and has been heaped with culinary accolades. It also has an enchanting lakeside setting. In summer, there is also a waterside dining terrace shaded by trees. The *menu dégustation* at F620 offers the chance to sample eight of the chef's specialities. Last orders: lunch 2pm; dinner 9pm. Set menus from F450; à la carte around F700.
Hotel has sail-boards and rowing boats and arranges water-skiing; lake swimming; pretty lakeside and mountain walks; tennis courts 500m, and golf 2km

LAKE ANNECY

🏨 |○| 7/10 ▭ ££

Hôtel Chappet, Bout-du-Lac, Doussard, 74210 Faverges.
Tel: 50.44.30.19
Closed November 15–February 1; restaurant closed
Monday and Thursday evening except during July and
August
Dbl rm F320

This simple hotel stands alone on a small promontory at the
south-west corner of the lake. Recently renovated bedrooms
are comfortable and well-furnished; all have en-suite bathrooms. A major attraction is its large, tree-shaded dining
terrace which looks out over the lake to the Pointe Chéni-
vier on the far side. Gisèle and Pierre Gessner provide
traditional regional fare at reasonable prices. The restaurant's
popularity makes reservations advisable, especially on Sundays. Last orders: lunch 3pm; dinner 9.30pm. Set menus from
F110; à la carte around F220.
Hotel arranges scuba-diving, water-skiing; sailing boats, sail-boards
and pedalos for hire; tennis courts and riding 100m

LAKE ANNECY

🏨 |○| 19/23 ▭ ££

Hôtel du Lac, Duingt, 74410 St-Jorioz.   Tel: 50.68.90.90
Closed November 4–February 1; restaurant closed
November 4–Easter
Dbl rm F290–F360

Comprising two pink-washed buildings, this lakeside hotel
has been recently redecorated. The light, airy bedrooms are
popular with families, and 12 have balconies overlooking the
lake. Half the restaurant's tables have lake views and, in
summer, meals are served on a tree-shaded terrace by the
water's edge. Fish is a speciality. Half-board obligatory in July

and August. Last orders: lunch 2pm; dinner 9pm. Set menus from F115; à la carte around F200.
Water-skiing, windsurfing and boat trips arranged by the hotel, sunbathing lawn and small private beach for lake swimming

LAKE ANNECY

🍴 🛏 ££

Auberge du Lyonnais, 14 Quai de l'Eveché,
9 Rue de la République, 74000 Annecy.
Tel: 50.51.26.10
Closed June 16–23 and November

This flower-decked restaurant is in the pedestrianized heart of old Annecy, where tiny canals are crossed by wrought-iron bridges. It is a friendly informal place and Henri Bruchet prides himself on his cooking and his staff who are always ready to translate the menu. In fine weather tables are arranged on the pavement giving clients a good view of the water rushing through a nearby lock. The menus offer plenty of choice but the emphasis is on fish and seafood. Last orders: lunch 2pm; dinner 10pm. Set menus from F100; à la carte around F200.
Boat trips around lake depart from Thiou canal in Annecy

LAKE ANNECY

🍴 **5/10** 🛏 £££

Le Belvédère, 7 Chemin du Belvédère, 74000 Annecy.
Tel: 50.45.04.90
Closed three weeks in November, Sunday evening
and Monday
Dbl rm F170–F210

Situated high above Annecy, on the road to the Montagne du Semnoz, this restaurant has panoramic views of the lake and Veyrier mountains. Fish and seafood dominate Jean-Louis Aubeneau's menus and his culinary skills are much appreciated by locals. In summer, meals are also served on a terrace. Bedrooms are simply but comfortably furnished; three have attached bathrooms. Last orders: lunch 2pm; dinner 9.30pm. Set menus from F200; à la carte around F300.

LAKE ANNECY

IOI ⊟ ££

Super Panorama, 7 Route du Semnoz, 74000 Annecy.
Tel: 50.45.34.86
Closed for five weeks during December–January

The terrace of the Super Panorama has a magnificent bird's-eye view of the lake and its mountainous backdrop. The traditional cooking is reasonably priced for such a view. The café–bar is open all day for pastries, ice-creams and coffees. Last orders: lunch 1.45pm; dinner 9.30pm. Set menus from F100; à la carte around F160.

ANTIBES

⌂ IOI 27/37 ⊟ ££

Hôtel Royal, Boulevard Maréchal–Leclerc, 06600
Antibes.   Tel: 93.34.03.09
Closed November 5–December 10; restaurant closed
Sunday evening and Monday October–June
Dbl rm F360–F550

A reasonably priced seafront hotel is a rare find in Antibes. This small hotel is the oldest in the resort and has a prime location overlooking the beach and the old walled town. Bedrooms are comfortable and clean with double-glazed French windows opening on to small wrought-iron balconies. Fifteen have air-conditioning. Its ground-floor restaurant, Le Dauphin, has a canopied dining terrace separated from the seafront promenade by a small road. Half-board obligatory July 1–September 20; F330–F440 per person. Last

orders: lunch 1.30pm; dinner 10pm. Set menus from F135 (children F55); à la carte around F230.
Private beach with café–bar; windsurfing and water-skiing; tennis courts (10 minutes on foot) boat trips to Cannes and islands

ARBOIS

🏠 |○| <u>12/22</u> 🍽 ££

Moulin de la Mère Michelle, Les Planches, 39600 Arbois.
Tel: 84.66.08.17
Restaurant closed to non-residents in January
Dbl rm F350–F600

The river Cuisance rushes past the stone walls of this 300-year-old mill, restored by its owners 11 years ago with great attention to detail. Many of the public rooms and bedrooms are furnished with antiques. A neighbouring building, which is as old as the mill, has recently been converted to provide a further 12 bedrooms. Five of the restaurant's tables have river views, and the waterside dining terrace is almost within the spray of the Cuisance as it thunders over a 30ft drop alongside. Last orders: lunch 1.30pm; dinner 9pm. Set menus from F135; à la carte around F300.
Swimming pool and tennis court in grounds, fishing (permit F20 a day)

ARBOIS

|○| 🍽 ££

Le Caveau d'Arbois, 3 Route de Besancon, 39600 Arbois.
Tel: 84.66.10.70
Open all year

Perched above the river Cuisance, like a house on stilts, this restaurant serves traditional Jura cuisine in a light, airy setting which gives the impression of eating in a garden. Popular dishes include chicken supreme with mild Comté cheese and pink trout in spinach. Children's games room. Last orders:

lunch 1.30pm; dinner 9pm. Set menus from F70; à la carte around F150.
Lovely riverside walk past Louis Pasteur's home to Arbois

ARCIS-SUR-AUBE

IOI ▭ £

Le Saint Hubert, 2 Rue de la Marine, 10700
Arcis-sur-Aube.   Tel: 25.37.86.93
Closed for a week in February, August 4–24, Friday
evening and Saturday except during July

The appeal of this simple restaurant on the banks of the river
Aube lies in its open-air terrace, in use from May to Sep-
tember. It is a particularly pleasant place for a waterside lunch.
The traditional regional cooking includes exotic salads and
Troyes *andouillettes* or tripe sausages. Last orders: lunch
2.30pm; dinner 9pm. Set menus from F54 (children's menu
F37); à la carte around F120.

ARDRES

IOI ▭ ££

La Frégate, Le Lac, 62610 Ardres.   Tel: 21.35.40.16
Closed three weeks in January
Off N43 from Ardres follow signs for Le Lac

On the banks of a large lake just north of Ardres, this
restaurant is an appealing place to stop for breakfast, lunch
or dinner on the way to or from Calais. The long, conservatory-style dining-room is filled with owner–chef Monsieur
Limousin's copies of Impressionist paintings, which he does
in his precious spare time. There is a large, gravelled, waterside terrace for meals and drinks in summer. Simple traditional fare including fish, crêpes, omelettes and patés. Open
9am–9pm in summer for snacks and drinks. Last orders for
meals: lunch 2pm; dinner 9pm. Set menus from F57; à la
carte around F130.

Pedalos, rowing and motorboats for hire, fishing (permit F10 a day),
lakeshore walks

AUBIGNY-AU-BAC

IOI ⊟ ££

L'Ermitage, 59265 Aubigny–au–Bac.   Tel: 27.89.22.22
Open all year; closed Monday
Follow signs for 'Plage'

Set above a sandy lakeside beach just outside Aubigny–au–
Bac, this tall, white mansion contains a smart restaurant with
large windows offering panoramic views of the lake. It opens
9am–7pm for breakfast, lunch, and afternoon tea, which can
be taken on the beachside terrace in fine weather. On
Saturday evenings and Sunday afternoons, there are din-
ner-dances, with bands, costing F150. Classic French
dishes. Set menus from F80; à la carte around F120.
Pedalos, rowing boats, pony-rides, children's playground

AULT

IOI ⊠ £

Chez Arlette, 31 Rue de St-Valery, 80460 Ault.
Tel: 22.60.40.93
Open all year; closed Monday October–May

This simple, family–run restaurant, situated on the cliff–edge,
looks out over the Channel. Off the tourist trail, it serves
appetizing homemade fare, offering just one menu for F80.
In the afternoons, it operates as a café–bar. Last orders: lunch
2pm; dinner 9pm.
Good walks along shingle beach and sand-dunes

AUXERRE

🏨 🍴 14/25 🛏 ££

Le Maxime, 2–5 Quai de la Marine, 89000 Auxerre.
Tel: hotel 86.52.14.19; restaurant 86.52.04.41
Open all year; restaurant closed December 20–January 7
and Sunday October 15–June 15
Dbl rm F430–F580

This charming, family-run hotel sits below Auxerre's cathedral on the banks of the river Yonne. Its pleasantly decorated bedrooms have good views of the river which is filled with barges and pleasure boats in summer. The restaurant is quaintly rustic with exposed beams and copper pots on the wall. Fish is a speciality with lobster kept live in a tank. Ten tables overlook the river. Last orders: lunch 2pm; dinner 9.30pm. Set menus from F150; à la carte around F350.
Convenient base for exploring historic Auxerre on foot; day-trip cruises along Canal du Nivernais, canoes for hire

AVALLON

🏨 10/11 🛏 ££££

Château Vault–de–Lugny, Vault–de–Lugny, 89200
Avallon.   Tel: 86.34.07.86
Open mid–March–mid–November
Dbl rm F700–F2200
5km from Avallon on Vézelay road.

One of the most beautiful chateau–hotels in eastern France, it is the ultimate in luxury. Surrounded by a wide moat, its courtyard shelters peacocks, geese and ducks who are keen to share guests' breakfast – which can be served under the trees. The castle dates back to the 13th–century crusades and its 11 guest rooms are richly decorated in a baronial style which displays the taste and flair of its charming owners, the Matherat-Audan family. Guests can dine in the hotel for around F250 and the family is happy to accommodate any special

requirements or diets, and use only home-grown vegetables.
Tennis court, marked footpaths, hot-air balloon flights

AVALLON

🏠 ⏺ 12/27 🛏 ££

Moulin des Ruats, Vallée du Cousin, Pontaubert,
89200 Avallon.   Tel: 86.34.07.14
Closed November 15–February 15
Dbl rm F350–F580
Avallon 4km

This slate-roofed villa stands on the banks of the tree-shaded
river Cousin in pretty countryside between Avallon and
Vézelay. Bedrooms are comfortable but simply furnished
and several have large wooden verandahs. The star attraction of this country inn is its conservatory restaurant which
looks directly over the river. In summer, meals are also served
on a gravel riverbank terrace shaded by tall trees. Fresh
seasonal produce served with light sauces in the modern
style. Last orders: lunch 1.30pm; dinner 9pm. Set menus
from F150 (lunch), F240 (dinner); à la carte around F300.
Fishing, riverside walks; bicycle and canoe hire at Avallon

AVIGNON

⏺ 🛏 ££

Le Bercail, Ile de la Barthelasse, 84000 Avignon.
Tel: 90.82.20.22
Closed November 1–March 31

On an island in the river Rhone, this modest, informal
restaurant serves simple Provençal fare, grilled meat and
fish, and pizzas. Its main attraction is a large waterside
terrace, shaded by plane trees, which looks over the river
towards the city and the famous Pont d'Avignon. Last orders:
lunch 2.30pm; dinner 11pm (later during Avignon's Festival

of Theatre and Dance which takes place during July and early August). Set menus from F115; à la carte around F110.

BAIX

🏨 🍽 **4/15** 🛏 £££

Hostellerie La Cardinale, Quai du Rhone, Baix, 07210 Chomerac. Tel: 75.85.80.40
Closed January 1–February 29
Dbl rm F750–900

Set in a peaceful glade on the banks of the Rhone, this 17th-century manor has been converted into an exclusive retreat. The spacious bedrooms were renovated three years ago in a tasteful classic French style and many contain antique furnishings. Although the restaurant has no river views, breakfast, lunch and dinner are served on its two terraces, overlooking the glade and river. The menus include plenty of sea and freshwater fish as well as lamb and chicken. The fine cooking is complemented by a good wine list featuring many Rhone valley wines. Last orders: lunch 2pm; dinner 9pm. Set menus from F140; à la carte around F300.
Hotel swimming pool, fishing, canoe hire nearby

BAZEILLES

🏨 🍽 **10/20** 🛏 £

Auberge du Port, 08140 Bazeilles. Tel: 24.27.13.89
Closed last two weeks of August, December 21 for a month; restaurant closed Saturday lunch and Sunday evening all year, Friday evening October–April
Dbl rm F250
Bazeilles 1km north

This hotel is in a peaceful location on the banks of the river Meuse. Bedrooms are nicely furnished – all with attached bathrooms – and offer good value. The restaurant serves traditional French dishes with specialities including duckling with cherries and lamb with wild mushrooms. Six tables have river views and in fine weather both meals and drinks are served on a waterside terrace. Last orders: lunch 2pm; dinner 9.30pm. Set menus from F110 (F160 weekends); à la carte around F250.

River swimming, fishing, good base for visiting Bazeilles, Sedan and Bouillon chateaux, riding stables nearby

BEAULIEU-SUR-MER

🏨 15/35 ▭ ££

Hôtel Frisia, 2 Boulevard Café Gauthier, 06310 Beaulieu-sur-Mer.   Tel: 93.01.01.04
Closed October 31–December 22
Dbl rm F460–F550

This modern, white seafront hotel overlooks Beaulieu's marina and a scenic stretch of coast ending in the sheer cliffs of Cap d'Ail. Bedrooms are simply furnished and those with sea views have sliding doors opening on to wrought-iron balconies shaded by canopies. A promenade and quayside road separate the hotel from the marina. There is a small garden at the rear as well as a sunbathing terrace on the roof. Breakfast only.

Small sandy beach; boat and fishing trips from the harbour, wind-surfing and water-skiing; tennis club

BESANÇON

🍽 ▭ £££

Le Chaland, Pont de Bregille, Promenade Micaud, 25000 Besançon.   Tel: 81.80.61.61
Closed first two weeks of August, Sunday evening and Monday

It could almost be Paris. A *bateau mouche* glides past and the buildings lining the river Doubs are just as elegant as those in the capital. Le Chaland occupies a boat moored in the heart of the city, and serves fresh seasonal produce such as salmon tartare, pigeon and turbot with mushrooms in the local *vin jaune*. Impeccable decor and service complement the beautiful view over the river and towards the citadel, high on a crag above the city. Last orders: lunch 2pm; dinner 10pm. Set menus from F125 (lunch), F150 (dinner); à la carte around F280.

River cruises to citadel, lovely walks around city, clock museum

BONNIEUX

🏠 🍽 4/9 ▭ £££

L'Aiguebrun, Relais de la Combe, 84480 Bonnieux.
Tel: 90.74.04.14
Open end March–end November; restaurant closed
Wednesday and Thursday lunch
Dbl rm F480–F500

This 150-year-old Provençal house is a haven of peace and tranquillity, disturbed only by the sound of the cascade and stream in the garden. Guests are assured of a friendly welcome from Madame Ferraris. Bedrooms and public rooms are elegantly decorated with antiques and paintings. The restaurant serves only fresh seasonal produce and, in summer, there is a terrace for lunch which overlooks the stream. Last orders: lunch 2pm; dinner 10pm. Set menus from F225; à la carte around F275.

Remains of Roman bridge in grounds, convenient base for touring Provence

BOUILLAND

🏠 🍽 5/26 ▭ £££

Hostellerie du Vieux Moulin, Bouilland, 21420
Savigny-lès-Beaunes.   Tel: 80.21.51.16
Closed mid-December–mid-January; restaurant closed
Wednesday and Thursday lunch

Dbl rm F380–F800
On D2 outside Bouilland

This old mill sits beside a rushing stream a few miles north of the Autoroute du Soleil's Beaune by-pass. The bedrooms have all been recently renovated and are handsomely furnished. Some are in an annexe with baby-listening facilities for anxious parents. Just three in the main mill overlook the stream where trout for the table are held between grilles. Facilities also include a swimming pool, sauna, gym with weights and a billiard room. The restaurant has a very good reputation, serving imaginative dishes based on fresh market produce. Make a reservation for one of the three tables overlooking the stream and gardens, which are illuminated at night. Last orders: lunch 2pm; dinner 9pm. Set menus from F190; à la carte around F350.
Riverside walks, ruins of 11th-century St Marguerite abbey near village

LAKE BOURGET

▥ |O| 18/20 ▭ ££££

Hôtel Ombremont, 73370 Le Bourget-du-Lac.
Tel: 79.25.00.23
Closed end November–mid-March; restaurant closed
Wednesday and Saturday lunch except
June 15–September 15
Dbl rm F850–F1300
Hotel signposted on N504

This small exclusive hotel, standing in beautiful grounds running down to the shore, has splendid views across the lake to Mont Revard. Bedrooms are bright, spacious and luxurious, some having small balconies. The dining-room has good water views and, in summer, tables are arranged on a first-floor terrace overlooking the landscaped gardens, swimming pool and lake. Half-board is obligatory mid-June–mid-September from F1560 for two. Last orders: lunch 2pm;

dinner 9.30pm. Set menus from F195; à la carte around F450.
Heated swimming pool, sauna, gymnasium and billiards room;
water-skiing, windsurfing, fishing and boat trips to l'Abbaye de
l'Hautecombe arranged; tennis 2km; riding and 18-hole golf course
8km

LAKE BOURGET

🏠 ℺ 8/12 ▭ ££

La Terrasse, Bourdeau, 73370 Le Bourget-du-Lac.
Tel: 79.25.01.01
Hotel and restaurant closed October 15–March 1,
Sunday and Monday nights out of season
Dbl rm F300–F380

Bourdeau is a pretty village on the slopes of the wooded
Mont du Chat and this simple, traditional hotel offers basic
accommodation with magnificent views over the lake to
Mont Revard behind Aix-les-Bains. The conservatory-
style restaurant, which has panoramic views of the lake,
serves traditional regional dishes. Last orders: lunch
1.30pm; dinner 9pm. Set menus from F90 (children F50);
à la carte around F250.
On lake: swimming and fishing; windsurfers, sailing boats and
rowing boats for hire; water-skiing; boat trips around lake from Le
Bourget and Aix-les-Bains

LAKE BOURGET

🏠 ℺ 10/14 ▭ ££

Weekend Hôtel, Rue du Colonel Bachetta, 73420
Viviers-du-Lac.   Tel: 79.54.40.22
Closed December 1–January 5; restaurant closed
Monday except during July and August
Dbl rm F200–F290

Robert Charvet and his wife have turned this rather plain
hotel on the south-east shore of the lake into an attractive

place to stay. Bedrooms are reasonably spacious and have been attractively modernized; all have en-suite bathrooms. Six of the lake-view rooms have small balconies. Madame Charvet speaks very good English and is happy to organize water-skiing, windsurfing and sailing, or translate the menu. The restaurant, Au bord du Lac, has panoramic lake views and serves traditional regional fare, with the emphasis on freshwater fish. There are moorings for private boats visiting the restaurant. Last orders: lunch 2pm; dinner 9.30pm. Set menus from F95; à la carte around F200.

LAKE BOURGET

⦿ ⊟ £££

Auberge Lamartine, Route du Tunnel du Chat, Bourdeau, 73370 Le Bourget-du-Lac.
Tel: 79.25.01.03
Closed December 2–January 20, Sunday evening and Monday

Situated high above the lake, this charming restaurant combines a gastronomic treat with a breathtaking view, especially from its terrace which is used whenever it is sunny. The decor is simple but elegant: white-washed walls, rustic furniture, and starched, white table linen. Perch and *lavaret* (a fish from the salmon family) and *omble chevalier* (char fish), for which Lake Bourget is famous, are specialities. In the autumn, there is a special game menu. Last orders: lunch 2pm; dinner 9.30pm. Set menus from F220; à la carte around F300.

BRIANCON

🏛 ⦿ 10/18 ⊟ £

Le Mont Prorel, 5 Avenue René Froger, 05100 Briançon.
Tel: 92.20.22.88

Open all year
Dbl rm F170–F250

This Alpine chalet-style hotel is situated in the centre of
Briançon, next to the departure point for the Prorel cable-
car that takes skiers and summer walkers up to the peaks of
the Serre Chevalier. Bedrooms are comfortable and well-
equipped; nine have en-suite bathrooms. Those at the back
of the hotel have balconies overlooking the fast-flowing
Guisanne river. Only window tables in the restaurant have
views over the river. Half-board is obligatory during school
holidays and costs F170–F220 per person. Last orders: lunch
1.30pm; dinner 9pm. Set menus from F95; à la carte around
F160.
Kayaks and mountain bikes are available for hire and rafting trips;
good marked footpaths, municipal tennis courts, Olympic swimming
pool, skating rink

BUFFON

🏨 🍴 ⅗ 🛏 £

Le Marronier, Buffon, 21500 Montbard.   Tel: 80.92.33.65
Hotel closed December 15–April 1; restaurant closed
Tuesday evening and Wednesday except
June 1–September 15
Dbl rm F80–F180

A quiet road separates this hotel from the Canal de Bour-
gogne. Bedrooms are small and, as the price suggests, very
simply furnished with showers and washbasins only. The
restaurant offers four good value menus which feature traditional regional dishes. Inside window tables have water views
and there is also a terrace seating around 30 for meals and
drinks in fine weather. Last orders: lunch 2.30pm; dinner
10pm. Set menus from F60; à la carte around F120.
Tow-path walks, 18th-century Buffon forge and model workers'
village, Flavigny artisans' village 15km

CALOIRE

🍴 ▭ ££

Verdier-Riffat, La Mure, Le Pertuiset, Caloire, 42240
Unieux.   Tel: 77.35.75.25
Open all year; closed Tuesday evening and Wednesday
A72 exit Firminy 4km

Peacefully situated high above the river Loire, this restaurant
faces the village of Le Pertuiset and is linked to it by a splendid
modern bridge across the river. The red-tiled dining terrace,
shaded by tall horse chestnut trees looks over the river, as do
many of the inside tables. An imaginative gourmet menu
features some unusual dishes such as turbot baked in Champagne and *assiette Verdier-Riffat* which includes *foie gras*,
salmon, fish paté and regional *charcuterie*. Last orders: lunch
2pm; dinner 9.30pm. Set menus from F89; à la carte around
F200.
Fishing; windsurfers for hire; boat trips to St Victor dam

CANNES

🏨 🍴 48/430 ▭ ££££

Hôtel Martinez, 73 Boulevard de la Croisette,
06400 Cannes.   Tel: 93.94.30.30
Closed mid–November–mid–January; restaurant
closed Monday lunch and Tuesday lunch
Dbl rm F2150–F2990; ask about discounted *forfait
soleil* packages.

Cannes boasts many luxury hotels, but the Martinez has the
added attraction of a swimming-pool on a terrace overlooking the Croisette. Built in 1929, in Art Deco style, bedrooms
are luxuriously appointed and decorated in blues and pinks.
Its highly acclaimed restaurant, La Palme d'Or, has panoramic views of the bay from its dining terrace. Gourmet
cooking based on fresh market produce. Last orders: lunch

2pm; dinner 11pm. Set menus are available from F280; à la carte around F520.

Swimming pool; private beach; tennis courts; watersports organized by hotel

CANNES

🏨 50/64 🛏 £££

Hôtel Splendid, 4 Rue Félix Faure, 06400 Cannes.
Tel: 93.99.53.11
Open all year
Dbl rm F708–F938

This 19th-century hotel stands beside a tree-shaded Provençal garden which also contains a boules park and the resort's flower market. Bedrooms are comfortably furnished, air-conditioned and soundproofed; 25 have balustraded balconies which are shaded by canopies. Sea-view rooms look out over the old port of Cannes and the casino. There is no restaurant, but breakfast is served in the rooms.

CANNES

IOI 🛏 ££

Plage Le Voilier, Boulevard de la Croisette,
06400 Cannes.   Tel: 93.94.25 46
Open all year; closed evenings except firework nights, July 14, August 15 and 24

On the beach in front of the Carlton Hotel, this is more of a restaurant on the beach than a beach-restaurant. It is run by Maurice Amzallag and his English wife Gill who serve simple salads with as much panache as a four-course meal. Its pleasant ambience and inventive classic cooking, based on fresh market produce, have earned it a loyal local following. There is always a large choice of unusual salads (costing F35–F145) and pasta dishes on the menu. Last orders for lunch 4pm; cold food and salads 5pm. Sun-loungers F80 a day.

CANNES

IOI ▭ £££

Ondine Plage, Boulevard de la Croisette, 06400 Cannes.
Tel: 93.94.23.15
Lunch only; closed November 15–December 15

Yellow-and-white umbrellas shade customers from the sun
at this beach-restaurant opposite the Miramar. It is well-
respected for the high quality of its food, which includes
raw fish and carpaccio salads. Open 9am–7pm for drinks, ice-
creams and pastries. Last orders: lunch 4pm. A la carte F180–
F300 for two courses.

CAP D'ANTIBES

▥ IOI **79/100** ▱ ££££

Hôtel du Cap-Eden Roc, Boulevard Kennedy, 06602
Cap d'Antibes.   Tel: 93.61.39.01
Closed October 15–mid-April
Dbl rm F2300–F3000

Believed to be the palatial hotel described in F. Scott Fitzgerald's *Tender is the Night*, this is one of the most exclusive
establishments on the French Riviera. Superbly situated in
secluded gardens at the end of the rocky Cap d'Antibes, it has
drawn what Fitzgerald called 'the notable and fashionable
people' since it opened in 1870. Most of its luxuriously
appointed bedrooms have sea views, as does its celebrated
restaurant, the Eden Roc, which sits above the rocky shore.
Last orders: lunch 3pm; dinner 10pm. No set menus; à la
carte around F450 (lunch), F600 (dinner).
Heated swimming pool; five tennis courts, beach cabins on private
rocky beach, watersports in association with nearby club

CAP D'ANTIBES

🏚 🍽 <u>18/18</u> 🛏 £££

Don Cesar, 46 Boulevard de la Garoupe, 06602
Cap d'Antibes.　Tel: 93.67.15.30
Open Easter–November 15
Dbl rm F650–F1050

This small intimate hotel opened just a couple of years ago, in a prestigious location on the Cap d'Antibes. The light, airy interior is attractively decorated in pastels, brightened by floral prints. All bedrooms are air-conditioned and have sliding doors opening on to ground-floor patios or first-floor balconies which overlook the bay of La Garoupe. Its imaginatively designed swimming pool overflows on to rocks. Both the cocktail bar and the restaurant have good sea views. In summer, meals are also served on the swimming-pool terrace. Fish and seafood dominate menus. Last orders: lunch 1.45pm; dinner 9.45pm. Set menus are available from F200; à la carte around F350.
Fishing trips and car excursions organized by hotel; sandy beach 10 minutes on foot; watersports and sailing in Antibes port

CAP D'ANTIBES

🍽 🛏 ££

Chez Joseph, Plage de la Garoupe, 06602 Cap d'Antibes.
Tel: 93.61.36.52
Open Easter–Sept 30; lunch only

Situated on the Plage de la Garoupe, a beach of fine sand near Pointe Bacon, this is a cheerful beach-restaurant with green-and-white striped umbrellas and sun-loungers at the water's edge. These can be rented for F55 a day. The menu concentrates on fish and Provençal specialities. Last orders for lunch 3pm. A la carte around F150. Open 9am–6pm for drinks and ice-creams.

Water-skiing 500m; volleyball in the sea; swimming pontoons; sailboards and pedalos for hire

CARRY-LE-ROUET

IOI ▭ ££££

L'Escale, Promenade du Port, 13620 Carry-le-Rouet.
Tel: 42.45.00.47
Closed November 1–January 31, Sunday evening and
Monday (Monday lunch only during July and August)

Built on a series of flower-decked terraces overlooking the
small seaside resort of Carry-le-Rouet, this highly acclaimed
restaurant has spectacular views of this attractive wooded
stretch of coastline to Cap Croisette, which lies beyond
Marseille and its islands. The atmosphere is relaxed and dress
informal. The menus are mouth-watering and include dishes
such as langoustines poached in herb butter and orange juice
and sea bass in a mustard and paprika sauce. Last orders: lunch
2.30pm; dinner 10pm. Set menus are available from F280; à
la carte around F400.
Supervised bathing beaches, bicycle hire and riding nearby

CASSIS

▥ IOI **25/35** ▭ £££

Les Roches Blanches, Route Port-Miou, 13260 Cassis.
Tel: 42.01.09.30
Closed mid-December–end January
Dbl rm F460–F700

This attractive hotel overlooks the bay of Cassis, a ten-
minute walk from the heart of Cassis, a Provençal fishing
port which has retained much of its charm. Bedrooms are
modestly but comfortably furnished, 15 with private balconies. A friendly informal atmosphere pervades the public
areas. The restaurant has expansive sea views. In fine weather, meals are also served on a sea-view terrace. Classic

Provençal cooking. Last orders: lunch 2.30pm; dinner 9.30pm. Set menus from F160; à la carte around F200.
Private swimming pool; sand and shingle coves; hotel arranges fishing and scuba-diving trips and sail-board hire

LA CELLE

🏨 ℐ𝒪𝐼 <u>10/10</u> ▭ ££

Mas de la Cascade, La Celle, 83170 Brignoles.
Tel: 94.69.01.49
Open all year
Dbl rm F310–F490

A good overnight stop, this former tile factory offers a very warm welcome. Set back from a fairly busy road, it overlooks a fast-flowing stream. Bedrooms are full of character and furnished with antiques. Restaurant tables next to the large picture windows have the best views over the tree-shaded stream and, in fine weather, dinner is served on a garden terrace. Varied and inventive regional menus. Last orders: lunch 2pm; dinner 9.30pm. Set menus from F115; à la carte around F200.

CHABLIS

ℐ𝒪𝐼 ▭ ££

Le Vieux Moulin, 18 Rue des Moulins, 89800 Chablis.
Tel: 86.42.47.30
Closed Sunday evening and Monday December 1–April 1
A6 exit Auxerre 12km

Straddling the little river Serein, this restaurant is arranged on two floors and has space for 140 diners. More than half the tables have views over the mill-race that runs beneath the building. Monsieur Lecoeur serves hearty Burgundian dishes, notably poached eggs in a rich red wine sauce, scorpion fish in Chablis, and *andouillettes* (chitterling sausages). Last orders: lunch 1.30pm; dinner 10pm. Set

menus from F59 (weekdays), F98 (weekends); à la carte around F130.
Pretty walk along Promenade du Patis beside Serein, Chablis Wine Festival in third week of November, vineyard tours

CHAMONIX

🏨 **10/20** ▭ ££

Hôtel de la Vallée Blanche, 36 Rue du Lyret, 74400 Chamonix.   Tel: 50.53.04.50
Open all year
Dbl rm F320–F590

Guests are warmly welcomed by the hotel's Irish owner, Patricia Byrne. The homely bedrooms, half with views over the river Arve, are furnished with pretty fabrics and hand-painted Tyrolean furniture. There are also 14 new suites overlooking the river Avre which can sleep up to four people. The owner is building a typical Irish pub with a waterside terrace, importing authentic furnishings from Ireland. No restaurant.
Winter skiing and, in summer, organized canoe, kayak and rafting trips down river; fishing in nearby lakes, mountain-biking, resort swimming pools and tennis courts, ice-skating

CHARIX

🏨 ❘○❘ **1/6** ▭ £

Auberge du Lac Genin, Lac Genin, Charix, 01130 Nantua.   Tel: 74.75.52.50
Closed October 15–December 1; restaurant closed Sunday evening and Monday
Dbl rm F110–F180
A40 exit Sylans 20 minutes

This simple inn is has an idyllic setting on the grassy shore of a natural lake. Pine forests lead down to the water's edge, and the silence is remarkable. Bedrooms are simple but well-appointed although only one has an en-suite bathroom. The restaurant can seat 100, and serves regional food grilled over an open wood fire. Sausages cooked in foil with red wine are a speciality. There is also a large terrace overlooking the lake for meals and drinks used whenever the weather is fine. Last orders: lunch 2pm; dinner 9pm. Set menus from F58; à la carte around F110.

Fishing (permits sold in hotel); lake swimming; pleasant walks around the lake and in the nearby Bois de Puthod and Foret du Fouget

CHATILLON

△ 4/8 ⊟ £

Chez Yvonne, Chatillon, 39130 Clairvaux-les-Lacs.
Tel: 84.25.70.82
Closed November 1–March 15, Sunday evening and
Monday except during July and August
Dbl rm F200–F225
On D39 2km Café of Chatillon

All the tables in this lively restaurant, decorated in pinks and lilacs, look out over the river Ain. In fine weather, meals and drinks are served on its three flower-decked waterside terraces. Fish dominates the menu with specialities including crayfish with truffles, trout *meunière*, with almonds and local wine, and fresh salmon. The bedrooms have recently been given a facelift and brightened with floral fabrics. The bar is open all day for snacks, drinks and ice-creams. Last orders: lunch 1.30pm; dinner 9pm. Set menus from F85; à la carte around F120.

Trout fishing (day permits sold); windsurfers, pedalos and rowing boats for hire on Lac de Chalain 3km

CHAUMONTEL

🏠 6/20 🛏 ££

Château de Chaumontel, 21 Rue André Vassord, Chaumontel, 95270 Luzarges   Tel: 1.34.71.00.30
Open all year
Dbl rm F430–F450

This pretty turreted chateau is surrounded by a wide moat which winds away across a park containing beautiful floral displays. Bedrooms are tastefully decorated in period style with antique furniture and parquet floors covered in Persian rugs. The restaurant has an intimate, cosy ambience and, in fine weather, meals are served on a garden terrace, but neither has views over the moat. Last orders: lunch 1.30pm; dinner 9.30pm. Set menus from F154; à la carte around F250.
Walks in 20-acre grounds

CHENECEY-BUILLON

🏠 🍴 5/10 🛏 £

Hôtel Gervais-Pape, Chenecey-Buillon, 25440 Quingey.
Tel: 81.60.31.55
Closed January 15–February 28; restaurant closed Tuesday
Dbl rm F90–F170

Standing on the tree-shaded banks of the river Loue, this 70-year-old hotel has been run by three generations of the Gervais-Pape family, and has the feel of a traditional French family hotel. Bedrooms are large with sturdy old-fashioned furniture; only two have en-suite bathrooms. The restaurant comprises three dining-rooms serving hearty regional fare. In fine weather, you can dine on a waterside terrace seating 50. Last orders: lunch 2pm; dinner 9pm. Set menus from F83; à la carte around F110.
Tennis courts, river swimming, riverside walk to Chenecey limestone caves

CHENNEVIERES-SUR-MARNE

IOI ⊟ ££££

L'Ecu de France, 31 Rue de Champigny, 94430
Chennevières-sur-Marne.   Tel: 1.45.76.00.03
Closed September 2–9, Sunday evening and Monday

This former post-house, on the banks of the river Marne, has
a facade dripping with statuary and geraniums. It is beautifully
situated on the riverbank and overlooks a wooded islet.
There are two dining-rooms, a large ground-floor room in
the style of a hunting lodge, and a bright salon upstairs which
has a conservatory extension overlooking the river. In fine
weather, meals are also served on a waterside garden terrace.
Classic French cooking with some inventive twists. Last
orders: lunch 2pm; dinner 9.30pm. No set menus; à la carte
around F250.

LA CIOTAT

⌂ 4/6 ⊟ ££

Le Revestel, Corniche du Liouquet, 13600 La Ciotat.
Tel: 42.83.11.06
Closed February
Dbl rm F280

This convivial restaurant is popular with the locals and has
good sea views through the trees. In summer, meals and
drinks are served in the pretty garden. Traditional Provençal
cooking. There are six simply furnished bedrooms; half-
board is obligatory June–September and costs F255 per
person. Last orders: lunch 1.30pm; dinner 9.30pm. Set
menus from F138; à la carte around F300.
Nearby sandy beach, sailing boats and sail-boards for hire

COLMAR

🏠 🍽 **18/31** ⬜ £££

Le Maréchal, 4–6 Place des Six Montagnes Noires,
68000 Colmar.   Tel: 89.41.60.32
Open all year
Dbl rm F500–F750

Ideal for a romantic getaway, this pretty hotel sits on the river Lauch in the heart of Colmar's *Petit Venise* district. Many of the bedrooms are handsomely furnished in Louis XV style with four-poster beds and exposed beams. Water-view rooms look out over the river which is lined with half-timbered houses. There are three richly decorated dining-rooms, but the best water views are from what is known as the Salle Jean Sebastian Bach. There is also a canopied waterside terrace for meals and drinks in summer. Last orders: lunch 2pm; dinner 10pm. Set menus from F150; à la carte around F350.
Good base for exploring Colmar's medieval quarter and Renaissance mansions; music festival in July

CONDE-STE-LIBIAIRE

🍽 ⬜ £££

La Vallée de la Marne, 2 Quai de la Marine,
Condé-Ste-Libiaire, 77450 Esbly.   Tel: 1.60.04.31.01
Closed August 1–21; Monday evening and Tuesday

This tastefully decorated restaurant comprises three dining-rooms. Eight tables have views over the river Marne; in summer, customers can enjoy aperitifs on the waterside terrace. Gastronomic cuisine based on fresh seasonal produce, especially fish and, in winter, game. Last orders: lunch 2pm; dinner 9.30pm. Set menus from F135; à la carte around F240.
Walks along the riverbank and the Marne canal

CONDRIEU

🏨 🍽 7/25 ▭ £££

Hostellerie Beau Rivage, 69420 Condrieu.
Tel: 74.59.52.24
Open all year
Dbl rm F620–F820

A warm welcome is assured at this comfortable hotel which stands in landscaped gardens leading down to the river Rhone. Bedrooms, appealingly decorated in different styles, are furnished with antiques. Several have private balconies, and seven enjoy commanding views over an attractive stretch of the river. Picture windows in the elegant dining-room which sits on the river bank make the most of the water view. Last orders: lunch 2pm; dinner 9.30pm. Set menus from F180 (lunch), F275 (dinner); à la carte around F350.
Walks along the banks of the Rhone, Pilat National Park 6km, vineyard tours

CONTREXEVILLE

🏨 🍽 15/31 ▭ ££

Campanile du Lac, Route des Lacs, 88140 Contrexéville.
Tel: 29.08.03.72
Open all year
Dbl rm F258

This small motel-style establishment sits alone on the banks of a beautiful lake on the outskirts of Contrexéville, famous for its mineral springs and spa treatments. Bedrooms are simply furnished, all with en-suite bathrooms, and two rooms are equipped for the disabled. A brasserie, with a lakeside terrace seating 200, serves Alsatian specialities, snacks, drinks and ice-creams from noon to midnight. There is also a more formal restaurant offering inexpensive regional specialities. Last

orders: lunch 2pm; dinner 10pm. Set menus from F77; à la carte around F110.
Kayaks, canoes and pedalos for hire, lake swimming, fishing with permit May–Sept, lovely walks around forested lake shore

LA CROIX-VALMER

🏨 🍴 30/40 ▭ £££

La Pinède, Route de Gigaro, 83420 La Croix-Valmer.
Tel: 94.54.31.23
Open May 1–October 20
Dbl rm F650–F1080

On a secluded and unspoilt stretch of coastline, this modern hotel is surrounded by pine trees and vineyards. The spacious bedrooms are tastefully decorated with floral fabrics and cane furniture and have patio doors which open on to small individiual verandahs. Tree-shaded lawns lead down to the restaurant which sits on the edge of the hotel's private sandy beach and specializes in fish and seafood. Last orders: lunch 3pm; dinner 9pm. Set menu F150 (lunch), F210 (dinner); à la carte around F250.
Private swimming pool; hotel pedalos and sail-boards for hire; tennis court, coastal path to Cap Lardier

LE CROTOY

🍴 6/6 ▭ ££

Chez Mado, Quai Léonard, 80550 Le Crotoy.
Tel: 22.27.81.22
Open all year
Dbl rm F280

This congenial restaurant is arranged on two floors, and window tables have unimpaired views over the bay of the Somme. The French drive long distances to enjoy a relaxing Sunday lunch or dinner in its homely dining-rooms which are filled with antique furniture and plate. Freshwater fish and seafood and homemade puddings are the order of the day. There are two open-air verandahs and a terrace where breakfast, drinks, ice-creams and seafood platters are served. The six bedrooms are spacious and also furnished with lovely old furniture. Last orders: lunch 2.30pm; dinner 10pm. Set menus from F80; à la carte around F200.

Beach with sun-loungers, sail-boards and bicycles for hire, steam-train ride from Le Crotoy to St-Valery

CRUSEILLES

🍴 💳 ££

L'Ancolie, Parc des Dronières, 74350 Cruseilles.
Tel: 50.44.28.98
Closed Christmas and three weeks in February
A41 exit Allonzier 7kms

L'Ancolie's attractive location, on the banks of Dronières lake, is not matched by its angular modern construction. But the interior is bright and airy and most tables have a good view of the small lake – which is popular with local fishermen. In summer, meals are also served on a lakeside terrace. Good regional home cooking. Last orders: lunch 2pm; dinner 9pm. Set menus from F98 (lunch), F145 (dinner); à la carte around F200.

DOLANCOURT

🏨 🍴 8/16 💳 ££

Moulin du Landion, Dolancourt, 10200 Bar-sur-Aube.
Tel: 25.27.92.17
Closed December and January
Dbl rm F320–F350

This old watermill straddles a small stream which runs through the pretty garden. It is a simple, homely place. Bedrooms are cheerfully decorated and all have private balconies overlooking the stream or garden. In the rustic dining-room, 12 tables look out through large picture windows over the mill, its water-wheel and the stream. In fine weather, meals are served on a waterside terrace which has recently been added. The cooking has a good local reputation. All the fish served in the restaurant is taken fresh from the river, and bread, jams and *foie gras* are made on the premises. Last orders: lunch 2pm; dinner 9pm. Set menus from F100; à la carte around F270.

Swimming pool in garden, good lake and river fishing

DUNKERQUE

○| ⊟ ££

Le Don Quichotte, 2 Rue de Flandre, Malo-les-Bains, 59240 Dunkerque.   Tel: 28.63.16.32
Open all year; closed Monday and Saturday lunch

On the seafront at Malo, Dunkerque's beach resort, this first-floor restaurant has a commanding view of the Channel. Appealingly decorated in pink and white, it is popular with local residents and has a convivial atmosphere. The cooking is a mixture of regional favourites from Toulouse and Spanish dishes such as *paella* and *zarzuela*. Last orders: lunch 2pm; dinner 10.30pm (later at weekends). Set menus from F112; à la carte around F150.

Dunkerque is the ferry port for Ramsgate; musée des beaux arts containing Delftware and Flemish paintings from 16th century

ELINCOURT-STE-MARGUERITE

🏛 ○| 13/55 ⊟ ££££

Château de Bellinglise, 60157 Elincourt-Ste-Marguerite.
Tel: 44.76.04.76
Open all year
Dbl rm F770–F1250
Off D142 north of Elincourt

The turrets of this beautiful Renaissance manor, set in 650-acre grounds, are reflected in its lake. It was turned into a military hospital during the Second World War and, after restoration, opened as a country house hotel in 1975. The cheaper rooms are in Le Valois, an annexe in the park, but it is worth paying up to occupy one of the gorgeous bedrooms, each decorated in a different style, in the chateau itself. The public rooms are the epitome of comfort, and its gourmet restaurant occupies three dining-rooms; window tables in two of them have lake views. Last orders: lunch 2pm; dinner 9pm. Set menus from F195; à la carte around F350.

Tennis court, bicycles for hire; excursions to Compiègne forest and chateau, Senlis and Chantilly

ENFONVELLE

🏚 ⁏◯⁏ 6/9 🛏 ££

Moulin de l'Achat, Enfonvelle, 52400
Bourbonne-les-Bains.   Tel: 25.90.09.54
Closed January 1–March 1
Dbl rm F280

This old watermill turned country inn is situated in one of the prettiest parts of the Vosges mountains, a land of green rolling hills and picturesque medieval villages. Bedrooms are cosy with antique beds and furniture, and six have lovely views of the river. The restaurant is rustic in style with stone walls, heavy exposed beams and a smell of hay and leather. Monsieur Arends makes guests feel very much at home. Meals and drinks are served from 7am–midnight, non-stop. Good home cooking including a special eel paté. Set menus from F90; à la carte around F120.

Hotel facilities include swimming pool, tennis court, bicycles and riding stables

ENGHIEN-LES-BAINS

⁏◯⁏ 🛏 ££££

Duc d'Enghien, 3 Avenue de Ceinture, 95880
Enghien-les-Bains.   Tel: 34.12.90.00

Closed January 1–10, August, Sunday evening and
Monday
Train from Gare du Nord takes 20 minutes

Situated in a casino at this 19th-century spa, just north of St-
Denis, this acclaimed restaurant attracts many Parisians who
come for the racing and gambling. The dining-room is
elegantly decorated in *belle époque* style; seven inside tables
have lake views. In fine weather, meals are also served on a
lakeside terrace. Michel Kéréver's gastronomic cooking
includes specialities such as pigeon and *foie gras* salad, and
lobster ravioli with wild mushrooms. *Menu dégustation* F460;
à la carte around F550.
Lakeshore walks, pedalos available for hire

ERONDELLE

� 5/8 ⌷ ££

Manoir de la Renardière, Erondelle, 80580 Pont Rémy.
Tel: 22.27.13.00
Closed January and February
Dbl rm F300–F400
On Huppy-Liercourt road, 4km from D901

This small Victorian mansion has a commanding view over
the lakes of the Somme valley from its peaceful hill-top
location. Hélène Thaon d'Arnoldi extends a warm welcome to guests and advises reserving weekends a month or
so in advance. The bedrooms, recently redecorated using
English Sanderson fabrics, are furnished with antiques and
have a homely appeal. The Blue Room has a large first-floor
balcony and guests can also stay in a log cabin in the grounds
with a large bay window overlooking the lakes. Breakfast is
more like brunch with homemade *brioches* and breads, jams,
eggs and fresh orange juice. A 'light supper' is also served, on
advance request, comprising fish and seafood dishes, cheese,
pudding, coffee and wines for F250.

Trout and eel fishing; owner organizes tour of lakes by rowing boat and bird-watching and mountain bike tours with lunch at country inns

ETAPLES

IOI ▭ ££

Aux Pecheurs d'Etaples, Quai de la Canche, 62630 Etaples.   Tel: 21.94.06.90
Closed January

Owned by the local fishermen's co-operative, this convivial modern quayside restaurant is guaranteed to receive the best catch of the day. It sits above a fish market and half the tables look out over the river Canche, busy with fishing craft. Frequented by local residents, it is a treat for lovers of fish with particularly delicious grilled sole, and monkfish with wild mushrooms. Last orders: lunch 2pm; dinner 10pm. Set menus from F90 (children F39); à la carte around F140.

EVIAN-LES-BAINS

▥ IOI 10/12 ▭ ££££

Les Prés Fleuris, Route de Thollon (D24), St Paul, 74400 Evian-les-Bains.   Tel: 50.75.29.14
Open May 1–September 30
Dbl rm F850–F1200

Situated among the summer pastures high above Evian, this intimate chalet-style hotel has panoramic views of Lake Geneva. Its simple wooden structure belies the luxury inside, and all bedrooms have private terraces. Chef Roger Frossard has earned a good local reputation for his imaginative interpretations of traditional dishes. In fine weather, lunch and high tea are served on the lawn which also has a splendid view of the lake. Last orders: lunch 1.30pm; dinner 9.30pm. Set menus from F250; à la carte around F400.

EVIAN-LES-BAINS

🏨 ⑩ 80/158 🛏 ££££

The Royal Hôtel, 74500 Evian-les-Bains.
Tel: 50.26.85.00
Closed December 15–January 31
Dbl rm F960–F2420

'Health, fitness, sports and self-discovery' is what this exclusive hotel promises. Set in a landscaped park, on a wooded hillside above the spa, it has splendid views of Lake Geneva. An oasis of pampered luxury, it offers every conceivable fitness programme and meets all dietary requirements. There is a children's club with supervised activities which is free for guests. There are several restaurants and all have lake views. Le Barbecue Piscine offers a buffet lunch for F220 and its gastronomic restaurant, Le Café Royal, serves *nouvelle cuisine*. Last orders: lunch 2.30pm; dinner 9.30pm. Set menu F340; à la carte around F400.
Indoor and outdoor swimming pools, tennis courts, gymnasium, sauna and fitness classes, windsurfing, water-skiing and sailing on the lake arranged by hotel, nearby riding, and 18-hole golf-course.

EZE

🏨 ⑩ 4/8 🛏 ££££

Le Château Eza, 06360 Eze-Village.   Tel: 93.41.12.24
Closed November 1–March 31
Dbl rm F1200–F2500

Château Eza, formerly the residence of Prince William of Sweden, clings to a rocky hilltop more than a thousand feet above the sea. It is exhilarating to stand on its terrace and peer down over a swathe of the coastline far below. Eze-Village itself is a beautifully restored medieval settlement, with narrow streets of honey-coloured stone houses. In high season, it attracts hordes of day trippers. The Château Eza has only eight bedrooms, which are filled with handsome antique furniture, tapestries and oriental rugs. The names of the rooms indicate their decorative style – Camelia, Renaissance and Suite du Prince. Window tables in the dining-room and its dining terraces have magnificent sea views. The cooking enjoys a very good reputation. Last orders: lunch 2pm; dinner 10pm. Set menus from F150 (lunch); F510 (dinner).

Sandy beach and watersports at Eze, 20 minutes by car

EZE

🏨 🍽 <u>20/20</u> 🛏 ££££

Château de la Chèvre d'Or, Rue du Barri, 06260 Eze-Village.   Tel: 93.41.12.12
Closed January 6–March 1; restaurant closed Wednesday March 1–Easter
Dbl rm F1500–F2500

This chateau–hotel occupies the ruins of a hilltop castle which fell into disrepair almost a thousand years ago. The interior reflects its medieval past with heavy timbers, tiled floors and the use of rich colours. Bedrooms, arranged in several village houses, are spacious and furnished with antiques. All the rooms, the swimming-pool terrace, and its acclaimed restaurant, La Chèvre d'Or, have breathtaking sea views. In fine weather, meals are served on a terrace. There is also a grill for simpler fare. Last orders: lunch 2.30pm; dinner 10.30pm. Set menus from F350 (lunch) F560 (dinner); à la carte around F500.

EZE

🏨 🍽 <u>40/40</u> 🛏 ££££

Le Cap Estel, Bord de Mer, 06360 Eze.   Tel: 93.01.50.44
Closed November 1–March 15
Dbl rm F1410

A secluded and exclusive retreat, Le Cap Estel sits on a small rocky promontory surrounded by five acres of landscaped gardens with exotic palms and tall pines. The interior is graceful and it has a refined, rather than a flashy, style. Each of the gorgeous bedrooms has a balustraded balcony or private terrace. One of its most attractive features is an indoor swimming pool, built out into the Mediterranean as if part of the bow of a ship. On top of it sits a larger outdoor pool. In fine weather guests can dine on the tree-shaded terrace, which has lovely sea views. Half-board is obligatory June–September and costs F1175–F1600 per person. Last orders: lunch 2.30pm; dinner 9.30pm. Set menus are available from F350; à la carte around F400.
Private beach with scuba-diving and water-skiing

FILLIEVRES

🏨 🍴 **5/10** 🛏 £

Auberge du Vieux Moulin, Fillièvres, 62770 Le Parcq.
Tel: 21.47.93.42
Open all year
Dbl rm F180

This inn overlooks a mill-pond in the Canche valley. Bedrooms are very simply furnished, but clean and comfortable enough for an overnight stay; only four have en-suite bathrooms. The ground-floor restaurant has French windows opening on to a gravel courtyard beside the river. Good home cooking based on fresh market produce including trout from the river. Last orders: lunch 2pm; dinner 8pm. Set menus from F70; à la carte around F90.

FLAGY

🏨 🍴 **5/10** 🛏 ££

Hostellerie du Moulin, 2 Rue du Moulin, 77940 Flagy.
Tel: 1.60.96.67.89

Hotel and restaurant closed September 12–24,
December 19–Jan 21, Sunday and Monday nights
Dbl rm F250–F425

This half-timbered mill on the banks of the Orvanne river
dates from the 12th century. Entered through a tiny door, it
has the feeling of a cosy country cottage. Guests are warmly
welcomed by Claude and Jacqueline Scheidecker who run a
very professional operation. The bedrooms have heaps of
rustic charm and are furnished with antiques. The restaurant
serves classic French dishes and is very popular with locals.
Six tables have views over the river; in winter, a fire is lit in its
massive range. Last orders: lunch 2.15pm; dinner 9.15pm.
Set menus from F160; à la carte around F220.
Fishing; Fontainebleau forest and chateau 23km

FONCINE-LE-HAUT

🍽 ▤ ££

Restaurant de la Truite, 39460 Foncine-le-Haut.
Tel: 84.51.90.07
Open all year; closed Tuesday evening except June–August

This rustic inn makes an ideal lunch stop on a tour of the
Jura's lakes and mountains. Part of its dining-room is built on
stilts out over the river Saine and seven tables have fine river
views. Traditional Jura dishes, especially using river trout.
The adjoining bar is popular with locals. Last orders: lunch
1.30pm; dinner 9.30pm. Set menus from F70; à la carte
around F120.

FONTAINE-DE-VAUCLUSE

▦ 🍽 3/12 ▤ £

Le Parc, Rue des Bourgades, Fontaine-de-Vaucluse,
84800 L'Isle-sur-la-Sorgue.   Tel: 90.20.31.57
Closed January 2–February 15; restaurant closed Wednesday
Dbl rm F250

Famous for its resurgent stream, Fontaine–de–Vaucluse was also the home of the 14th–century Italian poet Petrarch. This unpretentious hotel has a tranquil setting on the banks of the river Sorgue, just outside the village. Bedrooms are modestly furnished but clean and quiet. In summer, meals are served on a pleasant riverside terrace. Imaginative regional cooking. Last orders: lunch 2pm; dinner 9.15pm. Set menus from F95; à la carte around F160.

Pleasant riverside walks, canoe-hire for trip down to L'Isle-sur-la-Sorgue

FONTAINE-DE-VAUCLUSE

○ 5/5 ⊟ ££

Hostellerie Le Château, Quartier Petite Place,
Fontaine–de–Vaucluse, 84800 L'Isle–sur–la–Sorgue.
Tel: 90.20.31.54
Closed Tuesday evening and Wednesday; lunch only January and February
Dbl rm F170

Situated in the heart of the village, this convivial restaurant has a superb view of the source of the river Sorgue. All tables have water views and, in fine weather, meals are also served on a flower-decked balcony overhanging the river. Traditional regional cooking. Bedrooms are simply furnished with shared bathrooms. Last orders: lunch 1.45pm; dinner 8.30pm. Set menus from F110; à la carte around F250.

FOUCHERES

○ 4/7 ⊟ £

Le Relais des Fouchères, Route Nationale 71, 10260
Fouchères.   Tel: 25.40.71.11
Open all year
Dbl rm F150

The dining-room of this simple roadside inn occupies a conservatory on the edge of the river Seine. It serves

traditional regional cuisine, and all tables have views over a
pretty wooded stretch of the river. Bedrooms are comfortable and clean; four have en-suite bathrooms. Good for an
overnight stop on a journey across Champagne. Last orders:
lunch 1.30pm; dinner 9.30pm. Set menus from F69; à la carte
around F140.
Pedalos, rowing boats and canoes free for guests

FRISE

⊨ 3/3 ⇝ £

La Ferme de l'Ecluse, 1 Rue Mony, Frise, 80340
Bray-sur-Somme.   Tel: 22.84.59.70
Open all year
Dbl rm F240

Almost surrounded by water, this characterful farmhouse sits
amid the Somme's lakeland. Young farmers Michel and
Annick Randjia enjoy taking in guests – who have their
own separate entrance and sitting-room – and sharing their
love of the area with their visitors. The recently renovated
bedrooms are prettily decorated and furnished. A good
home-cooked dinner, served *en famille*, costs F80.
Fishing on the lake can be arranged for F35 per person per day

GERARDMER

🏨 |○| 22/32 ⇝ ££

Beau Rivage, Esplanade du Lac, 88400 Gerardmer.
Tel: 29.63.22.28
Closed October 10–December 20; restaurant closed
Wednesday lunch except during August
Dbl rm F280–F450; apartments sleeping 2–6 people
F1760–F4310 per week

In a popular resort for winter and summer sporting holidays,
this attractive modern hotel is situated on the lake's shore just
before you enter the town. Bedrooms are comfortable and

well-equipped, many with balconies offering panoramic lake
views. The apartments contain kitchenettes and are good
bases for families. The restaurant has good lake views and,
in the summer, you can dine outdoors on a terrace. Last
orders: lunch 2pm; dinner 8.30pm. Set menus from F98; à la
carte around F140.

*Heated swimming pool, sauna and Jacuzzi on premises. On lake:
fishing (day permits sold), swimming from beaches, sailing, windsurfing, kayak, canoe and pedalo hire, forest walks along marked
trails*

GERARDMER

🚪 🍽 9/11 🛏 £

Chalet du Lac, 97 Chemin de la droite du Lac,
88400 Gerardmer.   Tel: 29.63.38.76
Closed October 1–31; restaurant closed Friday
October–May
Dbl rm F237

This pretty, family-run chalet has a homely appeal. It stands
on its own beside the lakeshore and has excellent views over
placid waters framed by the forested Vosges mountains. The
comfortable bedrooms are prettily furnished, seven with en-
suite bathrooms. Five rooms have French windows opening
on to wooden balconies. All tables in the conservatory-style
dining-room have excellent lake views. Good regional home
cooking. Last orders: lunch 2pm; dinner 9pm. Set menus
from F65; à la carte around F150.

Boats trips around lake

GERARDMER

🍽 🛏 £

Auberge au Bord du Lac, Chemin du Tour du Lac,
88400 Gerardmer.   Tel: 29.63.44.98
Closed mid-November–mid-December

Set high on the south ridge of the lake, this simple restaurant and café has the most spectacular views of the lake, especially from its open-air terrace. The interior is rustic in style, and the extensive menus chiefly comprise regional dishes, including a good quiche Lorraine. Open 8am–midnight for snacks and drinks. Last orders: lunch 2.30pm; dinner 10pm. Set menus from F85; à la carte around F120.

GERMIGNY L'EVEQUE

🏨 🍽 <u>6/10</u> 🚪 ££

Hostellerie Le Gonfalon, 2 Rue de l'Eglise,
Germigny-l'Evèque, 77910 Varreddes.
Tel: 1.64.33.16.05
Closed January, Sunday evening and Monday
Dbl rm F280–F340

This comfortable inn stands on a pretty stretch of the river Marne, 50km from Paris. Bedrooms are nicely decorated and those facing the river have French windows opening on to a covered terrace with tables and chairs. The restaurant has a very good local reputation and specializes in fish and seafood. Lobsters are kept live in a tank. Eight tables have river views and, in summer, meals are served on a waterside terrace. Last orders: lunch 2pm; dinner 9pm. Set menus from F240; à la carte around F250.

Fishing (permit needed), riverbank and forest walks, 9-hole golf course in village

GIENS

🏨 🍽 <u>27/45</u> 🚪 ££

Le Provençal, Place St-Pierre, Giens, 83400 Hyères.
Tel: 94.58.20.09
Open April 1–October 31
Dbl rm F440–F520

This typical Provençal seaside hotel sits on a promontory in the busy resort village of Giens. Both the rooms and the restaurant have splendid views of the wooded offshore islands of Porquerolles and Port-Cros. Bedrooms are pleasantly furnished, many with sliding doors opening on to balconies or larger terraces. Its cool garden, shaded by pine trees, contains a seawater swimming pool and tennis court, and there is sea swimming from a rocky platform. Half-board compulsory in July and August: F420–F540 per person. Last orders: lunch 2pm; dinner 9.30pm. Set menus from F140; à la carte around F270.

Watersports nearby, boat trips to islands from harbour at La Tour Fondue 10km

GIGOT

🏨 🍽 <u>7/15</u> 🛏 £

Hôtel de Gigot, Gigot, Bretonvillers, 25380 Belleherbe.
Tel: 81.68.91.18
Closed January
Dbl rm F90–F110
On D39 12km N of Fuans

This country inn is difficult to find, but discovery is reward enough. Beautifully situated on the floor of the Dessoubre valley, its simple rustic bedrooms, some with showers, offer very good value. Seven look out over the river to green pastures and the conifer-covered hills of the Jura. The bar is popular with locals, and ten of the restaurant's tables have river views. Last orders: lunch 2.30pm; dinner 9pm. Set menus from F50; à la carte around F120.

Scenic lake, the Cirque de Consolation, 6km

GIVET

🏨 <u>10/20</u> 🛏 ££

Hôtel Val St Hilaire, 7 Quai des Fours, 08600 Givet.
Tel: 24.42.38.50

Closed December 20–January 5
Dbl rm F320

Alongside the river Meuse near the Belgian border, this attractive hotel, which opened last July, has views over a pleasant stretch of river full of swans and bordered by a promenade. Bedrooms are light and airy and immaculately maintained. Breakfast only. Window tables in the next-door restaurant, Les Mouettes, have similarly good views.
Boat cruises along Meuse from Givet to Dinant in Belgium

GOLFE-JUAN

IOI 🍽 £££

Nounou, Boulevard des Frères Roustan, 06220
Golfe-Juan.   Tel: 93.63.71.73
Closed November 17–December 25 and Sunday
evening and Monday except during July and August

There are plenty of beach-restaurants to choose from along this stretch of sand, but the genial Monsieur Esmiol makes this a friendly and relaxing place to stop for lunch. Despite the busy coast road, which runs behind the restaurant, the beach is surprisingly quiet and there is private parking for customers. All tables in the enclosed dining-room have sea views and, in fine weather, meals are also served on a small terrace shaded by colourful parasols. Seafood cuisine, especially *bouillabaisse*, grilled lobster and crawfish. Last orders: lunch 1.45pm; dinner 10pm. Set menus are on offer from F165; à la carte around F350. Sun-loungers F60 a day.
Private beach; watersports and sailing from marina in Golfe-Juan

GOUVIEUX

🏠 IOI **10/22** 🍽 ££

Hostellerie du Pavillon Saint-Hubert, Avenue de
Toutevoie, 60270 Gouvieux.   Tel: 44.57.07.04

Closed mid-January–mid-February
Dbl rm F250–F320

Set in a peaceful spot on the wooded banks of the river Oise, this pretty, old hostelry has a warm, friendly atmosphere. Bedrooms are decorated in traditional rustic style with flower-sprigged wallpaper and handsome old furniture. The dining-room is well-furnished and, in summer, meals are also served on a waterside terrace. Refined cuisine based on fresh market produce. Last orders: lunch 2pm; dinner 9.30pm. Set menus from F120; à la carte around F200.
Convenient base for touring the chateaux, abbeys and forests of Senlis, Chantilly and Compiègne; golf and riding nearby

GRENOBLE

🏨 ⅠⅠ 35/58 ▭ ££

Rive Droite, 20 Quai de France, 38000 Grenoble.
Tel: 76.87.61.11
Closed December 23–January 3
Dbl rm F295

Close to Grenoble's historic centre, this hotel is conveniently situated with plenty of parking space – a rarity in this town. From the bedrooms on the upper floors there are commanding views over the river Isère to the distant Belledonne mountains. Bedrooms are very comfortable and tastefully decorated. A good base for exploring the city and surrounding countryside. No river views from the restaurant. Last orders: lunch 2pm; dinner 10pm. Set menus from F80; à la carte around F150.
Cable-car up to Fort de la Bastille departs from behind the hotel

GROSLEE

ⅠⅠ ▭ ££

Penelle, Port de Groslée, Groslée, 01680 Lhuis.
Tel: 74.39.71.01

Closed January 1–February 10, Monday and Tuesday
On the crossroads of the D60 and D19

Set against an impressive mountainous backdrop, this rather
plain restaurant has superb views along the Rhone and the
long Groslée bridge that crosses it. In fine weather, meals and
drinks are also served on a terrace with a view stretching for
several miles down river. Menus are unadventurous but
reasonably priced and it is advisable to book or arrive early
for Sunday lunch. Last orders: lunch 1.30pm; dinner 9pm.
Set menus from F80; à la carte around F140.

GUEBWILLER

🏨 ¶○¶ 32/77 ▭ £

Hôtel du Lac, Rue de la République, 68500 Guebwiller.
Tel: 89.76.63.10
Open all year; restaurant closed Monday
Dbl rm F190–F250

Set against hills, this pleasant modern hotel with Relais
annexe and a pizzeria is built on the banks of a small artifical
lake. Bedrooms are tastefully furnished, all with modern en-
suite bathrooms, and 15 have balconies overlooking the lake.
The restaurant serves regional fare, including young boar in
season, and meals and drinks are served on a lakeside terrace
in summer. Open 7am–1am. Last orders: lunch 2.30pm;
dinner 9.30pm. Set menus from F47 (lunch), F70 (dinner);
à la carte around F110.
Swimming pool and tennis court on premises, lake fishing, conve-
nient for touring Route du Vin and historic Alsatian villages

GUERNES

🏨 ¶○¶ 4/7 ▭ £

Auberge du Bac, Rue du Bac, Guernes, 78520 Limay.
Tel: 1.34.77.35.36

Open all year; restaurant closed Monday October–March
Dbl rm F160

On a beautiful peaceful stretch of the river Seine, this country
inn provides a warm welcome and good value. Bedrooms are
charmingly rustic but very simply furnished with shared
bathrooms. The restaurant serves good home cooking, especially fish. In summer, meals and drinks are served on a
riverbank terrace. There are swings for children. Last orders: lunch 2.30pm; dinner 10pm. Set menus from F120; à
la carte around F130.
Fishing (with permit), long riverbank walks

ILLHAEUSERN

🛏 🍽 ££££

Auberge de l'Ill, Illhaeusern, 68150 Ribeauvillé.
Tel: 89.71.83.23
Closed February, Monday and Tuesday (open Monday
lunch May–October)

This celebrated Alsatian restaurant, owned by the Haberlin
brothers, has been heaped with culinary accolades. It occupies a pretty house just feet from the river Ill and the planned
addition of 11 bedrooms should be ready for guests this
summer. Through the floor-to-ceiling windows all tables
enjoy a beautiful painterly scene of the serene river shaded
by weeping willows. In summer, aperitifs and coffee are
served in the garden. The ultimate in creative Alsatian
cooking. Salmon soufflé is a particular speciality. Reserve
well ahead. Last orders: lunch 2pm; dinner 9pm. Set menus
from F440 (lunch) F560 (dinner); à la carte around F600.

L'ISLE-ADAM

🏨 🍽 ⚓ 🛏 ££

Le Cabouillet, 5 Quai de l'Oise, 95290 L'Isle-Adam.
Tel: 1.34.69.00.90

Closed February; restaurant closed Sunday evening and
Monday
Dbl rm F280–F380

This attractive, ivy-covered establishment stands beside a
stone bridge over the river Oise. Both rooms and restaurant
have lovely views over two islets in the river. Bedrooms are
comfortably furnished, all with en-suite bathrooms. Part of
the restaurant occupies a covered first-floor terrace. The
imaginative menus are based around fresh market produce,
especially freshwater fish and seafood. Last orders: lunch
2pm; dinner 9.30pm. Set menus from F215; à la carte
around F350.
*Riverside walks, beach for river swimming in summer, fishing (with
permit), tennis courts nearby, riding 5km*

LES ISSAMBRES

IOI ⊟ ££££

Le Saint Pierre, RN 98, 83380 Les Issambres.
Tel: 94.96.89.67
Closed December 15–January 15 and Tuesday (lunch
only during July and August)

Situated on a cliffside between St-Tropez and Fréjus, this
conservatory-style restaurant has splendid sea views on three
sides. The decor is plain but the ambience is convivial and, in
fine weather, meals are served on a terrace just a few feet from
the sea's edge. The brightly-lit coastline makes an impressive
vista for diners at night. Extensive menus with specialities
including seafood lasagne and mussels with spinach. Last
orders: lunch 2pm; dinner 10pm. Set menus from F210; à
la carte around F350.
Good cliff walks

ITTEVILLE

🏨 🍴 24/24 🛏 ££

Auberge de l'Ile du Saussay, 91760 Itteville.
Tel: 1.64.93.20.12
Open all year
Dbl rm F390–F490
Paris 30 minutes

A refreshing change from the traditional auberge, this beautifully designed establishment, which opened two years ago, stands on an island in the middle of a pretty lake on the river Essonne. The fashionably decorated bedrooms are bright and airy with small sitting areas that open out on to private terraces just a few feet from the water's edge. The restaurant has similar views over the wooded lakeshore and meals are served on a waterside terrace in fine weather. Last orders: lunch 2.30pm; dinner 10pm. Set menus from F160; à la carte around F250.
Fishing (with permit)

JOIGNY

🏨 🍴 17/29 🛏 ££££

La Côte Saint Jacques, 14 Faubourg de Paris, 89300 Joigny.   Tel: 86.62.09.70
Closed January
Dbl rm F1050–F1650

This smart hotel sits on the banks of the river Yonne on the outskirts of Joigny, a picturesque town beside the forest of Othe. The luxurious bedrooms are beautifully decorated in various styles. Some have imaginative glass-covered verandahs, others large balustraded terraces on which guests can relax and watch the river run slowly by. The elegant restaurant has no river views, but enjoys a very good reputation. Breakfast is sometimes served on the hotel's boat, which operates brunch cruises down the river. Last orders: lunch

1.45pm; dinner 9.45pm. Set menus from F620; à la carte around F550.

Indoor heated swimming pool, tennis court, four-person hotel boat for hire

JOYEUSE

◻ **16/16** ▭ ££

La Guaribote, Route de Valgorge, Le Gua, 07260 Joyeuse.
Tel: 75.39.55.12
Closed November 10–weekend before Easter
Dbl rm F220–F270
Take D203 from Joyeuse to hamlet of Le Gua, 12 km

Set in a chestnut grove amid wild and spectacular scenery near the Ardèche gorges, this 13th-century olive mill is just the place for those who like to get off the beaten track. It has been painstakingly converted by the multi-talented and enterprising owner–chef Hervé Garnier. Monsieur Garnier, who is a licensed pilot, will give guided tours of the spectacular countryside from the air. Most of the tables in the delightful restaurant, which has a wall of sliding glass doors, overlook the river Beaume. Refined and inventive dishes using fresh local produce. The comfortably furnished bedrooms are contained in handsome modern timber chalets in the grounds. All have good en-suite bathrooms and balconies or private terraces. Last orders: lunch 1.30pm; dinner 9.30pm. Set menus from F98; à la carte around F160.
Fishing; swimming in river from pebble beach; canoe and kayak rental nearby; very good walking country

JUAN-LES-PINS

🏨 ◻ **27/45** ▭ ££££

Belles Rives, Boulevard du Littoral, 06160 Juan-les-Pins.
Tel: 93.61.02.79

Open Easter–October 15
Dbl rm F1000–F2380

On the edge of a resort dominated by monotonous high–rise hotels, the Belle Rives has an enviable location on the seashore between Juan-les-Pins and the more residential Cap d'Antibes. Built in the 1930s, the hotel has retained its period charm and style. Both the rooms and restaurant have panoramic views over the bay towards the Iles de Lérins. The bedrooms are decorated with flair, air-conditioned and have modern marble bathrooms. Half board is obligatory during July and August. Innovative versions of classic French dishes are served in the dining-room and on the terrace. Last orders: lunch 3pm; dinner 10pm. Set menus are available from F290 (children F110); à la carte around F300. The hotel's beach restaurant also serves lunch and dinner: à la carte around F200.
Private beach and jetty with water-skiing and windsurfing

LAFFREY

🏨 🍽 11/25 ▭ £

Hôtel du Grand Lac, Lac de Laffrey, Laffrey, 38220 Vizille.   Tel: 76.73.12.90
Open all year; restaurant open May–September only
Dbl rm F130–F270

A good base for a family holiday, this small hotel stands on the banks of Laffrey lake, the largest of several natural lakes just south of Vizille. Bedrooms are simply but pleasantly furnished, some with basic facilities for cooking. The restaurant's large windows afford expansive views over the wooded shores of the lake and, in summer, tables and chairs are arranged on the grass leading down to the water. Traditional French cooking. Last orders: lunch 2pm; dinner 9pm. Set menus are available from F60; à la carte around F110.
Small beach in front of the hotel with pedalos, sail-boards, canoes and

rowing boats for hire; fishing (permits sold nearby); scenic drive along
the valley of the river Drac 5km away

LE LAVANDOU

🏨 🍽 <u>41/41</u> 🛏 ££££

Hôtel Les Roches, 1 Avenue des Trois Dauphins,
Aiguebelle Plage, 83980 Le Lavandou.   Tel: 94.71.05.07
Closed November 18–December 20; January 7–March 4
Dbl rm F1120–F1550

An oasis of luxury and tranquillity, this beautifully designed
hotel is built into the side of a cliff with terraced gardens
looking out over the Iles d'Or. Bedrooms are cool, elegant
and spacious, furnished with local Provençal fabrics and
antiques. The terrace bar and dining-room appear to be
suspended above the sea, and are filled with the bright light
of the Mediterranean. Interesting modern interpretations of
old Provençal recipes have earned the restaurant a very good
reputation. Last orders: lunch 2.30pm; dinner 10pm. Set
menus from F280; à la carte around F400.
Swimming pool, sea swimming off rocks, hotel boat for island
excursions and tuna fishing trips, all watersports can be arranged

LE LAVANDOU

🏨 🍽 <u>12/19</u> 🛏 ££

Hôtel Belle-Vue, Boulevard du Four des Maures,
St Clair, 83980 Le Lavandou.   Tel: 94.71.01.06
Closed November 1–March 31; restaurant dinner only,
closed Sunday
Dbl rm F310–F650

This delightful Provencal-style hotel is peacefully situated on
a hill above St-Clair beach and looks out over a sparkling blue
bay to Le Lavandou and the Iles d'Or. Bedrooms have been
appealingly renovated, and eight have large canopy-shaded
balconies. Window tables in the restaurant, which serves

traditional Provençal dishes, have good sea views. There is a terrace for breakfast and drinks. Last orders for dinner 9pm. Set menus from F160; à la carte around F250.

Sail-boards for hire, water-skiing and scuba-diving clubs in St-Clair bay, tennis courts nearby

ILE-DU-LEVANT

🏨 ○| <u>14/22</u> 🛏 ££

La Brise Marine, Héliopolis, 83400 Ile-du-Levant.
Tel: 94.05.91.15
Open May 1–Oct 15
Dbl rm F250–F390

This white-washed hotel with its blue shutters and flower-filled courtyard sits on a verdant hillside. Nudism is obligatory on most beaches, and the hotel is a favourite with naturists. Bedrooms are simply furnished but well-maintained. The restaurant, designed in the style of a Provençal farmhouse, has superb sea views. Last orders: lunch 2.30pm; dinner 10pm. Set menus from F94; à la carte around F130.

Sandy coves, sail-boards and sea canoes for hire, scuba-diving club, hourly ferries from Le Lavandou and Hyères

LONGECOURT-EN-PLAINE

🛏 <u>4/4</u> 🛏 £££

Château de Longecourt, Longecourt-en-Plaine, 21100 Genlis.   Tel: 80.39.88.76
Open all year
Dbl rm F650

The Comtesse Bertrand de Saint-Seine personally welcomes guests to this handsome turretted chateau that has been her family's home since 1680. She speaks little English but is a charming lady. Although in the village, the chateau is surrounded by a moat and has 90 acres of parkland, bordered by the Burgundy canal. It offers a relaxing old-style chateau

B&B experience that is unforgettable. Bedrooms are spacious but simply furnished, with old-fashioned fittings. The rococo salon, with its massive gilt mirrors and chandeliers, is the highlight of the house. Breakfast is included in the price and dinner can be provided if a day's notice is given.
Fishing in canal (with permit), good base for Burgundy wine-tasting excursions, nearby tennis courts

LOUHANS

🏨 🍴 **9/21** 🛏 ££

Moulin de Bourgchâteau, Route de Chalon, 71500 Louhans.   Tel: 85.75.37.12
Closed December 23–January 20; restaurant closed Sunday evening (October–April) and Monday lunch
Dbl rm F220–F260; apartment F600

Built in 1778 beside a natural pool on the La Seille river, this old flour mill was in use until 1973. It has been imaginatively converted into a hotel. Bedrooms are comfortable and well-appointed and all have en-suite bathrooms. The mill's thick stone walls are pierced by small windows, so only four tables in the restaurant have water views. Last orders: lunch 1.30pm; dinner 9pm. Set menus are available from F95; à la carte around F220.
Private fishing

LOYETTES

🍴 🛏 £££

La Terrasse, Place des Mariniers, 01360 Loyettes.
Tel: 78.32.70.13
Closed two weeks in February, Sunday evening and Monday

Menus change frequently at La Terrasse as talented owner–chef Gérard Antonin creates dishes around seasonal market produce. The restaurant occupies a conservatory-style terrace with sliding glass doors, making the most of its views of the fast-flowing river Rhone. In fine weather, there is a delightful waterside dining terrace. Creative French cooking with the emphasis on fish and game. Last orders: lunch 2pm; dinner 9.30pm. Set menus from F180; à la carte around F270.

LUMBRES

🏨 |◯| 12/24 ▭ ₤₤₤

Auberge du Moulin de Mombreux, 62380 Lumbres.
Tel: 21.39.62.44
Closed December 20–27
Dbl rm F580–F650

Peacefully situated in a park alongside the river Blequin, this hotel comprises a handsome, modern, brick building and, on the opposite bank, a restaurant housed in a converted 13th-century mill. Bedrooms are spacious and furnished with flair; ground-floor rooms are just feet from the river. The mill restaurant retains its rustic character, although only a few window tables have river views. In fine weather, drinks and pastries are served on a waterside terrace all afternoon. Inventive classic French cooking with seasonal fish and game. Last orders: lunch 2pm; dinner 9.30pm. Set menus from F220; à la carte around F275.

LYON

🏨 |◯| 49/179 ▭ ₤₤₤

Sofitel, 20 Quai Gailleton, La Presqu'Ile, 69288 Lyon.
Tel: 72.41.20.20
Open all year
Dbl rm F830

Part of the worldwide Sofitel chain, this modern hotel provides all the services and facilities expected of a large cosmopolitan hotel. Situated in the heart of Lyon on a prestigious island site between the Rhone and the Saone, the spacious bedrooms have commanding views of the river and city, especially those on the higher floors. Its Melhor bar and the Trois Domes restaurant, on the 8th floor, offer splendid city panoramas. Last orders: lunch 2.15pm; dinner 10pm. Set menus F200 (lunch) F240 (dinner and Sunday); à la carte around F330.

Bateaux mouches trips on the Rhone

LYON

IOI ▭ £££others

Nandron, 26 Quai Jean Moulin, 69000 Lyon.
Tel: 78.42.10.26
Closed August and Saturday

Lyon is justifiably renowned for its fine cuisine and Nandron is one of the city's several highly-acclaimed restaurants. The dining-room of this riverside restaurant is on the first floor and four window tables have good views over the Rhone. The Lyonnais take their food seriously, but explanations of the menu in English are given with enthusiasm and without being patronizing. Last orders: lunch 2pm, dinner 10pm. Set menus from F210 (lunch), F300 (dinner); à la carte around F400.

MAINTENAY

IOI ▭ £

Crêperie du Moulin, Maintenay, 62870
Campagne-lès-Hesdin.   Tel: 21.90.43.74
Closed December 15–January 15; open weekends only October–Easter

Set in a pretty rural countryside, the water-wheel still turns on this old mill, which serves excellent crêpes, galettes and, in May, fresh asparagus. Everything is fresh and homemade – even the jams. Five inside tables enjoy river views and, in

summer, meals are served on a lawn terrace overlooking the mill-pond. Last orders: lunch 3pm; dinner 10pm. Set menu F90; crêpes F15–F45.
Son et lumière on Thursday and Saturday at Valloires abbey 2km

MARCENAY-LE-LAC

🏠 🍴 4/18 ⊟ £

Le Santenoy, Marcenay-le-Lac, 21330 Laignes.
Tel: 80.81.40.08
Open all year
Dbl rm F175–F218

Overlooking a large artificial lake, this hotel is very popular with locals and serves up to 350 meals on a fine summer's day. Bedrooms are simply furnished, 12 with en-suite bathrooms. But the great attraction is its first-floor dining-room which has panoramic lake views and serves brasserie-style meals, using fresh market produce, until 11pm. In fine weather, drinks, snacks and full meals are also served on a terrace. Last orders: lunch 3pm; dinner 11pm. Set menus from F60; à la carte around F130.
Fishing (with permit), sail-boards and rowing boats for hire, riding stables nearby

MARSEILLE

🏠 🍴 17/17 ⊟ ££££

Le Petit Nice Passedat, Anse de Maldorme,
La Corniche J F Kennedy, 13007 Marseille.
Tel: 91.59.25.92
Open all year; restaurant closed Sunday in winter
Dbl rm F1000–F1700

Perched on a small bluff away from the bustle of Marseille, this white-washed villa is an exclusive retreat on the water's edge. Bedrooms are stylish and luxuriously furnished with choice antique pieces. All have views along the coast and across to tiny islands. The sea laps at the base of an open-air dining terrace next to the pool. The menus are seductive, offering refined modern versions of traditional Provençal recipes such as sea bass in virgin olive oil and langoustines with citrus fruits – this is the perfect setting for a romantic dinner. Last orders: lunch 1.30pm; dinner 10pm. Set menus from F300 (lunch), F390 (dinner); à la carte around F550. *Seawater pool; solarium; hotel arranges water-skiing, windsurfing and sailing*

MARSEILLE

IOI 🍽 £££

L'Epuisette, Vallon des Ausses, 13007 Marseille.
Tel: 91.52.17.82
Closed December 21–January 26, Saturday and Sunday
On road to Plages du Prado

Popular with locals, but generally missed by visitors to Marseille, this unprepossessing restaurant is just feet from the water on a rocky promontory overlooking a fishing village and offshore islands. Essentially a glass-sided bunga-low, it is a favourite with the city's fish lovers. Lobster is the speciality of the house, kept in tanks underneath the restau-rant. Last orders: lunch 2.30pm; dinner 10pm. Set menus from F140; à la carte F350.

MARSEILLE

IOI 🍽 £££

Aux Mets de Provence Chez Maurice Brun,
18 Quai de Rive Neuve, 13007 Marseille.
Tel: 91.33.35.38
Open all year; closed Sunday and Monday

Most restaurants in Marseille's old port are at street level, so water views are obscured by traffic, but this second-floor restaurant has a good view over the busy harbour. The prettily decorated dining-room has a timbered ceiling and, as it seats only 30, booking is essential. Run by Maurice Brun and his family, it specializes in traditional Provençal cooking and is a good place to try *bouillabaise*, a seafood casserole for the ravenous. Last orders: lunch 3.30pm; dinner 9.30pm. Gastronomic set menu F335; à la carte around F250.

MENTON

🏨 24/44 ▭ ££

Princess et Richmond, 617 Promenade du Soleil, 06500 Menton.   Tel: 93.35.80.20
Closed November 5–December 20
Dbl rm F440–F520

Hotels like the Princess et Richmond are a rare find on this stretch of the Riviera. An attractively designed modern hotel with a good central location in the resort, it is reasonably priced and run well by the Caravelli family who extend a warm welcome. The well-equipped bedrooms are decorated in fashionable pastel shades. All sea-view rooms have sliding glass doors leading on to canopied balconies. A road runs in front of the hotel but the traffic noise is not intrusive. There is also a roof terrace with sun-loungers, a welcome alternative to Menton's often crowded beach. Breakfast only.
Water-skiing, pedalos and sail-boards for hire 500m

MENTON

IOI ▭ ££

Imperial Plage, 5 Promenade de la Mer, 06500 Menton.
Tel: 93.28.29.65
Open May 5–September 5

Caskets full of plants decorate the terrace of this beach restaurant which is shaded by a bamboo canopy and green parasols. A friendly, informal ambience pervades both the din- ing-room and the terrace grill which are run by an Austrian/

Alsatian couple who speak good English. Open 9am–midnight for drinks. Last orders: lunch 2.30pm; dinner 10.30pm. No set menus; à la carte around F150. Sun-loungers F50 a day.
Children's play area; facilities for water-skiing and windsurfing

MERRY-SUR-YONNE

IOI ⌷ £

Restaurant des Rochers, Merry-sur-Yonne, 89660
Chatel Censoir.   Tel: 86.81.04.04
Open mid–March–mid–November; closed Monday
evening and Tuesday

In the shadow of towering limestone cliffs, this simple restaurant sits on the banks of the Nivernais canal. Popular with pleasure boaters, around 200 patrons can be seated in the various dining-rooms and on the terrace. Most tables have excellent views of the canal and the river, which converge here. Simple, good value menus. Open 8am–1am. Last orders: lunch 1.30pm; dinner 9pm. Five-course set menu F120; à la carte around F100.

MESSEY-SUR-GROSNE

⌷ IOI ⅖ ⌷ £

Moulin de la Chapelle, Messey-sur-Grosne, 71940
St-Boil.   Tel: 85.44.00.58
Hotel and restaurant closed February, Tuesday and
Wednesday nights except during July and August
Dbl rm F115–F190

Set in tranquil countryside, this simple hotel is bounded by a river, a pond and a mill-race. Bedrooms are fairly basic, three with en-suite bathrooms. The bright, airy restaurant serves fresh seasonal produce. Twelve window tables have pleasing views of the river. Last orders: lunch 1.30pm; dinner 9pm. Set menus from F55; à la carte around F120.
Fishing on private lake

METZ

🏠 🍴 **19/36** 🛏 ££

Hôtel du Theatre, Rue du Pont St–Marcel, 57000 Metz.
Tel: 87.31.10.10
Open all year; restaurant 'Pont St–Marcel' closed Sunday
evening and Monday
Dbl rm F460

In one of the oldest parts of Metz, this imaginatively designed
hotel opened two years ago as part of a redevelopment plan
for the old port of St–Marcel. Bedrooms are decorated in a
smart modern style. Only four look out over the river
Moselle, the rest have a view over a former dock. Its two
restaurants, the Pont St–Marcel and the Bistrot du Port, have
splendid views of the river itself, and both have waterside
dining terraces. Last orders for both: lunch 2pm; dinner
11pm. Set menus from F88 (Pont), F158 (Bistrot); à la carte
around F180 (Pont), F220 (Bistrot).
*Ideal for exploring the historic old city on foot, lots of cultural
activities, boat trips on the Moselle*

METZ

🍴 🛏 £££

Restaurant du Maire, 1 Rue du Pont des Morts,
57000 Metz.   Tel: 87.32.43.12
Closed two weeks in February, August 25–September 9,
Tuesday evening and Wednesday

One of the most respected restaurants in Metz, part of its
dining–room occupies a conservatory that overhangs the
river and has lovely views of the Pont des Morts and the
castle. In summer, meals are also served on the waterside
terrace below. Gourmet cooking with the emphasis on fish
dishes. Last orders: lunch 1.45pm; dinner 10pm. Set menus
from F180; à la carte around F300.

MONCOURT-FROMONVILLE

🏨 🍽 **5/12** 🛏 £

Hostellerie des Trois Sources, 125 Rue Grande,
Moncourt-Fromonville, 77140 Nemours.
Tel: 1.64.28.94.75
Hotel open all year; restaurant closed Monday evening
and Tuesday
Dbl rm F200–F220

This characterful inn used to be a stopover for barges and
their horses. Madame Lefèvre provides a warm welcome, and
public rooms are decorated with African carvings and local
watercolours. Bedrooms are simply furnished; four have
small en-suite bathrooms. The vine-covered dining terrace
has a pretty view of the canal. Good home cooking using
only fresh local produce including fresh fish which the
owners smoke themselves. Last orders: lunch 2pm; dinner
9pm. Set menus from F150; à la carte around F200.
Steam-train rides, forest and chateau at Fontainebleau

MONTBENOIT

🍽 **4/6** 🛏 £

Hôtel du Saugeais, Maisons du Bois, 25650 Montbenoit.
Tel: 81.38.14.65
Closed November 1–15 and Monday
Dbl rm F230
On D437, Montbenoit 4km

Situated in the upper reaches of the Doubs valley, this
wooden chalet-style restaurant has the sort of Alpine views
associated with Austria. Five tables in the rustic dining-room
have river views, and specialities include locally smoked ham
and beef, and trout cooked in Arbois wine. There are six
simply furnished but very cosy bedrooms; all have en-suite
bathrooms. Last orders: lunch 2pm; dinner 9pm. Set menus
from F55; à la carte around F100.
Riverside walks, fishing (permit F25 a day)

MONTIGNY-SUR-LOING

🏨 🍽 <u>12/12</u> 🛏 £

Le Vanne Rouge, 77690 Montigny-sur-Loing.
Tel: 1.64.45.82.10
Closed mid-January–February 20; restaurant closed
Sunday evening (October–April) and Monday
Dbl rm F220–F250

This half-timbered hotel, located on the banks of the river
Loing in the heart of a picturesque village, looks out over a
very attractive stretch of river and an islet. The bedrooms are
decorated in a traditional French style with flock wallpaper
and dark wooden furniture and all have en-suite bathrooms.
Its restaurant is popular with the locals and, in summer, meals
are served on the waterside terrace, which is shaded by trees.
Last orders: lunch 2pm; dinner 9.30pm. Set menus from F85;
à la carte around F220.
Canoes for hire, pretty riverside walks

MONTMERLE-SUR-SAONE

🏨 🍽 <u>8/21</u> 🛏 ££

Hôtel du Rivage, 12 Rue du Pont, 01090
Montmerle-sur-Saône.   Tel: 74.69.33.92
Hotel and restaurant closed November 15–December 15
and Monday night except June 15–September 20
Dbl rm F250–F350
A6 exit Belleville 4km

Situated on the banks of the river Saone beside a bridge, eight
of the bedrooms, prettily decorated with Laura Ashley-style
fabrics, look out over the river. In summer, meals and drinks
are served on a lovely lamp-lit terrace set above the water
with room for 120 diners. *Petite friture* (small Saone fish fried
in oil), eels and frog's legs are some of the delicacies on the
reasonably priced menus. Last orders: lunch 2pm; dinner
9pm. Set menus from F85; à la carte around F200.

MONTMORT-LUCY

⌂ ⁍◎⁍ 17/17 ▭ £££

Château d'Etoges, Etoges, 51270 Montmort-Lucy.
Tel: 26.59.30.08
Closed February 1–15
Dbl rm F450–F900

This handsome 17th-century chateau, surrounded by a wide
moat, has been completely renovated by its charming owner,
Anne Filliette-Neuville, who grew up here. Several of the
bedrooms are extremely spacious and retain all their original
woodwork, high ceilings, and period furniture. There are
eight tables in the elegant restaurant, which specializes in
traditional regional cooking, but they have no views of the
moat. An enchanting base for exploring Champagne's vineyards. Last orders: lunch 2pm; dinner 9.30pm. Set menus
from F160; no à la carte.
Walks in 50-acre grounds, many ponds for fishing on property

MORET-SUR-LOING

⌂ ⁍◎⁍ 12/20 ▭ ££

Auberge de la Terrasse, 40 Rue de la Pecherie, 77250
Moret-sur-Loing.   Tel: 1.60.70.51.03
Hotel open all year; restaurant closed Sunday evening
and Monday
Dbl rm F250–F355

This captivating medieval town, where artist Alfred Sisley
spent his last years, provides a scenic backdrop to this waterside inn. Most of the bedrooms have recently been redecorated, but only eight have en-suite bathrooms. Water-view
rooms look out over the river Loing, which flows immediately below. Half the restaurant's tables have good river views
and at weekends drinks are served on the waterside terrace
below. Last orders: lunch 2pm; dinner 9pm. Set menus from
F95 (weekdays), F140 (weekends); à la carte around F200.

*Son-et-lumière performances in Moret on Saturdays from late June—
end August*

MOUTHIER-HAUT-PIERRE

🏠 🍴 <u>23/23</u> 🛏 ££

La Cascade, 25920 Mouthier-Haut-Pierre.
Tel: 81.60.95.30
Closed Nov 15–February 15
Dbl rm F235–F295

Perched like an eagle's eyrie high on a cliff, this hotel is close
to the source of the river Loue. Its bird's-eye view over the
river valley, thick with conifers, is among the most dramatic
in the Jura. The bedrooms are comfortably furnished and
most have balconies with river views, where breakfast can be
served. Window tables in the restaurant also look out over
the Loue. French regional cooking: trout with wild mushrooms in *vin jaune*, the local wine, is a particular speciality.
Last orders: lunch 1.45pm; dinner 9pm. Set menus from
F100; à la carte around F150.
*Trout fishing (day permit F35), canoes and kayaks for hire,
impressive gorges at Nouailles*

LA MULATIERE

🍴 🛏 ££££

La Mère Guy, 35 Quai Jean Jacques Rousseau, 69350
La Mulatière.   Tel: 78.51.65.37
Closed August; Sunday evening and Monday

This quayside restaurant, by the Pont de la Mulatière just
south of Lyon, was a river fishermen's auberge back in the
18th century. Now it is one of the city's most elegant establishments, with magnificent views of the confluence of the
Rhone and the Saone, both from window tables in the
dining-room and from the riverside dining terrace. Roger
Roucou's cooking is widely praised, and his relatively

inexpensive business lunch menu is served with the same panache as his more elaborate creations. Last orders: lunch 1.30pm; dinner 9pm. Set menus from F250 (lunch with wine), F250 (dinner); à la carte around F350.

NANTUA

▥ ⏁◯ <u>27/50</u> ▭ ££

Hôtel de l'Embarcadère, Avenue du Lac, 01130 Nantua.
Tel: 74.75.22.88
Closed December 20–January 20, first week of May;
restaurant closed Monday
Dbl rm F230–F310

On the outskirts of Nantua, the hotel's functional exterior belies the comfort of the bedrooms and elegant simplicity of the first-floor restaurant. Bedrooms are bright and spacious; half of them overlook the lake and sailing boats moored at pontoons beside the hotel. The restaurant has good lake views through its picture windows and is popular with locals. Traditional French cooking. Last orders: lunch 1.45pm; dinner 9pm. Set menus from F105 (children's menu F50); à la carte around F200.
Lake swimming, sail-boards and canoes for hire

LA NAPOULE

⏁◯ ▭ £££

Brocherie II, Port La Napoule, La Napoule, 06210 Mandelieu.   Tel: 93.49.80.73
Closed January and Monday evening and Tuesday
October–May

The plain exterior belies the warm welcome found at this harbourside restaurant which overlooks La Napoule's marina. Although it sits firmly on dry land, its design conveys the impression of dining on a houseboat, with two flaming torches marking its gangplank entrance. In fine weather, meals are also served on a large terrace which has splendid views over the ranks of smart yachts and the sea beyond. Menus focus on seafood and there is a shallow pool stocked with lobsters for the table, who like to line up unnervingly on its sides. Last orders: lunch 2.30pm; dinner 11pm. Set menus are available from F180; à la carte around F250.

NEVERS

🏨 🍴 32/60 💳 ££

Hôtel Loire, Quai de Médine, 58000 Nevers.
Tel: 86.61.50.92
Open all year; restaurant closed December 15–January 15
Dbl rm F395

This modern hotel stands on stilts just feet from the Loire. It has magnificent views over the river, which is crossed by an old sandstone bridge. The bridge is far enough away for traffic noise to be hushed. Bedrooms are comfortably furnished, and most dining-room tables have expansive river views. Traditional French cooking, using fresh market produce. Last orders: lunch 1.30pm; dinner 9.30pm. Set menus from F120; à la carte around F200.
Canoes for hire; swimming pool opposite hotel

NICE

🏨 38/65 💳 ££££

La Pérouse, 11 Quai Rauba-Capeu, 06300 Nice.
Tel: 93.62.34.63
Open all year; grill open May 1–September 30
Dbl rm F875–F1250

Finding a peaceful and secluded hotel can be a problem in the busy port of Nice, but La Pérouse, which sits beneath the chateau at the end of the Baie des Anges, is an exception. Set in terraced gardens planted with lemon trees and aloes, it provides both a tranquil retreat and a panoramic view of the

Nice waterfront. Bedrooms and apartments are luxuriously appointed. All sea-view rooms have private terraces or balconies. There is also an attractive swimming-pool terrace and, in summer, an open-air grill is set up in the gardens.

Sights of old Nice; on Cimiez hill Marc Chagall and Matisse museums, Franciscan monastery and Roman baths; Nice Carnival before Lent; Jazz Festival and Festival of Folk Traditions in July; boat trips along coastline

NICE

IOI ▭ ££

Ruhl Plage, Promenade des Anglais, 06000 Nice.
Tel: 93.87.09.70
Closed October 30–December 15 and Monday
December–March
Opposite Hotel Meridien

Ruhl Plage is reputed to be the best beach-restaurant in Nice. Customers can eat on the terrace under blue and white striped umbrellas or on the sun-loungers which can be hired for F55 a day. Menus are varied and surprisingly reasonably priced. A popular choice is *salade Nicoise*, a combination of tuna, tomatoes, haricot beans, olives and hard-boiled eggs. Menus change daily according to what is available in the market. Open until 7pm; only salads and cold meals served after 5pm; à la carte around F100–F150.

Shallow pool for children; sail-boards, jet-skis and pedalos for hire

NICE

IOI ▭ £££

Chez les Pecheurs, 18 Quai des Docks, 06300 Nice.
Tel: 93.89.59.61
Closed November 1–mid-December; Wednesday all year;
Tuesday evening in winter; Thursday lunch in summer

This quayside restaurant has unobstructed views of the colourful harbour, busy with fishermen unloading their catch. Ten inside tables have water views and there is a pavement terrace for meals in fine weather. Popular with locals and visitors alike, it serves fish and seafood only, with specialities including *bouillabaisse* and *bourride*. Last orders: lunch 2pm; dinner 10pm. Lunch set menu F170; à la carte around F270.

NICE

IOI ▭ ££

Beau Rivage, Quai des Etats-Unis, 06300 Nice.
Tel: 93.80.75.06
Open mid-April– mid-September

This beach-restaurant has an enclosed dining-room as well as a terrace. It enjoys a good reputation locally and offers a varied menu including fish, fresh pasta, hamburgers and low-calorie meals, as well as the chef's dishes of the day which are based on fresh market produce. In high season, there is live music in the evenings. Open 9am–6pm for snacks and ice-creams. Sun-loungers F70 a day. Last orders: lunch 2.30pm; dinner 10.30pm. Dinner set menu F160; à la carte around F150.
Children's play area; sail-boards, jet-skis and pedalos for hire

ORCHAMPS-VENNES

▥ IOI 10/10 ▭ £

Hôtel de la Source, Cirque de Consolation, 25390
Orchamps-Vennes.   Tel: 81.43.55.38
Closed January and February
Dbl rm F130–F200

Few places in the Jura mountains offer better water views than this small hotel and restaurant on the Cirque de Consolation, high in the Dessoubre valley. Bedrooms and dining-room look out over a waterfall as it thunders into the valley to join the river Dessoubre. Good regional cooking, including

freshwater fish and ham smoked on the premises, and an English translation of the menu. Bedrooms are basic, only two with en-suite bathrooms. There is a terrace for drinks and snacks, served all day. Last orders: lunch 2pm; dinner 10pm. Set menus from F80; à la carte around F110.
Fishing (day permits F310); beautiful walks down valley to 17th-century Notre Dame Abbey

ORGEVAL

🏚 🍽 8/14 ▭ £££

Moulin d'Orgeval, Rue de l'Abbaye, 78630 Orgeval.
Tel: 1.39.75.85.74
Open all year; restaurant closed December 20–30
Dbl rm F720

This extremely comfortable hotel has an enchanting water-side setting in beautifully landscaped grounds. The spacious, fashionably furnished bedrooms look out over a stream that flows through an ornamental lake complete with islands reached by small bridges. Second-floor rooms enjoy the best water views. There are similarly good views from the dining-room and its canopied, waterside terrace. Traditional regional dishes using only fresh seasonal market produce. Last orders: lunch 3.30pm; dinner 10.30pm. Set menus from F195 (weekday lunch), F230 (dinner); à la carte around F250.
Heated outdoor pool, fishing (no permit needed); riding 2km, two golf courses 3km; good base for visiting Versailles and Giverny

ORNANS

🏚 🍽 9/31 ▭ ££

Hôtel de France, 51–53 Rue Pierre Vernier, 25290 Ornans.   Tel: 81.62.24.44
Closed December 21–February 1; restaurant closed Saturday and Sunday November 1–April 1
Dbl rm F350

Gustave Courbet's home town is like something from a medieval canvas, with old houses overhanging the swift-flowing river Loue, which is framed by towering limestone cliffs. Within sight of the river and a 17th-century bridge, but separated from it by the main road through town, this old coaching inn provides simple, comfortable accommodation, although river views are limited. The regional cooking is refreshingly innovative and includes a trout soufflé and pigeon with wild mushrooms. However, the ground-floor dining-room has no view of the river. Last orders: lunch 2pm; dinner 9pm. Set menus from F130; à la carte around F200.

Excellent fly-fishing and guests can use owner's private stretch of water 8km away for F80 a day; canoes and kayaks for hire nearby

PARIS

🏨 15/20 💳 ££

Hôtel du Palais, 2 Quai de la Mégisserie,
Place du Chatelet, 75001 Paris.   Tel: 1.42.36.98.25
Open all year
Dbl rm F280–F380

This 1930s hotel stands in the heart of Paris and looks across the Seine towards the Conciergerie and Notre-Dame Cathedral on the Ile de la Cité. A scruffy narrow staircase leads up to the hotel, but three of the four floors have recently been renovated. Rooms are simply but attractively furnished with beautiful old gilt mirrors and comfortable new beds. Most rooms have shower cabins, but five have no en-suite bathrooms. Room Six has the best views of the river. No restaurant.

PARIS

🏨 28/33 💳 £££

Hôtel du Quai Voltaire, 19 Quai Voltaire, 75007 Paris.
Tel: 1.42.61.50.91

Open all year
Dbl rm F520–F690

Just along from the Musée d'Orsay, this hotel looks out across
the Seine to the Louvre on the opposite bank. In the past,
guests have included Baudelaire, Richard Wagner and Oscar
Wilde. Now it is popular with French visitors. Bedrooms are
spacious and comfortable, all with en-suite bathrooms,
although the hotel would benefit from a facelift. The dou-
ble-glazing cuts down traffic noise, but do not expect this to
be a quiet location. The best river views are from bedrooms
on the second floor and above.

PARIS

🏠 12/18 🛏 ££

Les Rives de Notre Dame, 15 Quai St-Michel,
75005 Paris.   Tel:1.43.54.81.16
Open all year
Dbl rm F415

Occupying a 16th-century house on the edge of the Latin
quarter, this hotel should have been renovated over the
winter and prices may go up. Currently bedrooms are on
the small side, most with exposed beams, but are clean and
comfortable. All double rooms have tiny bathrooms and
double beds; there are also six single rooms with shower
cabins. Rooms with water views look out over the *bouqui-
nistes* stalls, Ile de la Cité and Notre Dame across the river.
Those on the top floor among the eaves have splendid views
over the roof-tops as far as the Louvre further along the
Seine.

PARIS

🍽 🛏 ££

Clap 49, 49 Quai de Seine, 75019 Paris.
Tel: 1.42.09.01.70

Closed Saturday lunch and Sunday evening all year;
Sunday lunch October–April

This modern restaurant decorated in pale pinks and soft greys
has a cinematic theme, with photographs of film shoots on
the walls. Window tables in the upstairs dining-room, which
serves imaginative and freshly-prepared classic dishes, have
views of the barges in the Bassin de la Villette. On the ground
floor there is a smart brasserie–bar with a pavement terrace.
Brasserie open noon–11pm. Restaurant last orders: lunch
2.30pm; dinner 10.30pm. Set menus from F59 (lunch),
F78 (dinner); à la carte around F220.

PARIS

○| ⊟ £

La Mégisserie, 20 Quai de la Mégisserie, 75001 Paris.
Tel: 1.42.21.03.89
Open all year

Just along from the Louvre, this first-floor tea room has a glass
wall to make the most of its views over the Seine. A genteel
and relaxing ambience pervades it and service is friendly and
attentive, something which is increasingly rare at establishments in this heavily touristed zone. Imaginative salads and
savoury tarts, duck cassoulet and lasagne feature on the menu,
as well as an impressive range of puddings, ice-cream sundaes,
tarts and gateaux. Open 9.30am–7pm.

PARIS

○| ⊟ ££

Le Petit Poucet, 4 Rond-Point Claude Monet,
Ile de la Jatte, 92300 Levallois.   Tel: 1.47.38.61.85
Open all year

This authentic and completely renovated open-air Renoir-
esque dance-hall and café sits beside the Seine at the end of

the Ile de la Jatte. Built of wood, with large windows which make the most of its views of barges plying the river and the smart suburb of Neuilly across the water. The dining-room is prettily arranged and full of light and greenery. In fine weather, meals are served on a splendid open–air verandah. Traditional French dishes with the emphasis on fish and exotic salads. Last orders: lunch 2.30pm; dinner 11pm. Set menus are available from F110; à la carte around F230.

PARIS

IOI 🍽 £££

Les Pieds dans l'Eau, 39 Boulevard du Parc,
Ile de la Jatte, 92200 Neuilly.   Tel: 1.47.47.64.07
Open all year; closed Saturday lunch and Sunday

As its name suggests, this restaurant sits right on the water's edge overlooking luxurious houseboats moored alongside the Ile de la Jatte. It has an appealing interior – stone floor, antique fireplace and low ceilings – where traditional French dishes, especially fish, are served. Five inside tables have views of the Seine, and meals are also served on a terrace in summer. Last orders: lunch 2pm; dinner 10pm. No set menus; à la carte around F300.

PARIS

IOI 🍽 ££££

La Tour d'Argent, 15–17 Quai de la Tournelle,
75005 Paris.   Tel: 1.43.54.23.31
Open all year; closed Monday

This highly acclaimed restaurant has panoramic views of the Seine, where it branches to flow around the Ile de la Cité, as well as fabulous views over the roof-tops to either Sacré Coeur or the Arc de Triomphe, depending on where you are seated. An old copper lift takes guests up to the panelled dining-room which serves some of the best food in Paris. It also has the most famous wine cellar in France, which customers can visit by arrangement. There are 14 window tables; reservations should be made a day or so in advance for lunch and weekday evenings, but 2–3 weeks ahead for weekends. Last orders: lunch 2pm; dinner 10pm. Set lunch menu from F375; à la carte around F900.

PARIS

IOI ⊟ ££££

Le Vieux Galion, 10 Allée du Bord de l'Eau, 75016 Paris.
Tel: 1.42.24.14.00
Open all year

This mock galleon dating from the 1920s floats on the Seine next to the Bois de Boulogne and provides an unusual and very attractive setting for lunch or dinner. Decorated with fishing and nautical paraphernalia, it serves traditional French cooking with the emphasis on fish. Attached to the galleon is another boat on which, suspended above the water, is a dining terrace, open in fine weather. All tables have river views. Last orders: lunch 3pm; dinner 10.30pm. No set menus; à la carte around F300–F500.

LES PILLES

IOI ³⁄₉ ⊟ £

Auberge de L'Aygues, Les Pilles, 26110 Nyons.
Tel: 75.27.72.97
Closed January and Monday
Dbl rm F170–F230

This simple inn offers a slice of rural life in Provence. The restaurant and bar are popular with locals, so tourists are somewhat incidental and expected to make themselves at home. Menus, based on Provençal specialities, are limited but perfectly adequate for lunch or dinner while touring. There is an outdoor terrace for drinks overlooking the river

Aygues. Last orders: lunch 2.30pm; dinner 9.30pm. Set menus from F60; à la carte around F100.

PLOMBIERES-LES-DIJON

⦿ ▭ ££

Le Cygne, Lac Kir, 21370 Plombières-lès-Dijon.
Tel: 80.41.02.40
Closed Sunday evening and Monday October–March

Just outside Dijon, this new conservatory-style restaurant sits on the shores of Lake Kir. Imaginatively designed to make the most of its lakeside location, there is space for 300 diners inside its glass walls, and another 200 on the outdoor terrace. Innovative classical French cooking. In the evenings, there are jazz or blues concerts giving it a lively, up-beat atmosphere. Open 9am–1am for drinks; short brasserie menu served 11am–11pm. Last orders for full meals: lunch 1.45pm; dinner 10.30pm. Set menus from F70; à la carte around F160.
Pedalos, canoes, kayaks and sail-boards for hire on lake

POISSY

⦿ ▭ £££

L'Esturgeon, 6 Cour 14 Juillet, 78300 Poissy.
Tel: 1.39.65.00.04
Closed August and Thursday

Facing a picturesque group of islands in the river Seine, this waterside restaurant used to be a favourite meeting place for Impressionist artists including Monet, Matisse and Renoir. The airy conservatory-style dining-room is built around three old trees and looks straight on to the river so most diners enjoy good river views. It is a beautiful spot for dinner in mid-summer when the sun sets directly between two islands. Traditional French cooking. Last orders: lunch 2pm; dinner 9.30pm. No set menus; à la carte around F270.

POLIGNY

🏨 🍴 10/10 🛏 ££

Domaine Vallée Heureuse, Route de Genève, 39800
Poligny.   Tel: 84.37.12.13
Open all year; restaurant closed Wednesday and Thursday
lunch except during school holidays
Dbl rm F450

A stream thunders past this neat, cream building with its
refreshingly bright interiors, reflecting the good taste of its
owners, Bill and Danièle Lombard. Bedrooms are airy and
comfortable, decorated with original paintings by Madame
Lombard who is also the chef. There are two dining-rooms
serving light versions of traditional Jura dishes. Try the *palette
du peintre gourmand*, a selection of ten puddings. In summer,
there are two outdoor dining terraces overlooking the stream
where simple grilled fare is also available for lunch and dinner
with *plats du jour* costing F48. Last orders: lunch 2pm; dinner
9.30pm. Set menus from F120; à la carte around F270.
*Heated swimming pool and sauna, trout fishing (permits F100 a
week); nearby tennis courts and two golf courses*

ILE DE PORQUEROLLES

🏨 🍴 12/60 🛏 ££££

Le Mas du Langoustier, Ile de Porquerolles, 83400 Hyères.
Tel: 94.58.30.09
Open May 1–November 1
Half-board F687–F1115 per person (May and October);
full-board only June–September F975-F1425 per person
Ferry from La Tour Fondue, Giens or Le Lavandou

The Ile de Porquerolles is a conservation area, its Mediterranean vegetation and marine life protected by the govern-
ment, so this pleasant Provençal-style hotel is situated in an
especially idyllic and tranquil location. Madame Richard,
whose family once owned the island, prides herself on
setting high standards of service and food. Guests either fly

in by helicopter, or are collected from the ferry by one of the few vehicles permitted on the island. In fine weather, meals are served on a terrace shaded by olive trees which looks over a sandy cove. The restaurant, which has won several culinary accolades, is open to non-residents for lunch and dinner. Last orders: lunch 2pm; dinner 9.30pm. Set menus from F330; à la carte around F420.

Hotel arranges scuba-diving, bicycle and sail-board hire; two tennis courts

PORT-GRIMAUD

🏨 🍽 **48/48** 🚪 ££££

Hôtel Giraglia, Place du 14 Juin, Port-Grimaud, 83310 Cogolin.   Tel: 94.56.31.33
Open Easter–October 10
Dbl rm F950–F2310

This smart hotel overlooks the Gulf of St-Tropez and the canals of Port Grimaud, a replica of a Provençal fishing village which was built in the late 1960s. Bedrooms are pleasantly decorated in different styles, most with recently renovated balconies looking out either over the brightly painted fish-ermen's houses that line a canal or the beach and sea. Its restaurant, L'Amphitrite, serves modern interpretations of classic French and Provençal dishes. Meals are also served on the beachside terrace which contains a large new swim-ming pool. Last orders: lunch 2pm; dinner 10pm. Set menus from F195; à la carte around F350.

Private sandy beach with sun-loungers, sail-boards and catamarans for hire, boat trips around Port-Grimaud's canals; tennis courts nearby

RAMATUELLE

🍽 🚪 ££££

Chez Camille, Plage de Bonne Terrasse, 83350 Ramatuelle.   Tel: 94.79.80.38

Open April 1–September 30; closed Tuesday except
during July and August

Booking is essential at this lively restaurant, set in a small bay
near Pampelonne beach. The decor is simple but chic,
brightened with large arrangements of fresh flowers. All
tables look out over the pretty bay and, in fine weather,
meals are also served on the beachside terrace. Fish dominates the menus: *bouillabaisse* and grilled spiny lobster are
popular choices. Last orders: lunch 2pm; dinner 9.30pm.
Set menus from F200–F440; no à la carte.
Swimming from rocks, deckchairs for clients on beach

RAMATUELLE

IOI ▭ ££

Nioulargo, Plage de Pampelonne, 83350 Ramatuelle.
Tel: 94.79.82.14
Open April 1–October 10
Signposted from D93

This beach-restaurant and bar is a cut above the others on
Pampelonne beach. Popular with trendsetters from St-Tropez, its simple wooden tables are decorated with fresh flowers
and, in the evenings, subtle lighting and soft music create a
convivial ambience. It comprises two restaurants under the
same ownership: one serving French food, especially salads
and grills, is open at lunchtimes only; the other concentrates
on south-east Asian food and is open for dinner between June
20–August 31, otherwise lunch only. Last orders: lunch 4pm;
dinner 11pm. No set menus; à la carte around F150. In the
high season, there is also a snack bar for drinks and sandwiches on the beach. Sun-loungers are available for hire at
around F60 a day; parasols F30.
*Large sandy beach, watersports equipment for hire but no jet-skis
allowed*

REHAINVILLER

🏨 🍴 8/8 🛏 £££

Château d'Adomenil, Rehainviller, 54300 Lunéville.
Tel: 83.74.04.81
Closed February; restaurant closed Monday and Tuesday
lunch also Sunday evening November 1–April 5
Dbl rm F400–F800
Nancy 25 minutes drive

This elegant manor stands in landscaped grounds bordered by
the river Meurthe. Imaginatively converted, it is reminiscent
of an English country house hotel. Bedrooms are tastefully
decorated in different styles and furnished with choice
antique pieces. All overlook a large pond, as do the window
tables in the dining-room with its fine beamed ceiling and
parquet floor. Gourmet French cooking with the emphasis
on fish and specialities such as a salad of frogs' legs and plum
soufflé. Last orders: lunch 1.30pm; dinner 9.30pm. Set
menus are available from F200; à la carte around F350.
Fishing in pond; forest walks

REVIN

🏨 🍴 14/20 🛏 £

Le Francois I, Quai Camille des Moulins, 08500 Revin.
Tel: 24.40.15.88
Open all year; restaurant closed Saturday and Sunday
November–March
Dbl rm F200

The road from Givet to Charleville-Meziers runs behind this
pleasant town hotel which is separated from the river Meuse
by the promenade and car park below. Bedrooms are small
but comfortably furnished with French windows opening on
to small wrought-iron balconies. Most have pleasing views of
the river flowing through a forested ravine. The restaurant

has similar views, through large windows, and serves local
game including venison, boar and pheasant. Last orders:
lunch 2.30pm; dinner 9.30pm. Set menus from F60; à la
carte around F200.
Boat trips along the Meuse into Belgium

RIGNY

🏨 🍽 13/24 🛏 ££

Château de Rigny, Route de la Vallée de la Saône,
Rigny, 70100 Gray.   Tel: 84.65.25.01
Closed January 5–30
Dbl rm F495
Originally a 13th-century castle, Rigny was rebuilt in its
present style during the reign of Louis XIII and has retained
its historic character. A perfect place to relax for a few days,
the river Saone flows through the bottom of the garden and a
lily-pond adds to the watery view. Both the public rooms and
bedrooms are furnished with antiques and in room No.6
there is an elegant Chinese four-poster bed which was
brought to Europe by a French general at the end of the
First World War. The restaurant serves good regional cooking and eight tables have water views. Last orders: lunch 2pm;
dinner 9pm. Set menus from F100 (weekday lunch), F180
(dinner); à la carte around F250.
*Heated outdoor swimming pool, tennis court, bicycles, fishing in
pond and river (permit F20 a day), pretty riverside walks*

LES ROCHES-DE-CONDRIEU

🏨 🍽 11/18 🛏 ££

Hôtel Bellevue, 38370 Les Roches-de-Condrieu.
Tel: 74.56.41.42
Closed February and August 4–14; restaurant closed
Monday all year, Sunday evening October–March
and Tuesday lunch April–September
Dbl rm F190–F290

This ivy-covered hotel overlooks a yacht marina on the river Rhone. Three of the nicely decorated waterside rooms have small balconies with good views across this wide stretch of the Rhone to Condrieu on the far side. The restaurant's decor is typically French with dark wooden furniture, crisp white linen and, in winter, a roaring log fire. There are lovely river views from tables on the enclosed extension which overhangs the water. Traditional French cooking. Last orders: lunch 2pm; dinner 9pm. Set menus from F105; à la carte around F200.

Canoes, sailing boats and windsurfers are available for hire at nautical centre; Gallo-Roman city of Vienne and Mont Pilat regional park nearby

ROQUEBRUNE-CAP-MARTIN

IOI ▭ £££

Sporting du Cap, 48 Avenue Winston Churchill, Roquebrune-Cap-Martin.   Tel: 93.35.63.07
Open all year; closed Sunday evening November 1–March 31

The coast road runs behind this appealing restaurant which is feet from the sea on Cap-Martin. Both inside tables and its tree-shaded terrace have splendid views of the coast around Menton. Its imaginative menus offer a wide choice of dishes including Italian favourites such as carpaccio and langoustine ravioli. Last orders: lunch 2pm; dinner 10pm. Set menus from F170; à la carte around F280.
Swimming from rocks below restaurant

RUOMS

IOI ▭ ££

Les Terrasses de l'Ardèche, Rue des Brasseries, 07120 Ruoms.   Tel: 75.39.74.34

Closed November 30–March 1, Tuesday evening and Wednesday except June–August

This convivial restaurant, very professionally run by Pierre and Mireille Magne, is a good lunch stop before tackling the spectacular Ardèche Gorges. In summer, meals are served on a large semi-circular terrace which seats 150 and has magnificent views of the river Ardèche as it falls over a weir and enters a narrow craggy gorge. Menus feature traditional French dishes with the emphasis on fish. None of the inside tables has a water view. Open all day from Easter to the end of September for drinks and ice-creams. Last orders: lunch 2.30pm; dinner 10pm. Set menus from F85 (children F65); à la carte around F200.

Fishing (day permits); canoes and kayaks for hire nearby; shingle beach for river swimming below restaurant; riding 1km

ST-GERVAIS-EN-VALLIERE

🏨 🍽 10/22 ⊟ £££

Moulin de Hauterive, Hameau de Chaublanc, St-Gervais-en-Vallière, 71350 Verdun-sur-les-Doubs.
Tel: 85.91.55.56
Closed December 22–January 31
Dbl rm F550–F850

This is one of seven large stone mills built by Cistercian monks along the river Dheune. Tastefully converted into a characterful hotel, bedrooms are comfortably furnished and have exposed beams. The mill-stream splits here to form a small island on which dining tables are set out during the summer, making it a popular venue for a romantic candle-lit dinner. There are also good views of the stream from eight inside tables. Traditional Burgundian cooking. Last orders: lunch 2pm; dinner 9pm. Set menus are available from F150 (lunch), F240 dinner; à la carte around F350.

Small heated swimming pool, fishing (no permit needed), tennis court, sauna, Jacuzzi and solarium; golf 7km

ST-HIPPOLYTE

🏨 ⋈ <u>12/15</u> ⊟ £

Le Bellevue, Route de Maiche, 25190 St-Hippolyte.
Tel: 81.96.51.53
Closed February 15–22, November 1–8; restaurant closed
Friday evening and Saturday lunch October–March
Dbl rm F200–F250

Aptly named, this hotel sits high on a ridge above St-Hippolyte, founded by the Romans, where the rivers Doubs and Dessoubre meet. Bedrooms are modern and bright, most with good views of the wooded valley below. It has a distinguished restaurant serving locally cured ham, fresh trout and carp. Last orders: lunch 1.30pm; dinner 9pm. Set menus are available from F78; à la carte around F180.
Free fishing permits for guests on half-board, river swimming in the Doubs

ST-JEAN-CAP-FERRAT

🏨 ⋈ <u>38/59</u> ⊟ ££££

Hôtel Bel Air du Cap Ferrat, Boulevard Général-de-Gaulle,
06290 St-Jean-Cap-Ferrat.   Tel: 93.76.50.50
Closed January
Dbl rm F950–F2000

Set on the tip of a peninsula and surrounded by a 14-acre semi-tropical garden, this palatial hotel has magnificent views of the coastline in both directions. Bedrooms are handsomely furnished with marble bathrooms; most with French windows opening on to small wrought-iron balconies. It has one of the largest and most beautiful pools on the Riviera, reached by a funicular. Built into the rocky foreshore it creates the illusion of dropping straight into the sea. On its terrace, the Club Dauphin restaurant, open 9am–7pm, serves buffet lunches, drinks and snacks under a white canopy. In the main building, Le Cap serves innovative French *haute cuisine*. In fine weather, meals are served on a pine-shaded terrace overlooking the sea. Last orders: lunch 2.30pm; dinner 10.30pm. Set menus from F260 (lunch), F400 (dinner); à la carte around F500.

Sea swimming from rocks, coastal footpath around Cap Ferrat, tennis courts, bicycles, 18-hole golf course nearby

ST-JEAN-CAP-FERRAT

🏨 🍴 **33/45** 🛏 ££££

La Voile d'Or, Port de St-Jean, 06230 St-Jean-Cap-Ferrat.
Tel: 93.01.13.13
Open early March–end October
Dbl rm F1250–F3100

This luxury hotel looks out over St-Jean-Cap-Ferrat's port, where brightly painted fishing boats jostle for berths with sleek white yachts. It combines intimacy with elegance, and rooms are filled with fine antiques. There are two swimming pools: one on a terrace set above the quay; the other on a private rocky beach. The light, airy dining room opens out to a garden terrace, and all the tables have picturesque views of the harbour. The cooking, which is a combination of classical French and regional dishes, has a good reputation. Last orders: lunch 2.30pm; dinner 10pm. Set menus from F350; à la carte around F500.

Swimming from rocks; watersports and sailing trips arranged by hotel

ST-JEAN-CAP-FERRAT

🏨 **20/20** 🛏 ££

Le Panoramic, 3 Avenue Albert I, 06230
St-Jean-Cap-Ferrat.   Tel: 93.76.00.37
Closed November 5–December 20
Dbl rm F495–F635

There are few moderately priced hotels with decent sea views in this exclusive corner of the Riviera, but Le Panoramic is one of them. Situated on a ridge above the port, it has splendid views of the verdant rocky coastline. Bedrooms are simply furnished and all face east, perfect for breakfast on the balcony as the sun rises. The hotel stands in a pretty garden and has the advantage of private parking. There is no restaurant but plenty of choice a short walk away.
Beaches and watersports a 5-minute walk; boat trips around coast from port

ST-JEAN-CAP-FERRAT

IOI ▭ ₤₤₤

Le Sloop, Port de Plaisance, 06230 St-Jean–Cap-Ferrat.
Tel: 93.01.48.63
Closed November 15–December 20, Wednesday
October–May, Wednesday lunch and Thursday lunch
June–September

Reputedly one of the best restaurants around the yacht marina, Le Sloop has a large waterside terrace. Popular with celebrities, especially from the music world, it specializes in fish. Traditional Provençal dishes, with good use made of fresh herbs, dominate the menus but there is also an interesting selection of Italian dishes such as crab and ricotta cannelloni. Puddings are delicious, often specially prepared to order, such as *gratin de pommes au marc de Provence*. Last orders: lunch 2pm; dinner 10.30pm. Set menus are available from F155; à la carte around F300. Reservations are essential.

ST-JEAN-CAP-FERRAT

IOI ▭ ₤₤

Le Vivaldi, Port de Plaisance, 06230 St-Jean–Cap-Ferrat.
Tel: 93.76.01.01
Closed November and Monday out of season

This cheerful informal restaurant can be found in a garden beside the marina and yachts are moored just a few feet away from its canopied terrace. The cooking is authentically Italian with freshly-made pasta in delicious sauces. Service is friendly and attentive. Last orders: lunch 2.30pm; dinner 11pm. Set menus are available from F135; à la carte around F190.

ST-JEAN-CAP-FERRAT

IOI ▭ ££££

Le Provençal, 2 Avenue Denis Séméria, 06230
St-Jean-Cap-Ferrat.   Tel: 93.76.03.97
Closed February, Sunday evening and Monday
October–Easter

Situated on a hillside above the port, this restaurant has a good local reputation. The elegant dining-room is decorated with trompe-l'oeil stencils and all the tables have sea views. In fine weather, meals are also served on a terrace, which has similarly good views of the coast and is protected from the road by a screen of flowering plants. Refined versions of classic French fish dishes such as St Pierre in fig leaves and lobster casserole. Last orders: lunch 3pm; dinner 11pm. Set menus from F350; à la carte around F600.

ST-MARTIN-BELLE-ROCHE

IOI ▭ ££

Port St-Nicholas, 71118 St-Martin-Belle-Roche.
Tel: 85.36.00.86
Closed January, Tuesday evening and Wednesday

Situated on a peaceful stretch of the river Saone, this restaurant has a great deal of charm. It serves good regional cooking including its speciality *les fritures de la Saône*, deep-fried river fish. Nearly all the tables have views of a lovely stretch of the

river, and there is a large waterside dining terrace which is open for meals during the summer months. Last orders: lunch 2.15pm; dinner 9.15pm. Set menus are on offer from F95; à la carte around F180.
River swimming

ST-PIERRE-DE-CHARTREUSE

▥ ⑪ 7/9 ▭ £

Hôtel du Guiers, St-Pierre-de-Chartreuse, 38380 St-Laurent-du-Pont.   Tel: 76.88.60.85
Closed weekdays November 16–December 25
Dbl rm F180–F200

The road to St-Pierre passes through the Gorge du Guiers Mort, affording beautiful vistas of pine forests clinging to the precipitous rockfaces. This characterful stone hotel offers good value for money. Visitors are warmly welcomed by the Scandolera family for whom nothing is too much trouble. Arrangements can even be made to pick guests up from the airport or station in Grenoble. Bedrooms are prettily decorated and all have en-suite bathrooms. Most look out over the river as it tumbles through the gorge. All the restaurant's tables have good water views and, in summer, meals and drinks are served on a waterside terrace below. Traditional regional cooking. Last orders: lunch is served all afternoon; dinner 10pm. Set menus from F85; à la carte around F200.
Fishing; riding and tennis nearby; marked walking paths; cross-country skiing in winter

ST-TROPEZ

▥ ⑪ 31/41 ▭ ££££

Résidence de la Pinède, Plage de la Bouillabaisse, 83990 St-Tropez.   Tel: 94.97.04.21
Open March 1–end October
Dbl rm F1300–F2500

This exclusive retreat stands in pine-shaded grounds and has a splendid view of St-Tropez across the bay. Bedrooms are handsomely decorated, most with spacious and well-equipped bathrooms. At the beginning and end of the season some of the smaller rooms are offered for just F750 a night. There is a pleasant terrace with a pool beside the hotel's private sandy beach. All the restaurant's tables have bay views. The menu offers a wide variety of traditional and regional dishes which have earned it critical acclaim, including pigeon with green lentils and baked red mullet. Last orders: lunch 3pm; dinner 10pm. Set menus from F270 (lunch), F450 (dinner); à la carte around F400.
Most watersports arranged by the hotel

ST-TROPEZ

IOI ⊟ £££

Le Girelier, Quai Jean-Jaures, 83990 St-Tropez.
Tel: 94.97.04.47
Closed January 1–March 15 and Thursday (lunch only July–September)

This quayside fish restaurant looks out over the old port, with yachts moored just feet away from its dining terrace. Both its decor and its customers are chic and trendy, but the atmosphere is friendly and informal. Fish soup, locally caught grilled fish and seafood are the order of the day. Last orders: lunch 2.30pm; dinner 11pm. Set menu available from F170; à la carte around F300.
Motorboat trips around the harbour; from Easter to mid-September daily services to Ste-Maxime, St-Raphael, Les Issambres, Port Cros and the Lérins islands

ST-TROPEZ

⌁ ⊟ £

Le Senequier, Quai Jean-Jaures, 83990 St-Tropez.
Tel: 94.97.00.90

Closed November 11–December 15

This lively café has a prime position on the quay and its terrace provides an ideal vantage point for watching the comings and goings in the port as well as the passing crowds. The café is busy from breakfast right through to the early hours of the morning and serves breakfast, sandwiches and *charcuterie*, as well as coffee, beer and ice-creams. Open 8am–2am during summer; until midnight in winter.

ST-VALERY-SUR-SOMME

🏚 🍽 <u>6/15</u> ⊟ ££

Le Relais Guillaume de Normandy, 46 Quai Romerel, 80230 St-Valery-sur-Somme.   Tel: 22.60.82.36
Closed January 1–20; restaurant closed Tuesday except during July and August
Dbl rm F240–F330

This red-brick mansion stands in a small park on the banks of the Somme estuary, looking across the bay to Le Crotoy. It has the feel of an old-fashioned family home, and the atmosphere is relaxed and convivial. The rooms, some furnished with antiques, have been completely renovated over the last year and now have smart modern bathrooms. Room No.1 is particularly attractive with a large terrace overlooking the bay and the open sea. The dining-room has floor-to-ceiling windows which also afford good bay views. Imaginative regional cooking including fish with seaweed and chicken with Camembert – an excellent and unusual dish. Last orders: lunch 1.30pm; dinner 8.30pm. Set menus from F80; à la carte around F120.
St-Valery is one of the more interesting places along the Calais-Dieppe stretch of coast and from here William the Conqueror set sail for England in 1066; pretty walks around estuary and ramparts of old town; steam-train rides around estuary to Le Crotoy

ST-VALERY-SUR-SOMME

🏨 ❚◯❙ <u>14/14</u> 🛏 £

Hôtel du Port et des Bains, 1 Quai Blavet, 80230
St-Valery-sur-Somme.   Tel: 22.60.80.09
Closed November 8–30
Dbl rm F120–F180

This ivy-covered inn sits on the quayside overlooking gaily
painted fishing boats anchored in the estuary. Bedrooms are
spacious, with creaky varnished wooden floors, old furniture
and handmade bedcovers. Only five have tiny en-suite
bathrooms with showers. Downstairs, the restaurant and
café are decorated in a similar rustic style. Very popular with
locals, it serves traditional seafood dishes and lamb fattened
on saltwater meadows. Window tables have good water
views. Last orders: lunch 2pm; dinner 9pm. Set menus from
F75; à la carte around F160.

ST-VICTOR-SUR-LOIRE

❚◯❙ 🛏 ££

La Presqu'ile, Le Bourg, St-Victor-sur-Loire, 42230
Roche-la-Molière.   Tel: 77.90.64.32
Closed two weeks in February and Tuesday October–May

Situated on the edge of a cliff above an artifical lake formed
by a dam on the upper reaches of the river Loire, this
convivial restaurant has a panoramic view of the lake. Inside
its bright, simply furnished interior, guests are offered good
home cooking, using fresh market produce. In summer,
there is also a terrace for drinks and ice-creams open 9am–
11pm. The traditional menu features hearty regional dishes
such as duck in pepper sauce. Last orders: lunch 2.15pm;
dinner 10pm. Set menus from F78; à la carte around F110.
*Interesting 11th-century fortified village; fishing (permit needed);
beach for lake swimming 1km; boat trips around lake stopping at
Graugent Island*

STE-MAURE

IOI 🖿 ££

Auberge de Ste Maure, 99 Route de Mery, Ste-Maure, 10150 Pont-Ste-Marie.   Tel: 25.81.06.85
Closed December 23–January 12, Sunday evening and Monday

This restaurant sits just feet from an attractive stretch of the river Melda, outside Troyes, and the floor-to-ceiling windows of the dining-room make the most of its location. In summer, meals are also served on a tree-shaded terrace. Imaginative menus based on fresh market produce and including fish and seafood. This is also the place to try the famous *andouillette de Troyes*, definitely an acquired taste, and Burgundian snails. Last orders: lunch 2pm; dinner 10pm. Set menus from F145; à la carte around F250.

STE-MAXIME

🏠 IOI <u>17/17</u> 🖿 £££

Hostellerie de la Belle Aurore, 4 Boulevard Jean Moulin, 83120 Ste-Maxime.   Tel: 94.96.02.45
Open mid-March–end-November
Dbl rm: F500–F1200

This small hotel sits on the rocky shore, feet from the sea, overlooking the St-Tropez Gulf in one direction and the resort of Ste-Maxime in the other. The comfortable bedrooms all have French windows opening on to small individual terraces. Below there is a pool set into a sandy terrace and a small jetty with steps into the sea. Half-board only, July–September, costing F750–F1250 per person. The glass-fronted restaurant has panoramic views of the bay and serves imaginative *haute cuisine* based on traditional Provençal recipes. There is also a small beach-restaurant for salads and grilled fish. Last orders in main restaurant: lunch 1.30pm;

dinner 10pm. Set menus from F210 (F350 June–September); à la carte around F350.
Watersports including windsurfing, water-skiing and jet-skis for hire on Ste-Maxime's sandy beach; tennis courts next door

LES STES-MARIES-DE-LA-MER

🏨 🍽 14/14 🛏 ££££

Le Mas de la Fougue, Route du Petit-Rhone, 13460 Les Stes-Maries-de-la-Mer.   Tel: 90.97.81.02
Open March 15–November 15
Half-board only; F900–F1200 per person

This plush, modern ranch with its white-washed walls and low red-tiled roof sits among the tall reeds and rushes of the Camargue marshes. Bedrooms are cool, light and spacious, with extremely luxurious bathrooms. All rooms open on to patios at the water's edge. It has a sophisticated but very informal ambience, with lots of rattan chairs in which to relax with a book or over a drink. All the restaurant's tables have views of the lagoon and, in fine weather, lunch is served on a waterside terrace. Last orders: lunch 2pm; dinner 9.30pm. Set menus from F220; à la carte around F300.
In hotel grounds: heated swimming pool, riding stables, tennis court; fishing in lagoon; beach 2km by road

LES STES-MARIES-DE-LA-MER

🏨 🍽 15/15 🛏 £££

Le Mas Sainte-Hélène, Etang des Launes, 13460 Les Stes-Maries-de-la-Mer.
Tel: hotel 90.97.83.29; restaurant Le Boumian 90.97.81.15
Open all year
Dbl rm F650

Water laps up to the door of this single-storey hotel which is beautifully situated among the marshes, reeds and meres of the Camargue. Ideal for keen birdwatchers or those in search of complete peace, birdsong is often the only sound to be heard. Bedrooms are handsomely furnished and all have sliding doors opening on to patios overlooking the Launes mere. There is no restaurant in the hotel, but nearby is Le Boumian, also owned by Noel Olivier, which serves popular Provençal dishes, with the emphasis on fish and seafood. Half its tables overlook the mere and there is a pool for hotel guests. Bar open from noon to midnight for snacks and drinks. Last orders: lunch 2pm; dinner 9.30pm. Set menus from F130; à la carte around F300. If Le Mas Sainte-Hélène is full, its sister hotel, Le Pont des Bannes (tel: 90.97.81.09), a collection of Camarguais ranchers' houses surrounded by waterways full of ducks and coots, is a livelier alternative. The rooms have less open water views but its terrace restaurant offers a better outlook.

Beaches 2km with sailing boats and sail-boards for hire, boat trips along coast, photo-safari jeep trips from hotels, cycle hire, tennis courts in village, riding on Camargue horses from hotels

SAMOIS-SUR-SEINE

IOI ▭ ££

Le Surcouf, 17 Quai de la République, 77920 Samois-sur-Seine.   Tel: 1.64.24.60.47
Open all year

This seafood restaurant is particularly appealing in summer, when customers can dine on its large flower-decked patio beside a quiet lane, or on a wooden terrace built out over the river. Inside tables are arranged on two floors, with the best views over this peaceful rural stretch of the Seine from the first-floor dining-room. The waterside terrace is open for meals, snacks and drinks April–October. Last orders: lunch 2.30pm; dinner 10pm. Set menus from F95; à la carte around F200.

Marked paths through nearby Fontainebleau forest, water-skiing, river swimming

SAUSSET-LES-PINS

🏨 🍽 42/42 🛏 ££

Hôtel Paradou Méditerranée, Le Port, 13960
Sausset-les-Pins.   Tel: 42.44.76.76
Open all year
Dbl rm F360–F450

Only a small road separates this modern resort hotel from the
sea. Opened last May, bedrooms are fashionably decorated
and air-conditioned, each with sliding doors opening on to
balconies giving good views of the fishing port and the open
sea. The conservatory-style restaurant turns into an open-air
patio in summer, and also has expansive sea views. Traditional French cooking, especially fish dishes. Last orders:
lunch 2pm; dinner 9.30pm. Set menus from F130; à la carte
around F200.
*Hotel swimming pool, safe sandy cove, glass-bottomed boat trips,
scuba-diving*

SAVINES-LE-LAC

🏨 🍽 20/23 🛏 ££

Hôtel Eden-Lac, 05160 Savines-le-Lac.   Tel: 92.44.20.53
Closed for a month from January 8 and November 15
Dbl rm F250–F330

This resort hotel stands alone on a wooded hillside above
Serre-Poncon lake, one of Europe's largest reservoirs. Bedrooms, decorated in browns and creams, are clean and well-
equipped. Most have expansive views of the lake and its
mountainous backdrop. The restaurant's good-value menus
are popular with the locals. Last orders: lunch 2pm; dinner
9pm. Set menus are available from F65; à la carte around
F100.
*Fishing (day permits sold), lake swimming from beach; catamarans,
sail-boards and pedalos for hire*

SCIEZ

🏛 ❙○❙ <u>8/20</u> ▭ ££££

Château de Coudrée, Sciez, 74140 Douvaine.
Tel: 50.72.62.33
Open May 1–October 31
Dbl rm F750–F1200

This ivy-covered chateau, in landscaped grounds beside Lake Geneva, dates back to the 12th century. It has been sensitively restored and inside the decor is unfussy and the furnishings pleasingly old-fashioned. Bedrooms are decorated in different styles, two with open lake views, the others glimpsing the water through trees. The beamed restaurant serves classic French cuisine. Last orders: lunch 2pm; dinner 9.30pm. Set menus from F180; à la carte around F300.
Heated swimming pool and lake bathing from small private beach; tennis court; boat trips around lake and over to Lausanne depart from port nearby

SEYSSEL

🏛 ❙○❙ <u>7/11</u> ▭ ££

Hôtel du Rhone, Quai de Gaulle, 01420 Seyssel.
Tel: 50.59.20.30
Closed January 5–31; restaurant closed Sunday evening and Monday lunch
Dbl rm F250–F280

The picturesque village of Seyssel straddles a quiet stretch of the Rhone, flanked by the mountains of Grand Colombier and Gros Fouq. This rather quaint, old-fashioned hotel is part of a terrace of old buildings on the right bank of the river. The bedrooms are cosy, decorated with busy floral wallpapers and patterned fabrics. A small road runs between the hotel and the river but carries little traffic. Classic French dishes are served in the restaurant where the four window tables have river

views. Last orders: lunch 2pm; dinner 9pm. Set menus from F95; à la carte around F225.
Fishing (with permit), watersports at leisure centre 500m

STRASBOURG

IOI ▭ £££

Maison des Tanneurs, 42 Rue du Bain-aux-Plantes, 67000 Strasbourg.   Tel: 88.32.79.70
Closed December 20–January 20, July 15–30, Sunday and Monday

Located in the picturesque old town, this restaurant occupies a 16th-century half-timbered house and has beautiful views of the river Ill and canals of the *Petite France* district. Traditional Alsatian dishes are served in the cosy dining-rooms with their beamed ceilings. Window tables on both floors have the best river views. Last orders: lunch 2pm; dinner 9.45pm. No set menus; à la carte around F250.
June music festival, son-et-lumière at 11th-century cathedral April– October, boat trips along Rhine, Ill and canals March–December

STRASBOURG

IOI ▭ £

Péniche Pourquoi-Pas?, Quai des Pecheurs, 67000 Strasbourg.   Tel: 88.36.71.31
Closed September, Saturday lunch and Sunday

This converted wooden barge sits on the river Ill in the centre of the city. Although port-hole views are limited, inexpensive seafood and grills are also served up on the deck terrace in fine weather, from which there are splendid views over the river Ill, the cathedral and the old city. Last orders: lunch 2pm; dinner 1am. Set menus from F45; à la carte around F150.

TAIN-L'HERMITAGE

📷 <u>10/10</u> ▭ ₤₤₤₤

Restaurant Reynaud, 82 Avenue Président Roosevelt,
26600 Tain-L'Hermitage.
Tel: hotel 75.08.07.96; restaurant 75.07.22.10
Closed January, August 15–30, Sunday evening and Monday
Dbl rm F400

Jean-Marc Reynaud's restaurant is recognized as one of the
best in the Rhone valley. The first-floor dining-room is
extremely elegant, and although only nine tables have river
views, in summer, meals are also served on a terrace with
panoramic views over a wide slow-moving stretch of the
river Rhone. The wine list includes many prized Rhone
valley vintages. Monsieur Reynaud has recently added accommodation across the courtyard. Bedrooms are stylishly
decorated and all have expansive river views. Last orders:
lunch 2pm; dinner 9.30pm. Set menus from F160; à la carte
around F300. Reservations essential.

TOULON

🏰 📷 <u>12/22</u> ▭ ₤₤

Hôtel La Corniche, 17 Littoral Frédéric Mistral,
83000 Toulon.   Tel: 94.41.35.12
Open all year; bistro closed Sunday; restaurant closed
Monday
Dbl rm F450–F490

Overlooking the old fishing port of St Louis, where fishermen still bring in their catch, this extremely comfortable and
welcoming hotel is owned by an Englishwoman, Rebecca
Suere, and her French husband, Patrick, for whom nothing is
too much trouble. Bedrooms are decorated with flair and
immaculately maintained. There is a restaurant built around a
protected pine tree, and a bistro, both of which enjoy

harbour views. Meals are also served on a quayside terrace in summer. The bistro serves meals until 12.30am; ideal for a late-night supper after driving down the motorway from Paris. Restaurant last orders: lunch 2.15pm; dinner 10.30pm. Set menus from F160; à la carte around F300.
Sandy beaches nearby with windsurfing

TREFFORT

🏨 ⏿⏣ ⚋⚊ ⊟ ££

Le Château d'Herbelon, Treffort, 38650
Monestier-de-Clermont.   Tel: 76.34.02.03
Closed January 2–February 15; restaurant closed Tuesday in low season
Dbl rm F285–F410

This 17th-century chateau, with a wood-shingled roof, is beautifully situated beside the peaceful Lac de Monteynard, reached down a small country lane. Restored by its present owners, it has spacious bedrooms that are simply but comfortably furnished. All have expansive views over the lake, which is set in an attractive hilly landscape. The restaurant retains much of its original character. It has a beamed ceiling and stone fireplace, which in winter contains a roaring fire. Only two tables have lake views but, in summer, meals are also served on a terrace overlooking the lake. Regional dishes based on fresh market produce, and home-smoked salmon.. Last orders: lunch 1.30pm; dinner 8.30pm. Set menus from F95; à la carte around F100.
Fishing (permits from village), lake swimming from beach; hotel canoe for guests

LES VANS

🏨 ⏿⏣ ⚋⚊ ⊟ £££

Château Le Scipionnet, 07140 Les Vans. Tel: 75.37.23.84
Closed November 15–March 1

Dbl rm F500–F585

This attractive 19th-century chateau was built by Odilon
Barrot, Napoleon III's prime minister. On a peaceful stretch
of the river Chassezac, it is an excellent base for exploring the
gorges, mountainous landscapes and Romanesque churches
of this beautiful region. Some bedrooms have been recently
renovated and redecorated in light pastel shades, others are
somewhat old-fashioned. Only those on the top two floors
have a river view, as trees obscure views from lower floors
and from the elegant dining-room. Last orders: lunch 2pm;
dinner 9.30pm. Set menus from F150; à la carte around F230.
*Swimming pool, private pebble beach for river swimming; fishing
(permits sold in village); tennis court; canoes, kayaks and mountain
bikes for hire 3km; riding 10km*

LES VANS

IOI ▭ ££

Chez Vincent et Michèle, Les Lauzasses-de-Casteljau,
07140 Les Vans.   Tel: 75.39.35.33
Closed January, February and Monday except June–August

This 15th-century fortified house has been renovated by
Vincent and Michèle Vors, who fell in love with its ruins
when they came to the Ardèche on holiday 15 years ago.
There are two dining areas. The convivial La Bastide occupies the great hall and serves traditional French dishes and
pizzas. Alternatively, in summer, you can dine at Le Lagon,
where tables are set out on terraces around the heated
swimming pool, imaginatively constructed among rocks.
The best views of the Chassezac river are from La Bastide's
small, first-floor terrace or from a new riverside terrace. La
Bastide open noon–11pm. Set menus from F88; pizzas F50.
Le Lagon last orders: lunch 1.30pm; dinner 8.30pm. Set
menus from F120 (F60 children); à la carte around F150.
*Heated swimming pool for clients of Le Lagon, pebble beach for river
swimming, beautiful countryside walks*

LA VARENNE-ST-HILAIRE

IOI ⊟ ££££

Le Pavillon Bleu, 66 Promenade des Anglais, 94210
La Varenne–St-Hilaire.   Tel: 1.48.83.10.56
Open all year

Situated on the banks of the river Marne, this beautiful restaurant enjoys a good reputation. All the tables in the bright, airy dining-room have views over a pretty, rural stretch of river – even though it is only 15 minutes from Paris by road or RER train. In summer, meals are also served on the waterside terrace shaded by weeping willows. Gourmet cooking, using only fresh market produce. Last orders: lunch 2.30pm; dinner 11pm. Set menus from F200, F300 (Sunday lunch); à la carte around F350.

VAUX

IOI ⊟ £££

La Petite Auberge, 2 Place du Passeur, Vaux, 89290
Champs-sur-Yonne.   Tel: 86.53.80.08
Open all year; closed Sunday evening and Monday

The wide river Yonne flows slowly by this small restaurant, separated from the riverbank by a narrow, quiet road. Five inside tables enjoy river views, and there is a small triangular terrace under a tree on the riverbank for aperitifs and coffees. On really warm days, Madame Mansour can be persuaded to serve meals on the terrace too. Imaginative, classic French dishes based on fresh market produce, including Burgundian specialities such as fricassée of snails with garlic. Last orders: lunch 2pm; dinner 10pm. Set menus from F140; à la carte around F250.

VILLEFRANCHE-SUR-MER

🏠 🍽 32/32 ▭ £££

Hôtel Welcome, 1 Quai Courbet, 06230
Villefranche-sur-Mer.   Tel: 93.76.76.93
Closed November 20–December 21; restaurant closed
Monday except June–August, no lunch served
Monday–Friday June 15–August 31
Dbl rm F450–F880

One of the nicest hotels on the Riviera in this price range, this former 18th-century convent has a prestigious location on the harbour front. For many years it was the home of writer and artist Jean Cocteau who said the best moments of his life were spent here. Opposite the hotel is the Chapelle St-Pierre, which was decorated by Cocteau. The hotel has recently been modernized and the bedrooms are light, airy and comfortably furnished. Most sea-view rooms have small balconies with views of the picturesque harbour and Cap Ferrat on the far side of the bay. A small terrace, which leads off the bar, is a popular place for breakfast or a drink over-looking the port. Very little traffic passes along the quayside road. The hotel's restaurant, Le Saint Pierre, is a delight. It has a good local reputation and most tables have harbour views. Last orders: lunch 2.30pm; dinner 10.30pm (midnight in season). Set menus from F165; à la carte around F280.
Boat trips from the harbour; small sandy beach 500m with wind-surfing and water-skiing facilities; pleasant walks around the harbour and picturesque streets

VILLEFRANCHE-SUR-MER

🍽 ▭ £££

La Mère Germaine, Quai Courbet, 06230
Villefranche-sur-Mer.   Tel: 93.01.71.39
Closed November 15–December 31

This is the most charming and convivial of the many restaurants that line the harbourside. Its visitors' book, full of comments from writers, celebrities and politicians, is a testament to the restaurant's enduring popularity. Fish and seafood dominate the menus with dishes including *bouillabaisse* with lobster, pan-fried turbot in saffron sauce, and poached crawfish with Hollandaise sauce. Last orders: lunch 2.30pm; dinner 10.30pm. Set menus are available from F190; à la carte around F320.

VILLEFRANCHE-SUR-SAONE

IOI ⊟ £££

Auberge du Faisan Doré, 686 Route de Beauregard, Pont de Beauregard, 69400 Villefranche-sur-Saône. Tel: 74.65.01.66 Open all year; closed Sunday evening and Monday except bank holiday weekends

Only a few minutes from the motorway, this traditional restaurant has a good local reputation. Inside tables have no river view but, in fine weather, most clients choose to eat outside on a large terrace overlooking the river Saône. Menus are based around fresh seasonal produce, and home-smoked salmon is always available. For F90 children can eat what appeals from the wide-ranging gourmet menus. Last orders: lunch 2.15pm; dinner 9.30pm. Set menus from F170; à la carte around F250.

VULAINES-SUR-SEINE

IOI ⊟ ££

L'Ile aux Truites, 6 Chemin de la Varenne, 77870 Vulaines-sur-Seine.   Tel: 1.64.23.71.87 Closed December 21–February 1, Wednesday and Thursday lunch

Set in a verdant garden full of small ponds, this restaurant, with its red walls and thatched roof, resembles a doll's house. It specializes in trout, which are kept in ponds and a stream that runs through the garden, and children are encouraged to catch their own fish for dinner. All the tables in its rustic interior have beautiful views across the river Seine to 19th-century mansions on the opposite bank. There is also a large dining terrace just feet from the river. Pink, river and fountain trout are cooked in a variety of ways and there are also grilled meat dishes. Last orders: lunch 2pm; dinner 10pm. No set menus; à la carte around F110.
Safe river swimming; boat cruises

WIMEREUX

🏨 🍽 6/13 🛏 ££

L'Atlantic, Digue de Mer, 62930 Wimereux.
Tel: 21.32.41.01
Closed January and February; restaurant closed Sunday evening and Monday except during July and August
Dbl rm F400

This small, attractively designed hotel stands on the promenade overlooking Wimereux's sandy beach. Bedrooms are nicely decorated and have recently renovated bathrooms. The bright, airy, first-floor dining-room serves imaginative dishes based on fresh market produce, especially fish. Lobsters are kept live in a tank. On the ground floor, there is a conservatory-style brasserie for breakfast. Light meals and drinks are served all day. In fine weather, the brasserie opens on to a promenade-side terrace. Excellent sea views from window tables on both floors. Restaurant last orders: lunch 2.30pm; dinner 9.30pm. Set menus are available from F110; à la carte around F200.
Safe sandy beach, watersports, riding on the beach

WINGEN-SUR-MODER

🏠 🍽 <u>18/23</u> 🛏 ££

Auberge d'Imsthal, La Petite Pierre, 67290
Wingen-sur-Moder.   Tel: 88.70.45.21
Open all year; restaurant closed November 20 for a
month, Monday evening and Tuesday
Dbl rm F300–F560

This attractive hotel is peacefully situated beside a small lake
and surrounded by woodlands. The recently renovated bedrooms are comfortable, some with balconies overlooking the
lake and the mountains beyond. All have modern en-suite
bathrooms and two rooms are equipped for disabled guests.
Ten tables in the rustic dining-room enjoy water views, and
menus offer an extensive choice of regional dishes. In summer, meals are also served on the lakeside terrace. Last orders:
lunch 2pm; dinner 9pm. Set menus from F75; à la carte
around F160.
*Lake swimming and fishing (free for guests), canal trips from
Phalsbourg and Lutzelbourg, excellent forest walks*

WISSANT

🍽 🛏 £££

La Sirène, Cap Gris Nez, 62179 Wissant.
Tel: 21.32.95.97
Closed mid-December–end January, Monday except
during July and August; September–April lunch only
except Saturday

Cap Gris Nez is the traditional departure point for cross-
Channel swimmers and this beachside restaurant has a marvellous panorama over the Channel, busy with ferries and
tankers. A pleasant, convivial place, it is popular with French
families, especially at Sunday lunchtimes. Fresh-water fish and
seafood, including grilled lobster, dominate the menus. Window tables have the best sea views and there is also a bar for

drinks and coffees, open 9am–11pm. Last orders: lunch 2pm; dinner 9pm. Set menus from F97; à la carte around F220.

YVOIRE

◻ 4/4 ▭ ££

Restaurant du Port, Yvoire, 74140 Douvaine.
Tel: 50.72.80.17
Closed November 12–March 1 and Wednesday in winter
Dbl rm F650–F750
Geneva airport 25km

This restaurant enjoys one of the best waterside locations in the picturesque medieval village of Yvoire. In fine weather, meals are served on a geranium-filled terrace with expansive views over Lake Geneva. The restaurant is popular both for its location and reputation, and it is advisable to book in advance, especially for the eight inside tables with lake views. Specialities include lake perch and *omble chevalier* (char fish). There are four new air-conditioned bedrooms, decorated in blues and yellows, with balconies overlooking the lake. Last orders: lunch 2pm; dinner 10.30pm. Set menus from F95 (lunch), F98 (dinner); à la carte around F150.
Fishing and windsurfing; pleasant walks

Index

The Family Welcome Guide 1993

Malcolm Hamer and Jill Foster

The *Family Welcome Guide* is the only comprehensive and authoritative guide to the best hotels, self-catering accommodation, pubs, restaurants and places to visit for parents and children.

Over 600 establishments are listed, with maps to help you locate them. Every one extends a friendly welcome to all the family, and provides the essential basic services: hotels with cots, high chairs, a free baby-listening service; pubs with separate family rooms; and restaurants with high chairs and special menus for children. If you are planning some sightseeing, this guide will help you pick the museums, stately homes, wildlife and theme parks with the best facilities for families.

Whether you are planning a meal or day out, a journey or a holiday, don't leave home without it!

'The entries in the guide are informative, practical and bear the stamp of honest, down-to-earth assessment.'   *Observer*

'An essential handbook for anyone planning a family outing.'
                                                            Parents Magazine

Fontana

Europe by Train 1993

Katie Wood and George McDonald

The bestselling classic, recommended by EUROTRAIN

Europe by Train is still the best value and most comprehensive book on the market for eurorailers. It contains all the essential, practical information required by students and those on a tight budget:

- Maximizing the benefits of rail passes
- Train networks and station facilities
- The best routes
- Local transport
- What to see
- Where to sleep
- What to eat
- Where the nightlife is

In addition to being fully revised and updated for 1993, this year's new edition of *Europe by Train* includes even more information on eastern Europe, plus details of all new passes and tickets.

'Excellent . . . a reliable guide to the systems of all European countries'   *Independent*

Fontana

One Summer's Grace

A Family Voyage Round Britain

Libby Purves

In the summer of 1988 Libby Purves and her husband Paul Heiney set sail in their cutter *Grace O'Malley* with their children Nicholas, aged five, and Rose, three. They sailed the 1,700 miles around Britain, from the offshore labyrinths of the sandy south-east to the towering stacks of Cape Wrath and back home through the North Sea. Her account of the voyage is a new classic of the sea.

'It is that rarest of all books on the yachting shelf – a work of acerbic realism. Libby Purves is wonderfully sharp on the woes of containing a marriage and a family inside their pressure-cooker of a small boat. Her portrait of coastal Britain in the 1980s is wise, affectionate and sceptical; her pleasure in our scary seas rings true because there is not a word of cant or overstatement in her story. This is how it is – and Miss Purves tells it beautifully'

Jonathan Raban

'A delightful book, warm, wise and candid' *Sunday Telegraph*

Fontana

The Anatomy of Thatcherism

Shirley Robin Letwin

The Anatomy of Thatcherism explains why, for the first time in British history, a prime minister's name has become synonymous with an idea and a political movement. Dr Letwin argues that Thatcherism has prompted a fundamental re-alignment in British politics by focusing on a moral agenda rather than on an economic doctrine or a political theory. She introduces a new term – 'the vigorous virtues' – to describe what Thatcherites have aimed to cultivate in individual Britons and in the country as a whole.

The Anatomy of Thatcherism is a bold and searching book about how Britain changed between 1979 and 1991. It challenges truisms about British politics, and is indispensable reading both for those who believe in the future relevance of Thatcherism and for those who want to demolish it. And it will be of particular interest to those concerned with the history of British politics, as it shows how Thatcherism arose out of, and confronted, trends that permeated Toryism for the entire twentieth century.

Fontana

Fontana Non-Fiction

Fontana is a leading paperback publisher of non-fiction. Below are some recent titles.

- ☐ EUROPE BY TRAIN Katie Wood & George McDonald £7.99
- ☐ CHEAP SLEEP GUIDE TO EUROPE Katie Wood £7.99
- ☐ ON THE WATERFRONT IN BRITAIN 1993 Alice Hart-Davis £8.99
- ☐ ON THE WATERFRONT IN FRANCE 1993 Gill Charlton £8.99
- ☐ HITCH-HIKER'S GUIDE TO EUROPE 1993 Ken Welsh £5.99
- ☐ FAMILY WELCOME GUIDE Malcolm Hamer & Jill Foster £5.99
- ☐ OBSESSIVE TRAVELLER David Dale £4.50

You can buy Fontana Paperbacks at your local bookshops or newsagents. Or you can order them from Fontana, Cash Sales Department, Box 29, Douglas, Isle of Man. Please send a cheque, postal or money order (not currency) worth the price plus 24p per book for postage (maximum postage required is £3.00 for orders within the UK).

NAME (Block letters)_____

ADDRESS_____

_____

While every effort is made to keep prices low, it is sometimes necessary to increase them at short notice. Fontana Paperbacks reserve the right to show new retail prices on covers which may differ from those previously advertised in the text or elsewhere.